"*The Social Justice Investor* understands the link between doing well and doing good, and it offers readers the tools and knowledge necessary to transform everyday financial decisions into social justice commitments."

—Stacey Abrams

"Money is a lever with which you can change the world. *The Social Justice Investor* is a treasure chest of valuable insights for readers who want to finance a more just society."

—Joanne Gan, head of Impact Investing & ESG, Treasury, PayPal

"This easy-to-understand book boils down financial concepts to everyday language so all of us can leverage our financial resources to drive positive change. *The Social Justice Investor* helps us finance the world in which we want to live."

—Matt Glatting, chief financial officer, NeighborWorks Capital

"A transformational road map for social justice investing, this book is a master class of personal finance activism."

—Jason Howell, CRP®, CPWA®, CSRIC®,
author of *Joy of Financial Planning*

"*The Social Justice Investor* teaches you how to be an intentional steward of your money. This insightful and practical book gives every person—even those who may not think of themselves as investors—the information and steps necessary to drive meaningful change in the trajectory of our planet, society, and financial system."

—Jennifer Novak, senior vice president,
Community Reinvestment Fund, USA

"*The Social Justice Investor* offers an exceptionally lucid, practical, and human-centered framework for transforming communities through impact investing. Longton seamlessly interweaves authentic and timely accounts of real-life investors within a hands-on road map to maximizing both financial earnings and justice outcomes."

—Milan Bhatt, senior manager,
Inclusive Economic Recovery and Growth, Clinton Global Initiative

"This book stands out as a bold new paradigm for incorporating social justice priorities into everyday wealth-building decisions. I'm excited to share with family members to help them understand what social justice investing is."

—Christina Szczepanski, CFA, president,
Lending and Investments, Reinvestment Fund

"Money is powerful and has always had the ability to change an individual's life, a child's outcomes, a family's fortitude, a community's vibrancy, and a nation's resilience. This book is a movement. It takes us on a journey today, putting money to work not only to create wealth but to provide the resources required to address problems and improve our communities. It reaffirms our power to make a difference."

—Dr. Christie Cade, PhD, board member, Bridging Virginia

"You will be inspired by the personal stories shared by the social justice heroes in this book who claim and wield financial power. Read about them, and then share this book with your friends, family, and neighbors. Together, dollar by dollar, we can change the world."

—Tina Poole Johnson, deputy director, Center for Impact Finance,
Carsey School of Public Policy, University of New Hampshire

The Social Justice Investor

Advance Your Values While Building Wealth,
Whether a Few Dollars or Millions

THE SOCIAL JUSTICE INVESTOR

ANDREA LONGTON, CFA

BROADLEAF BOOKS
MINNEAPOLIS

THE SOCIAL JUSTICE INVESTOR
Advance Your Values While Building Wealth, Whether a Few Dollars or Millions

The sections titled "Energy Boost" are from interviews provided to the author by the following individuals and used with their consent: Beth Bafford, Rachel Robasciotti, Morgan Simon, Phuong Luong CFP®, Leah Fremouw, Sonya Dreizler, Ebony Perkins, Lakota Vogel, John Holdsclaw IV, Bill Bynum, Dr. Riordan Ledgerwood, Christina Travers, Catherine Berman, Dr. Andrea Abrams, Fran Seegull, Janine Firpo, Dr. Stephanie Gripne, Monique Aiken, and Tanay Tatum-Edwards.

The "Energy Boost" titled "A Can of Worms—Enough Is Enough" is reprinted with permission of the author, Morgan Simon.

Library of Congress Control Number 2023037131 (print)

Cover image: Shutterstock_1748079425
Cover design: 1517 Media

Print ISBN: 978-1-5064-8757-1
eBook ISBN: 978-1-5064-8758-8

Contents

1.

What Is Social Justice Investing?

Nicole was stunned by the murder of George Floyd in May 2020. She protested police brutality and racial injustice through demonstration marches and Congressional letter campaigns. It wasn't enough; she wanted more change.

So Nicole joined her local NAACP chapter and met new friends who were using their *money* to advance racial justice. After researching the options, Nicole purchased a $500 investment product that finances Black-owned businesses. After three years, Nicole reviewed the investment's returns statement to discover her initial investment was now valued at $575 (15% financial return) and had contributed to the investment's collective creation of over 30,000 Black-owned businesses.

HOW CAN INVESTMENTS ADVANCE SOCIAL JUSTICE?

Many people feel intimidated by finance and investments.

That's intentional. Wall Street knows how powerful money can be. The traditional finance industry has made these concepts seem inaccessible for everyday people whose dollars actually keep the economy flowing.

Money finances the people and activities that transform a vision into reality. Just like a family's goal to buy a house is financed by a mortgage, an individual's goal to eliminate the racial wealth gap is financed by investments in Black-owned businesses.

Your money is a powerful tool that transforms intention into impact. Whether it sits in a savings account or a 401(k) retirement portfolio, your money finances *somebody's* vision. Social justice investing harnesses your money's power to finance the world in which *you* want to live.

What is social justice investing?

Social justice investing is putting money to work in a project, organization, or undertaking to both generate wealth and advance social justice. Investment returns are characterized by the twin goals of sustainable financial earnings coupled with social justice advancements. "Social justice" is defined by the investor's priorities. Common social justice priorities include combatting racism, gender inequity, climate crisis, and LGBTQ+ discrimination.

Each investor defines their own social justice priority

Whereas social justice refers to a fair and equitable division of resources, opportunities, and privileges in society, the practice of social justice *investing* is defined by three main tenets:

Every person has the right to reach their full potential.
Many people are shut out from reaching their full potential.
Social justice investors bridge the gap by investing in the potential of
    people.

Within this broad overview, each investor defines their own social justice priority. Some people may decide they would like to apply a climate justice lens broadly across their entire portfolio, investing in solar farms, companies focused on energy efficiency, and wind turbine manufacturing. Others may prioritize a more focused racial justice approach by moving their checking account to a Black-owned bank or pour their resources into creating a pathway for more Indigenous Americans to gain access to homeownership. Still others may use their capital to advance gender equity by investing in women-led companies.

There are many social justice causes and it can be overwhelming to consider them all at once. Instead, I encourage you to be thoughtful about the issues that feel most important to you and start there. You can always expand your focus as you gain confidence and knowledge, broadening your approach or going deeper into a particular topic.

This book will teach you how to build an investment portfolio tailored for your self-defined social justice priorities. Take the time you need to follow your instincts. Select the issues in which you're willing to invest your hard-earned money. After all, if you believe in it enough to invest your money, it's clearly important to you. This book teaches you how to invest that money with confidence and agency.

With balance comes stability

Social justice investors balance the desire to build financial wealth with their goal to create social change.

Whereas traditional investment culture emphasizes the single-minded pursuit of profit maximization, social justice investors target *sustainable* financial earnings coupled with social justice returns. Social justice investors reject Wall Street's tunnel vision on profit maximization. We've endured too many man-made financial disasters, felt the sting of deep recessions, and waded into deep and painful uncertainty about the ability to care for our family's financial concerns. We've witnessed the racial wealth gap widen, exacerbating tension, anger, and inequity within our country.

Wall Street culture isn't working for us.

Having lived through multiple periods of economic upheaval and uncertainty, a new investor era seeks a financial path that generates sustainable earnings rather than volatile extremes, and, more importantly, understands that long-term economic well-being requires widespread financial inclusion.

To that end, social justice investors crave stability in our economic well-being, both for themselves and everyone else. We reject the extreme volatility that undulates between manic financial growth and bottomless economic chasms. We want a more sensible approach to economic security. Instead of chasing a vision of immediate profit and overnight wealth at all costs, social justice investors seek a more lasting path with gentler economic cycles.

Will social justice investments build wealth for my family?

While we aren't chasing runaway profits, social justice investors are still focused on creating enough wealth to sustain their family's financial needs through a long-term horizon.

Just like their traditional counterparts, social justice investors begin their wealth creation plans by establishing a financial budget for expected and unexpected life events. Expected financial events may include a down payment for a home purchase, tuition for their child's education, and income during retirement. Budgets for unexpected financial events may cover unforeseen car repairs, health emergencies, sudden tax requirements, or job loss.

You'll learn how to assess your family's appropriate target for financial returns in later chapters.

After determining what is "enough" wealth to meet their financial needs, social justice investors target a corresponding financial return that sustains their budget. At the same time, moving away from profit maximization creates sufficient space for social justice returns to emerge.

Finding the right balance between financial earnings and social justice advances is a lifelong challenge. But it's work worth pursuing. After all, we've got to keep moving forward in our fight for equitable flow of investment.

Justice through respect

Justice is found in self-determination.

Investing in justice means connecting communities with the resources required to implement their plan and then getting out of the way. It means letting go.

Our secret sauce is listening to the communities that sit closest to the problems. Social justice investors restore an equitable flow of capital by asking the impacted communities for guidance on *what* to finance and *how*. Respect breaks down the barriers that otherwise keep dollars from creating real change.

This doesn't mean that you as an investor need to knock on doors and participate in community engagement interviews.

It does mean that you select products that reflect insights that professional social justice investors gleaned from those boots-on-the-ground conversations.

Don't worry. We'll cover the logistics in later chapters.

For now, it's your job to understand why it's important to listen to and learn from the people most impacted by social injustices.

Spoiler: it's because the people who sit closest to the problem always have the best insights to the solutions.

For example, consider the approach of Adasina Social Capital, a leading social justice investment firm.

Before Adasina chooses investments, the firm first asks the communities most impacted by injustice to explain what issues are important to them. For example, before choosing investments aligned with their gender justice values, Adasina talked to survivors of sexual harassment and women's rights activists, the community closest to this issue. In doing so, they discovered that the women most impacted were asking for an end to a corporate policy that they felt enabled serial sexual harassment at work: forced arbitration.

Forced arbitration requires workers, as a condition of employment, to sign an agreement that they will only settle disputes with the employer through private arbitration—with no judge, no jury, and almost no government oversight. The practice eliminates the option of going to court and legally prevents the employee from discussing the issue with anyone outside of the arbitration proceedings. Research has demonstrated that arbitration rulings favor employers, who likely benefit from maintaining ongoing relationships with arbitrators. When valid sexual harassment claims are routinely mishandled and employees are barred from publicly sharing their experiences, companies unintentionally protect serial harassers, silence victims, and create a culture of acceptance regarding sexual harassment.

After doing this research, Adasina realized that no other investors were advocating for an end to forced arbitration practices. While many people were trying to invest for gender justice, no one had really asked the most vulnerable communities what solutions would be most helpful. To make it possible for all social justice investors to choose investments that align with their gender justice goals, Adasina partnered with Grab Your Wallet and LedBetter to create the Force the Issue database. This database includes data for over 3,500 public companies, the full scope of regularly traded US public companies, and information about where they stand on the practice of forced arbitration.

Social justice investors can review the site to consider whether they want to continue any investments in companies that retain a forced arbitration policy for sexual harassment cases.

Since the creation of the Force the Issue database, more than 300 companies now report they do *not* use the practice of forced arbitration for sexual harassment. Those 300 companies impact more than 10 million employees. Social justice investors who use this data to choose their investments can see a tangible social justice return while feeling confident that they are supporting a solution self-determined by the impacted communities.

BEND THE ARC

Most people don't consider themselves investors, let alone social justice investors.

We've been collectively conditioned to assume that money is something that other people manage. We sock away our savings and keep our fingers crossed that we won't outlive our savings when we eventually retire. We draw a fence around our resources, separating our wealth from our social justice values.

We've started to believe that our resources and capacity don't hold a candle to the world's injustices.

Social justice investing isn't a magical fix. It's a tool—one that molds resources contributed by everyday people into real, authentic change. None of us can create an equitable world by ourselves and with our own limited resources. Instead, we can link arms with other social justice investors and collectively take small steps toward the world we want to live in.

We may even bend the arc of finance a little closer to justice.

Energy Boost: Nervous as Hell

Andrea Longton

Our power as investors is to finance the world in which we want to live. Unlike other personal finance books, this one will teach you basic tools of investing, applied through a lens of social justice.

I wrote this book because I'm on a mission to let investment money freely flow to people and places chronically disconnected from financial resources. I have raised more than $1 billion for investments into low-wealth communities across America. I work with community lenders that are deeply committed to racial and economic justice—which results in them being a critical source of capital for communities that are often left behind. This work means I spend most of my time using finance to pursue social justice.

And yet, I was nervous as hell to call my financial advisor, Becky, about my *personal* social justice investment goals. Despite my technical expertise, deep experience, and boots-on-the-ground knowledge of available social justice investment products and strategies, I was intimidated. I had to find the courage to push into a particularly taboo conversation—money and social justice—if I wanted to be proud of my financial assets as an extension of my values.

When Becky answered my call, I launched into the conversation before I could lose my nerve. "I want to invest according to my social justice values."

A long, uncomfortable pause followed. Becky remained composed, straightforward, and professional. "Well, okay. But I don't know what that means. And I'm not sure it's possible."

When I insisted, she asked me two questions: "What do you want and how will that work?"

What did I want? My goal was to make well-informed, strategic investment decisions that I was proud to financially support. My investment assets should be a powerful extension of my values, intentions, and commitments. I wanted financial returns that met my family's cash needs for expected and unexpected life events. I also wanted evidence of how my money created authentic social change.

Once I nailed down what I wanted, I jumped headlong into the "how." Blame it on the years of technical training and dry-as-dust bond math exercises, but I was *ready* for how to tackle a social justice investment portfolio. Once I had committed to my vision of prioritizing both financial and social justice returns, I worked with Becky to apply the same tools that any investor uses to achieve their specified objectives: I created an investment budget and went shopping for investment products that met my expectations. Then I kept an eye on how my investments performed over time.

Ready for a big secret that Wall Street never wants you to hear? You don't need intense investment training to be a social justice investor. You don't need intense investment training to be an investor, period! Rather, you need courage and community. Courage to stand up for what is right, even when established gatekeepers question whether it's possible. Courage to ask the tough questions. And community to help you find the best answers. Community to cheer you on while getting it done.

To be a social justice investor is to say: "I want my money to reflect who I am as a person. I'm marshaling all my resources—my time, talent, and treasure—to be the change I want to see in the world."

Once I found the courage to ask for what I wanted, I used the tools and knowledge at my fingertips to confidently walk through a budget, establish an investment strategy, and recommend specific products that met my expectations. When I ran into questions, I could easily call upon my network of professional social justice investors for guidance, advice, and new products to consider.

I realized that if *I* was intimidated, with my credentials and professional experience, people with a different range of expertise and experiences might not find the nerve to broach these conversations or the tools and knowledge required for this social justice approach to investing.

I wrote this book to give everyday investors confidence in their own agency as social justice investors, whether you have $100 or $100 million in your bank account.

Explaining investment tools through fictional characters and energy boosts

To make the technical content a little easier to digest, we'll learn by following the journeys of three fictional characters:

First, we'll discover how Angela, a 40-year-old mother of three who recently left her long-time teaching position, creates financial security with every $15 transaction in a DIY investment portfolio.

We'll learn how Tom, a 32-year-old man, designs his 401(k) to reflect his values.

And we'll explore how Nicole, a 55-year-old marketing executive in New York City, decides to use her accumulated wealth to create the change she wants to see in the world.

You'll also be energized by stories from real-life social justice investors who make everyday decisions to make the world a better place.

You are already a social justice investor

Your courage, coupled with the actionable steps in this book, will transform your money into financial assets that fight on your behalf to create a world in which no one is left out.

You have power.

Your dollars make a difference. Use them well.

2.

Are You an Angela, a Tom, or a Nicole?

Let's face it. Reading about finance and investment can be dry. Some might even say boring.

I get it.

To make these concepts more readable, this book follows three fictional characters as they work through everyday scenarios for people striving to build wealth while advancing social justice. Each character depicts one of the three most common investor types: DIY investors, 401(k) investors, and investors with accumulated wealth.

> Angela, our DIY investor, opens an online investment account to build wealth after she leaves her teaching position to become primary caregiver to her three young children.
>
> Tom, our 401(k) investor, shapes his 401(k) to reflect his personal values while saving for retirement.
>
> Nicole, an investor working with a financial advisor, decides to use her accumulated wealth to finance the world in which she wants to live.

We will follow Angela, Tom, and Nicole throughout the book as they work through their own "real life" applications of social justice investing. Please note that our trio of investors will feature more heavily in later chapters as we progress from ideas and concepts to decisions and implementation. The following stories introduce our characters at the beginning of their respective journeys.

Angela discovers DIY investing

Angela recently left her job as a third-grade teacher to manage her full-time workload as a 40-year-old mother of her three young children. One of her biggest anxieties about leaving her job was walking away from yearly contributions to her state-sponsored retirement pension.

To mitigate this risk, Angela takes her retirement plans into her own hands by contributing $15 every week to build a DIY investment portfolio in her spare time.

The only problem is . . . she doesn't really know how to invest money. We follow Angela as she works through a step-by-step plan that aligns her retirement savings with her financial and social justice goals.

Tom makes his 401(k) options work for him

Tom, a recently engaged 32-year-old man, just started a job as an account manager at a large manufacturing company in Cincinnati.

On his first day, the human resources (HR) manager, Tammi, hands him a stack of new employee paperwork to complete. He enrolls in medical, dental, and vision insurance; signs the employee handbook; and registers for direct deposit paychecks.

The last document is a list of investment fund options for the 401(k) retirement plan sponsored by his new employer. The 401(k) investment menu included 15 different fund options. The menu of options stretches on and on until the letters and numbers describing each approach blur together in an amorphous tangle of dots and dashes.

Tom pauses, unsure of how to proceed. While he'd love to strike the investment selections paperwork from his "to do" list, Tom isn't sure which of the investment options is right for him. Saving for retirement is important to him; he wants to take the time to get it right.

Rather than selecting a random approach, Tom asks for a few days to collect his thoughts and consider his options. Throughout the book, we follow his path to an unexpected destination.

Nicole embraces the power of accumulated wealth

Nicole, a 55-year-old marketing executive, lives and breathes New York City. She was born on Long Island, attended NYU for college, and has worked in

Manhattan for more than 30 years. As much as she loves her city, Nicole was horrified when 11 people were found dead in basements after torrential rains flooded the area in September 2021.

Skyrocketing rents have forced countless low-wealth families into window-less basements in order to afford housing in America's most expensive city. While cramped basement apartments are commonplace in New York City, some are illegally rented by landlords who overlook basic safety features like having more than one way to get out in an emergency. Unfortunately, these rentals are also a vital source of shelter for many low-wealth and immigrant families.

Nicole wanted these unsafe housing conditions in her beloved city to change. She thought, surely New Yorkers could rally behind the fact that every person deserves the right to safe, decent housing.

Nicole considered her options. She thought about writing a letter to her elected officials, but didn't know how to ask for appropriate legislation. She knew the problem, but didn't feel informed enough to demand any specific solutions. She donated to families who had lost everything in the basement flooding, and while she was glad the money could purchase food and replace basic clothing, Nicole wasn't satisfied with its limited scope. She wanted existing housing conditions to improve. She wanted to create real, long-term change. A crowdsourced donation wasn't going to address the root problems, just bandage the wound.

A colleague suggested she consider her investment portfolio. Nicole was surprised. Other than the standard annual check-in with her financial advisor, she hadn't peeked under the hood of her portfolio in years. Was it even possible to use her investments to create safe, affordable housing in New York City?

Nicole called her financial advisor to find out. After a thorough conversation, she updated her investment strategy to reflect her goals: maintain an investment portfolio that delivered a consistent financial return of 6% while choosing investments reflecting Nicole's belief that every person had the right to safe, affordable housing.

During a portfolio review, her financial advisor asked Nicole to consider investing in an exchange-traded fund (a basket of stocks often referred to by its acronym, ETF) that capitalized affordable housing developers. The ETF projected a financial return of 8% (exceeding Nicole's "sustainable" target of 6%) while projecting the collective creation of 1.5 million units of affordable housing in the next three years.

Nicole was immediately excited about the affordable housing ETF, but her financial advisor also asked her to consider another investment projecting 15% returns. The alternate investment was a rare opportunity to access an oil & gas hedge fund whose historic performance ranged from 9% to 25% returns, depending on market performance.

Although Nicole was tempted, she knew that the fund with an 8% yield was more than enough to achieve her financial goals. Both provided an opportunity to get high returns—but one investment's returns were purely financial in nature, while the other investment offered both financial and social justice returns.

Nicole was willing to wave away the potential for extreme wealth creation in order to stay true to her core objective: balancing her family's financial needs with opportunities to advance social justice. In doing so, she sidestepped the conventional propensity to chase high-risk, high-return investment opportunities.

Nicole is still unsatisfied with the unsafe housing conditions faced by low-wealth communities in New York, but she's proud of the small steps she continues to take to create a safer environment for the next generation of New Yorkers. This investment has even strengthened her confidence regarding her finances, and she has started thinking about whether there are other social justice issues she might want to apply to her portfolio.

Energy Boost: Everyone Deserves a Chance to Fly

Beth Bafford

In 2008, I quit a lucrative job at a top-tier investment bank in New York City to be an unpaid volunteer in an uncertain political campaign.

What can I say? From my first gig clipboarding in Union Square, I fell in love.

I loved the people, the passion, and the candidate's positions on issues that mattered to me. After a few weeks volunteering on weekend mornings and workday evenings, I was hooked.

I had never experienced such a powerful, bone-deep conviction to let go of my previous plans and follow a new path. Yet here I was, sitting on the subway on my way to work, preparing to hand in my resignation letter.

I had just finished a grueling two-year graduate rotational program at the bank. My boss, expecting a conversation about my preferences for a permanent position, was not prepared for my announcement.

Truth to tell, *I* was not prepared for my pronouncement.

The subway lurched into the next station. Nine more stops to go.

I desperately needed a surge of courage.

Fishing around in my bag, I pulled out my iPod and pressed play on the latest music I had downloaded. To my surprise, it started playing exactly the song I needed to hear. Headphones in my ears, Idina Menzel's "Defying Gravity" burst through the speakers.

I had to pinch my fingers together to stop the tears threatening to leak through my eyelashes. The music had broken through my perpetual cloud of doubts, encouraging my instinct to close my eyes and leap toward something bigger.

I relaxed into my seat, closed my eyes, and felt my resolve strengthen. The music filled my soul and carried me off the subway and into my office building.

Before I could lose my nerve, I knocked on my boss's door to ask if she had a moment.

"Of course!" She smiled warmly and welcomed me in her office. "I've got your paperwork ready. Let's discuss your next move."

Life seemed to freeze in that moment.

I could see two distinct paths ahead of me. One invited me to pull up a chair and dream about what I could do with the money and prestige that came with a high-power career at a Wall Street firm.

The other path trailed behind me, back out the door and toward an unknown, unpaid future.

But something had already changed within me. I was ready to leap.

I stepped forward and cleared my throat. "I know we planned to meet today to discuss my permanent placement at the bank, but I've decided to go in a different direction."

My breath had grown shallow and I had to pause to collect myself.

"I'm here to give you my two weeks' notice. I am incredibly grateful to have learned so much from you and my colleagues, but I am resigning my position."

My boss's face fell. Several moments sank in silence.

"I see," she finally said. "Do you mind sharing where you'll be going?"

It was not uncommon for younger associates to be poached by rival firms. Investment banks competed for talent and salaries were negotiable.

"I'm leaving to serve as a volunteer on a political campaign."

Never before nor after have I seen a face transform into a mask of pure shock.

We stared at each other for a few beats. Then she blinked and laughed.

"Well, I've never heard that one before!"

We both relaxed and I sat in the chair she offered.

"Who are you volunteering for? Will you receive any kind of payment or stipend?"

Leaning forward, I shook my head. "No, it won't be paid. I will be sleeping on friends' floors for a while and using my savings."

Now my boss looked concerned. "Aren't you worried about your financial future? Your career? What if it doesn't work out?"

Her concerns were valid. I was venturing into the unknown and leaving behind the world of corporate success.

"I'm terrified. But I know, with absolute certainty, that I'm meant to do this."

My boss's head moved abruptly backward, almost as though a wave of shock had blown across her face.

"What will you be doing? You never told me which campaign is worth leaving a job at the top of your field."

Now was my chance to smile. "I'm driving to Philadelphia this weekend to volunteer full-time for Senator Obama's run for president."

Shock transformed into disbelief before my eyes. "That's a long shot at best. Are you sure you want to give up a promising career to volunteer for a first-term senator who's up against Hillary Clinton? You don't even know if he'll win the primary election, let alone the general election!"

Somehow, her disbelief solidified my resolve. I planted my feet on the carpet, looked my boss in the eye, and felt conviction surge.

"This might be my best chance to fight for the change I want to see in the world. Ignoring this opportunity would be a much bigger risk for me."

I spent my last weekend as a Wall Street investment banker at Senator Obama's campaign headquarters in Philadelphia. When I walked into their makeshift offices to inquire about a volunteer position, the supervisor welcomed me to the team and directed me to a pile of clipboards and a list of phone numbers to start calling.

By the time I returned the following Monday, it felt like coming home.

My time on the campaign was defined by unpredictability. I climbed into 15-passenger vans with a backpack and phone charger without a clear idea of where I'd be sleeping that night. I ended up campaigning in New York, Virginia, Rhode Island, and Philadelphia before I was asked to take on a more permanent position as an organizer in Michigan, a critical battleground state.

I'm proud of the work we accomplished during the campaign and, later, at the White House.

I'm even prouder of the positive ripple effects that have been created by my former colleagues following the end of the Obama Administration.

President Obama's deep care for all Americans permeated throughout our collective culture. We were all trained in effective and meaningful community engagement, living by the motto "Respect. Empower. Include." Our work was straightforward: we talked to people about what they needed and their hopes for the future. My job was to listen and learn from the communities we hoped to serve. I listened to rural communities and urban communities, rich families and poor families.

So much of what people want is not about politics. Almost without exception, people want safety for their kids and food on the table. At the end of the day, we all want a community of people who know us and care for us.

The real work started on Inauguration Day and continued until President Obama left the White House in 2016. My colleagues and I fought every day for policies and systems for everyday people.

After eight years of fighting for hope and change, the people who worked for President Obama weren't willing to let go of our convictions.

We call it "The Obama Effect." It's fascinating to watch just how far the ripples extend in far-flung directions.

Personally, I carry "The Obama Effect" into my fight for an increased flow of affordable financing for everyday people. I want to see a financial system in which no one is left out. I'm incredibly grateful to have found a new home in Calvert Impact Capital, where I'm surrounded by like-minded colleagues dedicated to being the change we want to see in the world.

Leaving a dream job freed me up to walk along an unforgettable path.

Throughout the journey, I've learned time and time again that everyone deserves a chance to fly. The trick is conquering the fear of leaving the ground. My advice? Just do it. You only discover your wings by taking the leap.

Contributing Author Biography

Beth Bafford leads Calvert Impact Capital's strategy and new business development efforts to build financial products and services that accelerate private capital for the benefit of communities in the United States and around the world.

Prior to joining the Calvert, Beth was a manager in McKinsey & Company's Washington, DC, office where she focused mostly on US health-reform strategy for large health insurers, academic medical centers, and hospital systems. She has also worked as a special assistant at the White House Office of Management and Budget during the drafting and passage of the Affordable Care Act, as a regional field director for the 2008 Obama for America campaign, and as a senior associate at UBS Financial Services. Beth lives in Washington, DC, with her husband and four young children.

3.

Why Invest and Not Just Give?

What is an investment portfolio?

An investment portfolio is a collection of financial investments like stocks, bonds, exchange-traded funds, mutual funds, and other product types. Portfolios may also contain a wide range of assets including real estate, gold, art, and private investments. Many investors carry a small amount of cash and cash equivalents in their portfolio.

WHY INVEST?

You may ask yourself, "Why should I choose to build a portfolio of socially just investments as the most effective use of my money? What about the financial resources I've already allocated for social justice purposes?"

For instance, you might donate your money to the Red Cross to fund relief programs when natural disasters devastate entire cities. Or you might use your savings to purchase a plane ticket to Washington, DC, to protest discrimination faced by the LGBTQ+ community at a march on the national mall.

When assessing the impact of their financial interventions, people should consider the two major differences between investments and other financial interventions for social justice.

Reason #1: Investments finance sustained action

While donations fund a point-in-time emergency response, investments offer a reliable stream of funding for organizations that know how to transform your dollars into authentic change.

Philanthropic organizations use your dollars to defend against further erosion of rights, power, and quality of life. Like Nicole in our earlier example of severe flooding in New York City, financial donations respond to a problem that has already become an emergency.

On the other hand, when Nicole expanded her actions from donations to investments, she combatted housing injustice at its source—creating safe, affordable housing. In the aftermath of terrible flooding, Nicole was able to not only donate to people who were already in a housing emergency, but also invest in long-term solutions that would hopefully prevent these emergencies from reoccurring in the future.

Reason #2: Investments let you recycle your money over and over again

Unlike other financial interventions, the money you contribute via investments is expected to return to you. It usually comes back with more money than you put in.

This structural design is different than donations, where there is no expectation or obligation that your donation will be returned to you. No one expects a mother to repay the Red Cross for the blanket that covered her newborn son after she gave birth in a makeshift hospital. The airline will not be returning the cost of your ticket to the march in Washington, DC. Those costs are expenses that will not be recouped. You likely budgeted for those costs, but you also know resources are not infinite. Investments offer an opportunity to not only recoup your costs, but actually build financial wealth while supporting the social justice causes you care about.

When you donate, the money is gone forever, but when you invest, you can give and give and give using the financial earnings from previous investments.

Five more reasons to invest in social justice

Investments work on your behalf even when you're sleeping.

Investments finance work that continues even when public attention fades.

Investments fund boots-on-the-ground professionals who know how to transform your dollars into social change.

Investments build your financial wealth.

Investments are an effective tool to convert your intention into long-lasting impact.

Investments are vehicles for your money

Wall Street professionals often refer to investment structures as "vehicles" that drive your money to organizations that know how to send it back refueled with income, profit, and earnings.

Traditional investors drive their money to companies and organizations with the intention of recouping maximum profits. Their goal is to get the "vehicle" back fast with as much money as possible.

Social justice investors drive their money to organizations that know how to transform justice-motivated contributions into social change. After a specified period of time, the vehicle is returned with financial earnings, plus evidence of authentic, on-the-ground advances in social justice. Social justice investments create benefits for the investor, the on-the-ground professionals who transform your dollars into impact, and the impacted communities.

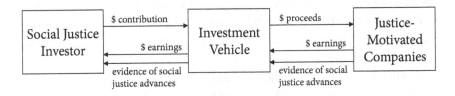

Traditional investments, on the other hand, follow the same general structure, but are designed such that the returns are exclusively defined as financial earnings:

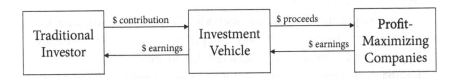

Let's consider an example of an investment vehicle that delivers sustainable financial earnings coupled with social justice returns.

Affordable housing company seeks justice-minded investors

Johnna ran into her boss's office with a freshly printed email in hand. "Dianne! The county just announced that the parcel of land in Aurora Hills has finally been approved for a housing development! Let's start pulling together the bid for our proposal!"

Johnna and Dianne worked for Affordable Housing Company (AffCo), an affordable housing developer with its headquarters in Arlington, Virginia, a close-in suburb of Washington, DC plagued by rising housing prices. Any homes available through its limited housing stock were quickly absorbed by buyers with deep pockets. It was not uncommon for houses to sell at 20% over the asking price after just three to five days on the market.

Anytime a new parcel of land became available for purchase, housing developers would race to compile competitive bids to win the site. In most cases, the rights to develop were won by the highest bidder. AffCo, which sought to build safe, decent housing for the county's low-wealth families, was typically outbid by mainstream developers whose luxury prices could offset the higher bid costs.

In this case, however, Arlington County put its finger on the scales. In an effort to expand affordable housing in the county, the local government had offered a tax credit as an extra incentive for developers who could keep the housing pricing below the county's average home prices. The tax credit lowered the overall costs of the project, which meant AffCo could better compete with the luxury housing developers.

Dianne and Johnna were determined to use this advantage to win the bid and build a housing development the owners would be proud to call home. Still, they needed to secure the financing to sew up the bid, so they set off to the bank to apply for a loan.

In the bank lobby, Dianne picked through the materials she had packed for the fifth time that morning.

"Okay, I've got our financial statements for the past three years, the letter from the county announcing the tax credit program, our plans for the Aurora Hills parcel, and examples from our latest developments."

Johnna smiled and patted the seat next to her. "Come sit down, Dianne. You've got everything we need." Her smile grew wider when she waved to Reggie, the loan officer assigned to AffCo.

"Good morning, ladies!" Reggie called. "Let's head to my office and get you sorted."

Reggie reviewed the statements, nodded his head to evidence of AffCo's extensive track record, and "Oohed" and "Aahed" over the pictures of new homeowners.

"This is all in good order. Falcon Bank is proud to support your work as a banking partner. What brings you here today?"

Johnna smiled. "We're here to discuss financing options for our bid on the Aurora Hills property. This development is about 15% larger than our most recent projects, so we'll need a bit longer loan. We're also hoping that our excellent track record will improve some of our financing terms. We're specifically looking to reduce our interest rate."

Reggie clicked his pen and began writing the highlights. "Yes, we've had quite a bit of interest in the Aurora Hills property. Even some of our individual clients have made inquiries about financing for pre-sales of the luxury homes."

Dianne's fingers tapped a silent rhythm on her legs. Competition from deep-pocketed developers was never a good sign. News that homeowners were making inquiries before they could even secure financing made her neck itch.

Reggie logged into his bank system to review the prevailing market rates. Frowning, he scribbled out a few notes. "Rates have been rising like crazy in the past few weeks. I don't know if I can go lower than the terms on the last loan. Give me a few minutes while I find my manager to ask. Maybe the tax incentive will give us a chance to make an exception."

Johnna and Dianne sat in nervous silence while they waited for Reggie's return. Without enough capital, they wouldn't be able to make a competitive bid, even with the tax credit lowering their overall expenses.

The wait seemed to stretch into hours, but Dianne's watch confirmed only 10 minutes had passed when Reggie returned with his manager, Seth.

Johnna's heart sank even as she plastered on her best professional smile.

Clearing his throat, Reggie introduced his manager and pulled his computer screen around to face Dianna and Johnna. "Unfortunately, we cannot offer you the lower rates you requested. In a rising rate environment, we have a responsibility to our clients and investors to remain competitive to other rates."

Dianne sighed. "I understand, Reggie. We'll just have to make it work with the rates we already have."

Reggie's eyes flickered to his notepad on the table.

Seth stepped in to support his loan officer. "Dianne. Johnna. I hope you know we deeply value you as clients and as community leaders. We see your incredible impact and appreciate your work to preserve and expand affordable housing in northern Virginia."

Johnna glanced at Reggie, who hadn't raised his eyes from the table.

Seth continued. "Unfortunately, we cannot honor the same rates we provided on your last loan with us. Market rates have risen too high and we will lose money if we offer you the rates you need to make your debt service payments."

Dianne's fingers froze their silent dance. "Wait. You mean we will have higher rates than our last deals? We can't afford that. It's not like we can pass the cost through to our customers."

Reggie frowned. Seth nodded contemplatively.

Johnna took a deep breath to steady her nerves. "Does our status as a long-time customer qualify us for an exemption?"

Seth shook his head and quietly answered. "We cannot offer any exemptions to any of our customers bidding for the same project. It could be seen as discriminatory."

Johnna nodded as she stood. "Dianne, please gather our materials. We'll have to regroup and discuss our options."

Seth stood and extended his hand. "Thank you for understanding. I hope that you'll consider our bank when you come up with the next iteration of your proposal."

Dianne and Johnna completed the expected niceties and moved toward the exit.

"Wait," said Reggie. "I'll walk you to the lobby and share our updated term sheet with you so you have all the information."

"Great. Thanks." Johnna was already out the door.

Halfway down the hallway, Reggie said, "Listen, Johnna. I'm really sorry about this. I am your biggest cheerleader and am extremely disappointed that we can't offer you the rates you need to get this project off the ground."

Reading Johnna's tight lips and quick walk, Dianne jumped in. "It's not your fault, Reggie. Thanks for doing what you can. We'll let you know where we land."

Reggie opened the door for Johnna and walked a few steps outside. "Johnna. Dianne. Here's the term sheet. It's been tailored for the Aurora Hills project to include the tax credit information."

Johnna blinked twice. "This is outrageous! The rates have doubled since our last project with you. And that was just last year! How on earth are we supposed to build affordable housing units with rates that have gone through the roof? You know construction costs have skyrocketed!"

Reggie looked around. "Please hear me. We've received inquiries from five other developers interested in the project. Market rates are rising and the other developers are able to accept the higher rates. It's impossible for us to justify offering you lower rates. Even if we were willing to risk a discrimination lawsuit, we can't cover the costs. The funding market would eat us for breakfast. Investors would never consider purchasing bonds at rates so low."

Johnna closed her eyes. "Thank you, Reggie. I understand. Thank you for the term sheet and this information. We'll be in touch when we have a chance to regroup."

AffCo lost the bid.

A luxury developer created a shiny new townhouse community in Aurora Hills. The average price of housing in Arlington increased. Low-wealth families near Aurora Hills watched the new development rise and braced for their own property taxes and rent payments to increase.

Tapping a new investor audience

Johnna and Dianne went back to the drawing board. After losing the bid, the senior leaders at AffCo met over lunch to discuss their financing options in the evolving market.

Johnna began the meeting by asking the big question: "How can we connect to capital that gets what we're trying to do?"

Dianne leaned in. "Not just that. We need investors who are willing to put up the financing required to get it done."

Stony silence engulfed the room. Pencils tapped against notepads.

AffCo's project manager, Steve, piped in. "I don't know how we're going to compete with the luxury developers. I fight every day to keep our costs down, but it's tough to compete with groups willing to pay double our construction budget. I don't know how to keep prices from rising."

"I hear you, Steve," Johnna replied. "Let's focus on the financing and see how it ripples out." She looked around the room, meeting each person's eyes in passing. "Does anyone have any ideas? Don't be afraid to think outside the box."

Dianne was doodling a series of stars and hearts on her legal pad. She did her best thinking with a pen in her hand. "Have you seen the new ETF product for affordable housing?"

Steve's head swiveled to Dianne. "What's an ETF?"

"An ETF is an exchange-traded fund. It's like a basket of stocks all combined into a single investment vehicle. We would join the ETF as one of the stocks along with other affordable housing companies. When investors purchase the ETF, they would be purchasing a piece of AffCo. The investor purchases the ETF with cash in exchange for a share certificate and an expectation for future returns. The cash is directed through the ETF into each of the ETF companies on a proportional basis."

Dianne walked to the front of the room and picked up a dry erase marker from the tray. "May I?" she asked Johnna, who smiled and nodded to the white board.

"Here's what it looks like."

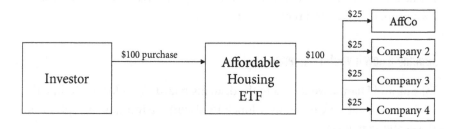

Dianne continued her explanation. "We would use the cash as capital to finance our next project. This money would be equity, so the investor receives financial returns that are based on our ability to generate profit."

Steve scratched his head. "Wouldn't that pressure for profit drive up our pricing?"

Dianne nodded, but Johnna jumped in. "I read somewhere that the affordable housing ETF advertises its returns as both financial and nonfinancial in nature. The investor goes in understanding that the financial returns are moderate in order to create space for nonfinancial returns like the development of affordable housing."

Johnna picked up another marker and started drawing arrows of her own. "That means that over time, we would send cash as financial returns to the investor through the ETF." Johnna turned to Dianne. "Do you think an 8% return is reasonable?"

Dianne nodded. "Yes, 8% is very reasonable given our historical performance. We averaged an 8.75% return over the past three years, but it's good to give a bit of cushion in case we hit unexpected turbulence. You should add it to the diagram."

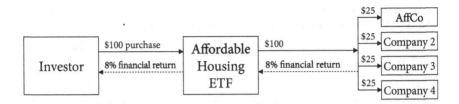

"We can't just offer financial returns if they're less than the market average. If we don't share how we're creating real change for the people who live in our housing sites, then the investor won't get the full picture of their investment's value. If they don't get the full picture, investors will gravitate toward highest-return investment options like the ones offered by luxury developers." Dianne drew an arrow under Johnna's and added the words "evidence of expanded homeownership."

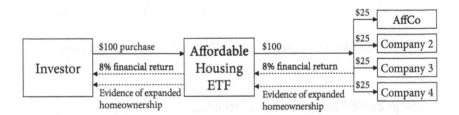

Steve, Dianne, and Johnna blinked at each other. Steve broke the silence. "Is that even possible? Why would investors buy that ETF? What financial returns could we offer? Would it be enough to compete with the other investment options?"

Johnna leaned against the wall, but Dianne tapped her marker against the "Investor" box on the white board. "It would depend on the intentions of the investor. If the investor wants to make real change, they'll have to consider lower-than-typical financial returns."

Johnna nodded. "Not only consider. They'd have to *prioritize* the nonfinancial returns in order to accept moderate financial returns."

Dianne's shoulders fell. "Who would prioritize nonfinancial returns?"

"Uh, people who understand that homeownership is a powerful driver of health and wealth for everyday Americans," said Steve. "Our projects create once-in-a-lifetime opportunities for families who are consistently shut out of homeownership, one of the primary tools for building wealth in America. You and I both know that the majority of our homeowners are people of color. Do you think they get any better responses than we did when they ask the bank for a loan?"

Dianne smiled, glancing around at her coworkers. "I know some people who get that. If we would be willing to make that choice, surely other people would too."

Johnna replaced the cap on her marker. "Dianne. Go figure out how to make this happen."

Fifteen months and many gray hairs later, Dianne announced that AffCo had successfully joined an affordable housing ETF traded under the name "HOME" (a hypothetical ticker created for illustrative purposes). She beamed around the conference room as she taped the press clippings to the white board. HOME was marketed as the nation's premier collection of affordable housing companies dedicated to creating homeownership opportunities for Black, Latinx, Native American, rural, and low-wealth communities across the country.

"Well, folks," Dianne grinned. "The cash spigot is open. Let's start building."

Energy Boost: Climate Justice Is Social Justice

Rachel Robasciotti

When I returned home from a week in Fiji, I expected to be jet-lagged and up at all hours as my body readjusted to life in San Francisco. Awake in the middle of the night, I unpacked my bags and settled into my pillows to post envy-worthy photos of my incredible trip. Mid-post, I was shocked to read a breaking news alert about the dam in Oroville, my tiny hometown in rural northern California.

I stared at my phone, unable to process the words that appeared on its screen.

"Oroville dam risk: Thousands ordered to evacuate homes."

My hand froze. Even as my eyes were trapped on the screen, the words blurred and my godmother's face floated to the top of my mind. Her house was in the direct flood path if the dam burst.

Clyme was the godmother who became a second grandmother to me. Growing up in the Southside of Oroville, Clyme was a bright light in our poor and segregated Black community. She was the one who taught me our town's history. How it was established around the major dam that was built there starting in the 1930s. How Black families migrated to Oroville from the American South for high-risk jobs building the dam. How the Black families building the town's physical and economic infrastructure were only allowed to live and buy homes in the Southside, the neighborhood with the highest risk for flooding from the very dam they were risking their lives to build.

Like many rural towns, unemployment in Oroville was very high. Good jobs were hard to come by and even harder for women. My community, with families primarily led by Black women, was chronically poor. Our community suffered from the kinds of problems that come from chronic resource deprivation. Growing up, my family was homeless multiple times and our neighborhood was not a safe or nurturing place for children to grow up.

But now that the dam was threatening to wash away the town, all I could think about was my godmother, whose arms had held me close during the hard times.

Still holding my phone, I blinked to reality when my home screen went dark. I jumped out of bed and started pacing my living room.

My mind was a frantic swirl of questions and panic. *Should I drive home? Is my family safe? Can I help?*

I wouldn't arrive for at least three hours and even then, I wasn't sure if I would be a help or a hindrance.

I decided to get more information first. I finally clicked the news alert and read more about Oroville's evacuation.

Traffic was one-way only: out. Out of town and out of harm's way.

I dropped my keys on the counter and sank down on my couch.

Fear, sadness, and anger rolled over me in waves.

With the racism, poverty, violence, drugs, and collective misery of the Oroville Southside where the Black folks were ghettoed, I had very mixed feelings about the idea of my childhood hometown being swept away.

Maybe all that water would wash away the pristine lake homes we were never allowed to enter; or the town's long history of white supremacy and bloodshed; or my grandmother's backyard littered with my aunt's used needles and her discarded, shoeless children.

But my godmother Clyme's front yard, the only safe place in my childhood world, would also be wiped off the map.

Grief welled within me.

This can't be happening, I thought miserably. *How did this happen?!*

The live news coverage filled in the gaps. I sat on my bed for hours, watching and listening to reports on the cause of the catastrophic infrastructure failure. Extreme weather fluctuations had stressed the aging infrastructure to a breaking point.

According to that evening's news anchors, officials expected a 30-foot wall of water to erase Oroville's Southside, just as the town's designers knew it would if ever the dam were to fail.

Now anger swelled.

Just as the residents of the 9th Ward saw during Hurricane Katrina, the poor Black neighborhood was the residential part of town with the greatest risk of flooding.

Once again, climate change hit the poorest, most marginalized communities first and hardest. And no one seemed to care. It was as if we as a society were willing to accept devastating losses of entire communities of people. Society was willing to devalue our existence because we were Black. Our lives were disposable.

I am not "okay" that certain populations take all the hits.

In that moment, watching Southside residents fleeing for safety, leaving their homes and community in the middle of the night, my grief and anger and sadness all rolled into a realization that transformed my understanding of social justice.

As a Black woman living in America, I never perceived climate justice as a priority issue. I figured that if Black and brown people were killed by police before they reached adulthood, what did it matter if the Earth didn't last another hundred years?

In February 2017, while frantically tracking down friends and family, I realized that Black and brown families would continue absorbing the hardest hits until we prioritize them and build a world where they are safe from climate change.

In that moment, I realized that climate justice *is* social justice, especially when the most vulnerable people become society's ultimate risk absorber. Climate justice is social justice when Black and brown families are intentionally placed in the path of catastrophic environmental damage, as they so often are.

Thankfully, the Oroville Dam only partially collapsed. The Southside is still there. Clyme's yard remains as the physical connection to my own history. My friends and family escaped the severe flooding.

Even after news crews moved on to cover other stories, my work fighting for social justice and climate justice didn't end. It was only beginning.

Contributing Author Biography

Rachel J. Robasciotti is the CEO and founder of Adasina Social Capital, an investment and financial activism firm that serves as a critical bridge between financial markets and social justice. Adasina Social Capital coined the phrase "social justice investing" and use it to describe their approach to managing investment portfolios. Rachel's passion for social justice investing is rooted in her background as a Black, queer woman and growing up in a community that struggled for safety and financial security within a rural town that was largely segregated. Among her many contributions, Rachel has been called upon to testify before the United States Senate regarding the state of financial markets. She is also regularly featured in the media as a leader in the financial industry for integrating issues of racial, gender, economic, and climate justice into investment portfolios.

4.

Reframing Returns

WHAT ARE RETURNS?

Returns are the measure of an investment's performance over time.

Whereas traditional investors define returns as the money made or lost on an investment, social justice investors define returns as sustainable financial earnings coupled with social justice advances.

Calculating financial returns

Calculating financial earnings is like measuring distance. Imagine inches along a ruler. Every dollar contributed is an inch. If you contribute 10 dollars, your contribution is 10 inches. If, at the end of three years, your investment has grown to 12 inches, the financial value of your investment has grown by 2 inches, or has demonstrated a positive 20% financial return. If at the end of the year the investment has shrunk to 8 inches, the financial value has declined by 2 inches, or has demonstrated a negative 20% financial return.

What are sustainable financial returns?

Financial earnings are critical for any investor interested in building wealth. Just because we have a twin goal of advancing social justice does not mean we can ignore or discount the financial implications of our investment selections.

Indeed, social justice investors should be finely attuned to the financial returns of their portfolios. We are regular people with everyday expenses.

We require financial earnings to pay for college tuition, down payments on new houses, and retirement plans.

When it comes to financial earnings, the difference between traditional investors and social justice investors is the concept of "enough."

Whereas traditional investors strive to maximize their financial profit, social justice investors target financial earnings that will *sustain* our cash needs throughout the course of our lives. In other words, social justice investors seek to generate sufficient cash to cover planned expenses as well as a reasonable financial cushion to cover unexpected life events.

Eschewing profit maximization goes against every fiber of Wall Street culture, whose collective rallying cry is "greed is good."

But social justice investors realize that Wall Street's promise of infinite returns is hollow. We have seen that this promise of maximizing profit at all costs means a lot for some and very little for everyone else. We want an economy that works for everyone.

Social justice investors purchase investments that reflect this financially sustainable approach.

HOW DO I KNOW WHAT IS "ENOUGH" FOR ME AND MY FAMILY?

The first thing you need to know is that everyone's financial situation is different. "Enough" for you may be "insufficient" for your neighbor.

The second thing you need to know? There is no simple answer. Having "enough" means generating sufficient financial earnings to cover expected life events (like retirement, college tuition, or opening a small business), plus some cushion in case of unexpected life events (like car repairs, celebrating the birth of a new child, or receiving a mountain of bills from a health emergency).

While you can work backwards to calculate the appropriate financial target for your initial assumptions, the challenge is our inability to predict the future. Life happens, derailing our carefully laid plans.

Traditional investors can short-circuit this human shortcoming by pursuing a single goal when they invest: make as much money as possible. Of course, then we fall into the vicious cycle of profit maximization where some people win big while others lose everything.

Successful investors aim for sustainable financial earnings by taking a step back to map out a budget of life events and plan their financial decisions accordingly. For instance, parents saving for their children's college tuition payments may deposit $100 each month in their child's college savings account. Others may set aside 6% of their salary each month in a 401(k) account to save for retirement. Still others may establish a DIY account to save money for a down payment on a home they'd like to purchase in the next three to five years. We adjust our financial plans as life happens and goals change.

Calculating an appropriate returns target depends on your risk tolerance as well as your time horizon. For instance, consider a young couple investing to pay for their newborn child's college tuition. A sustainable earnings target for them is one that enables their initial and ongoing investments to grow enough to cover college expenses 18 years down the road. The longer time horizon (18 years), coupled with a lower risk tolerance, means the couple can consider a lower risk, lower return potential offered from products like fixed-income securities.

At the same time, the young couple may also be saving for a down payment on a new home, which they hope to purchase by their child's fifth birthday. If they're starting from scratch, they may need to contribute higher volumes of cash into an investment account to accumulate enough wealth to afford a starter house. Given the shorter time horizon and the need to grow their money quickly, the couple will likely consider high-growth stocks and ETFs. While high-growth stocks offer a higher return, they are also considered higher risk than fixed-income positions.

This young family's definition of "enough" may be different from that of their neighbor, an 83-year-old retiree who's seeking to supplement his income through his investment portfolio. Our retiree may consider a 7% return from a mix of fixed-income positions and moderate-growth stocks to be enough to live comfortably.

"Enough" is relative. And a concept worth exploring with your financial partners.

For now, I encourage you to sketch out your financial life events on a blank piece of paper. Consider life events like a wedding, birth of a child, starting your own business, purchasing a house, buying a car, retirement, college tuition, or milestone travel events. Be sure to include a projected year by which you'll need funding from your investment portfolio.

In later chapters, we'll organize your financial events into an investment policy statement (IPS), also called an investor roadmap, which will help you determine an appropriate rate of financial return.

WHAT ARE SOCIAL JUSTICE RETURNS?

Social justice returns are evidence of authentic social change.

Whether you're investing in Black-owned small businesses to advance racial justice, buying stocks of companies that develop solar farms in low-wealth communities, investing in companies that pay a living wage to their hourly employees, or selecting an ETF that screens for companies that have adopted LGBTQIA+ equal employment policies, you as an investor need to see how your money is financing authentic social change.

The catch? Social justice returns are notoriously difficult to articulate.

Whereas financial earnings are linear and measured like inches along a ruler, social justice returns are expansive and measured like the volume of a balloon. When your dollars create authentic social change, they ripple out further than you will ever see or could possibly imagine.

Trying to gauge social justice returns with conventional investment tools is like trying to measure a balloon with a ruler: frustrating and wholly inadequate.

Social justice investors will do well to remember what James Clear taught us in his seminal classic, *Atomic Habits*: "In our data-driven world, we tend to overvalue numbers and undervalue anything ephemeral, soft, and difficult to quantify. We mistakenly think the factors we can measure are the only factors that exist. But just because you can measure something doesn't mean it's the most important thing. And just because you can't measure something doesn't mean it's not important at all."

Social justice returns cannot be neatly calculated in an Excel spreadsheet or comprehensively captured through a company's annual impact report. You may never know the full extent and ripple effects of the money you invested in a person that had previously been boxed out of the financial resources needed for success.

Consider how an investment in a childcare center expands to create positive social change for the families and community connected to it.

Authentic change creates positive ripple effects

Sandra Kingston and her daughters live in a two-bedroom apartment outside Boulder, Colorado. She earns a living as a bookkeeper at a local law office in downtown Boulder and commutes through 30 miles of traffic every day to keep her oldest daughter, a second-grade student, in the suburb's high-quality public schools. Her youngest daughter attends the Sunshine Daycare Center, the only affordable daycare center near Sandra's apartment. Most of the other parents hire nannies or send their children to the more expensive daycare that's closer to the local shopping district. The Kingston family maintains the financial balance of affording childcare, rent payments, and other living expenses—but the balance is a nudge away from teetering over.

Shortly after spring break, Sandra receives a note from the Sunshine Daycare Center notifying parents of a significant pricing increase in the next school year. The daycare center's lease payments are rising to reflect increased demand for retail space in the neighborhood. The popular shopping district's boundaries are creeping closer and retail shops are willing to pay a higher rate for the foot traffic of nearby shoppers.

Sandra is distraught. The family's financial perch was stable, but cannot withstand a significant increase in one of its biggest expenses—childcare. Without the affordability of Sunshine Daycare Center, Sandra will be forced to make some impossible decisions. She can't move any closer to downtown Boulder because the rent is too expensive and the schools aren't as good. She doesn't want to move further away because she'd have to find a new job, find money for moving expenses, and send her daughters to new, lower-quality schools. With similar expenses and potentially lower income, the family's housing options would deteriorate quickly.

Sandra has always considered her family as middle-income, but now realizes how tenuous her financial perch has been. She's terrified of being forced into a financial position that would teeter into hand-to-mouth conditions.

Fortunately, the Sunshine Daycare Center didn't give up on its own precarious financial conditions. Its owner, who was committed to her clients and her community, established a partnership with a community lender that applied a social justice lens to its investment decisions.

After meeting with Sunshine Daycare Center's owner and assessing the social justice impact of the service they provide to low-income families, the community lender provided a low-cost, long-term loan that enabled Sunshine Daycare Center to maintain its pricing structure to its families. In addition, Sunshine Daycare Center was able to partner with the community lender to hire more teachers from the community and offer extended hours to its students and their siblings.

The availability of earlier hours means that Sandra drops off both her daughters when the daycare center first opens, which cuts her morning commute in half. She arrives at the office earlier (and calmer with less traffic stress) and leaves on time, able to beat the evening commute and spend more quality time with her family.

The community lender invested in the potential of Sandra and other parents whose children attend Sunshine Daycare Center. It invested in the potential of the teachers hired to staff extended hours. And it invested in the potential of Sandra's children to attend a high-quality school and spend more time with their mom.

Social justice investments like the one to Sunshine Daycare Center create butterfly effects that ripple out, multiplying in impact far beyond the sightline of the immediate change.

Energy Boost: A Can of Worms—Enough Is Enough

Morgan Simon

This story is an excerpt from Morgan Simon's Real Impact: The New Economics of Social Change *(2017) and is reprinted with permission from the author.*

It was the summer of 2003. I was 20 years old and working in Sierra Leone under the auspices of the Special Court, the United Nations–sponsored body charged with trying to make sense of the 10-year civil war in that country. I was an economics and political science major at Swarthmore College, obsessed with the development field and dreaming of my eventual posting, perhaps under the auspices of USAID or the United Nations itself.

I had been matched with a local nonprofit called Green Scenery, led by Ashoka Fellow Joseph Rahall. My task was to evaluate, and suggest improvements to, a government-sponsored tree-planting program that had been recently launched, and was failing miserably for unknown reasons. It was not your typical human rights field assignment—but it is not every country where women have to worry about getting attacked when they go to collect firewood. And in the wake of mass migration to the "safer" city and coastal areas, as well as severe overharvesting during the war, the wood-collecting walk took women an average of six hours a day. Tree planting—and fast—was a huge priority for the Sierra Leone government, given that the vast majority of the population depended on firewood for their daily nourishment.

My work involved long stretches of time in rural areas, where people generally ate just once a day given the extreme poverty that still permeated the country: rice with greens and some dried fish around 3:00 p.m. each afternoon. If variety is the spice of life, I wasn't getting much of it—and certainly I was getting a much lower calorie count than my US-raised body was accustomed to.

One afternoon I was passing through Bo Town, the capital of Bo Province in the southeastern part of Sierra Leone. I stopped by a streetside vendor for lunch—you guessed it, rice, greens, and dried fish for 500 leones a plate at the time, about the equivalent of 20 cents. I then went to a local market to stock up on the provisions I would need before making my next trip to the countryside. As badly as I felt about "sneaking" food into my room, I would buy Weetabix and other treats so that I could have at least two meals a day, a tremendous luxury in the village.

A shiny object on the cart of a woman street vendor caught my eye—a can of tuna! Sad to say, I was pretty excited about the idea of a tuna fish sandwich.

And then I picked up the can. Clearly stamped on it were these words:

World Food Programme: Not for Sale
Gift from the Government of Japan

I asked the woman how much she wanted for the can: 2,500 leones, she said, or just over $1. I pointed out the "Not for Sale" label, and asked where she had gotten the can. She just smiled back and indicated that, though she spoke at least three languages fluently, she couldn't read the can. She just wanted to know if I was going to buy it or not, and if not, I should let her go on with her business.

She was a convincing saleswoman; I bought the can. With the 2,500 leones I paid for it, this woman could buy five heaping plates full of her and her children's preferred meal. Talk about a rational economics lesson: Clearly, selling the tuna was her best possible use of it.

Luckily for her, I, essentially an aid worker with a US dollar-denominated stipend, had disposable income with which to purchase it from her, since clearly no one else locally was going to pay 2,500 leones for a can of tuna that was supposed to be a free gift. So thankfully the government of Japan had donated excess tuna to the World Food Programme, which transported it a little more than halfway around the world to feed starving people, so that a streetwise woman could realize she could eat about thirty-five as many calories as it contained by selling it to a US aid worker.

Doing some very rough math on the equally rough ride back to the countryside, I calculated that the can of tuna generated at least one hundred times as much economic value for other people—including the Japanese fishermen, the government agents in Tokyo, and the World Food Programme office directors in Rome and Freetown—as it did for the supposed beneficiary. Presumably, the beneficiary of aid work is the one who receives the most benefit. It became crystal clear to me in that moment that if I pursued a career as an aid worker, the balance of my life's work was going to create much more value for those in power than those without it.

Contributing Author Biography

Morgan Simon has close to two decades of experience making finance a tool for social justice. In that time she has influenced over $150 billion and is a regularly sought-out expert on impact investing. Her book, *Real Impact: The New Economics of Social Change*, has been featured everywhere from Harvard Business School to the United Nations. She is a regular voice in the media and an active investor as founding partner of Candide Group, a registered investment advisor.

5.

Will My Investment Decisions Make a Difference?

Money is a tangible asset that lends itself to being easily measured, monitored, and molded. Think of money like clay: Cold and hard when sitting on a shelf, it has little value in and of itself. When an artist warms it between her hands and strategically molds it into a shape, it holds form and power. Molded into a bucket, it carries water. Sculpted into a brick, it transforms into shelter. When fired in a kiln, it is fortified and strengthened to last the test of time.

The clay in and of itself has minimal value. It is only when a person uses it as a resource to build with intentionality that it retains meaning and purpose.

You have that power.

Your investment decisions make a difference.

When enough people work together, they can shift the flow of capital toward justice.

Consider how investors significantly shifted the flow of capital away from the private prison and immigrant detention industry in the late 2010s and early 2020s.

When news of family separations at America's southern border began shedding more light on conditions inside private immigrant detention facilities, financial activists like Morgan Simon (author and cofounder of investment firm Candide Group) organized investment efforts for everyday investors to pull their money from the private prison and immigrant detention industry, which incarcerates nearly one tenth of the United States' total prison population and over 80% of immigrants in detention.

The two largest private prison companies, CoreCivic and Geo Group, issue debt and equity securities in the public capital markets to access capital necessary to cover expenses related to daily operations, as well as to finance expansions and new initiatives.

Private prisons are financed through the public capital markets. When they need cash to build the next detention facility, they ask investors to purchase a fixed income bond (where a bond is a loan to private prison operators from everyday investors) to be repaid over time. The operators get a loan and the investors are repaid principal plus interest. Shares of CoreCivic and Geo Group stock are often purchased through their inclusion within conveniently traded ETFs and mutual funds.

Private prison and immigrant detention companies repay their debt holders and distribute profit to their shareholders out of the revenue they earn by incarcerating people.

Private prisons earn revenue based on the number of incarcerated people living in their facilities. Private prison companies hold profitability as their core value and act accordingly. The more people incarcerated, the higher the revenue.

If the pursuit of profit is the lens through which the company makes decisions, then it would make perfect sense to do everything possible to dramatically increase the number of people incarcerated across the country, as this would increase demand for private prisons to absorb excess capacity from government-run campuses. An increased number of incarcerated humans directly translates into increased revenues and increased profit.

In fact, both CoreCivic and Geo Group explicitly identify a reduction in incarceration rates as a "material risk" (to their profitability) in their annual reports.

While private prisons are not the only reason behind the disproportionately high incarceration rate of Black and brown people, they are a significant contributing factor. Investing in private prisons has a negative effect on social justice in America.

Here's the kicker: Because private prisons view all decisions through a lens of profitability, investments in private prisons offer an attractive financial earnings return. You can make good money investing in private prisons.

Many investors are shocked to find they hold stock in private prisons in their 401(k) or retirement accounts. The companies use innocuous-sounding names that easily hide in a laundry list of run-of-the-mill organizations. Companies like Geo Group and CoreCivic lurk in the investment portfolios of everyday people who would be devastated to learn their dollars are used to fuel an industry that profits off human incarceration.

"CoreCivic" and "Geo Group" are not exactly exciting or even descriptive names. Their nondescript nature keeps investors from flagging the names as something worth exploring further. Instead, your eyes float from the name to the financial earnings history—boring name, high return, sounds great—before moving on to the next line.

Social justice investors took issue with the fact that positions in private prisons pervaded the industry, appearing in countless blandly titled investment funds.

Investors who are serious about ending police violence against Black Americans should recognize that investing in for-profit prison companies undermines those values. "If your portfolio includes private prisons," says Rachel Robasciotti, cofounder of Adasina Social Capital, "you are part of the problem. You can't passively sit there and let that conveyor belt move toward injustice."

"Want to work for racial justice? Organize, protest, vote, and spend with intention. **And stop giving your investment dollars to companies that exacerbate racial inequities.** When publicly traded companies employ these practices, the repercussions extend throughout the financial system."

Having been made aware of terrible conditions within private prisons and immigrant detention centers, social justice investors divested from (sold their existing investments in) for-profit private prisons. Investors searched through their individual stock positions for private prisons and asked their advisors to run a fine-tooth comb through any bundled investments like mutual funds and exchange-traded funds for private prisons hiding within a larger pool of diverse industries.

Everyday investors used their financial decisions to cut off private prisons from the capital needed for business expansion.

And it worked!

Social justice investors forced two of the country's largest for-profit private prison companies to tighten their financial belts by starving them of capital. An article in the *Financial Times* by Aziza Kasumov (August 8, 2020) noted that financial experts were shocked to observe how social justice investment strategies "actually work in that bottom-line sense of hurting the target economically." Their market value, which we know impacts profit for all shareholders, was being negatively affected.

The same article reported that, in 2019, the two largest for-profit private prisons in the United States were "changing their structure to slash debt, as rising pressure from social activists cuts their ability to reach capital markets."

The movement scaled, growing from everyday investors to Wall Street banks.

Large investment firms took note of their clients' values and followed suit. In March 2019, following a years-long public pressure campaign from social justice investors, JPMorgan Chase, Bank of America, and Wells Fargo announced that they would stop financing private prison companies.

Because social activists divested (sold) their previous purchases of for-profit private prisons, the companies didn't have access to the debt needed to run and expand their operations. Since they had been leaning on that debt for continued growth—which in turn was used to repay the initial debt—the private prisons have now had to eat into their cash accounts to repay debt. At the same time, they were unable to pay their investors as rich a dividend, making them less attractive investments to traditional investors who pursue the highest possible financial earnings returns.

With stock prices plunging and access to capital evaporating, the *Financial Times* article reported that "both companies are exploring asset sales." In other words, the financial position is so rough that the companies are making the hard decisions needed to stay afloat. It's the corporate equivalent of selling furniture to pay your mortgage.

Of course, the firms' chief executives cried foul.

The *Financial Times* article quoted Damon Hininger, CEO of CoreCivic, one of the largest publicly traded private prison operators in the United States, as saying that the cost of the company's capital has increased by its "incorrect" characterization as a "non-ESG [Environmental, Social, Governance] investment."

Personally, I can't read this quote without thinking of a sugar cookie declaring that it has been incorrectly characterized as a nonvegetable. After all, they both provide a body with calories.

In the same article, Geo Group's chief executive George Zoley also noted that "the current political rhetoric and mischaracterization of our role as a government services provider has created concerns regarding our future access to capital."

Spinning its role as a "government services provider" rather than a company that earns a profit for incarcerating individuals is a marketing spin. And the footwork isn't particularly fancy. Mr. Hininger calls the characterization of his firm as a "non-ESG investment" "incorrect." Mr. Zoley is a bit slicker, casting doubts by calling on the "current political rhetoric" as the boogeyman that would dare cast the for-profit private prison as anything other than a dutiful government services provider.

But it's not fair to paint the chief executives as blundering. They are experienced executives with an army of legal, operations, and marketing experts. Even as late as 2022, financial activist Morgan Simon was awaiting a court's ruling over a lawsuit filed against her by a private prison operator. The lawsuit against Morgan Simon and her firm Candide Group claims that certain of her statements on Forbes.com regarding their involvement in family detention and lobbying activities are "defamatory."

Social justice investors hit companies where it hurts. In their profits.

Our money is a powerful tool.

We make our money work to advance social justice. Our money makes a real difference to people who are impacted by decisions made by senior managers at large corporations.

It's only when social justice activists call out companies' pursuit of profit at the expense of people that investors take a second look. And then a third. Until social justice investors decide that they're just not interested in those particular profits.

When enough people direct their money into investments that fulfill their twin objectives of sustainable financial earnings and social justice advances, we collectively finance our vision of the world.

Money talks. What do you want yours to say?

Energy Boost: Insights from the Other Side of the Desk

Phuong Luong, CFP®

Before becoming a financial planner, I was a public school teacher in communities with stark income and wealth disparities. Then I worked in the nonprofit world as a trainer for financial coaches working with people living in subsidized housing before shifting gears to educate financial professionals. I've trained both nonprofit financial counselors and coaches, as well as financial planners working with wealthy clients. Now, I provide financial planning for folks managing wealth for the first time in their lives and who want to invest in line with their values.

My career has always cut across income and wealth spectrums. My mission, which began as a personal one, is to demystify personal finance and financial systems with a focus on closing racial wealth divides. As a result, education runs through everything I do. I want every person I work with to have confidence in themselves and their ability to make decisions about their money.

My career and work has always been guided by questions. *How can financial advisors help close gender and racial wealth divides? How does financial history relate to current economic inequality, both within the United States and globally? What is social justice investing?* Too often, I encounter clients who feel nervous when asking me questions about their financial goals. As a reminder for everyone reading this book: financial planners are paid (by you) to advise on how to reach your financial goals. It's our job to support you and provide strategies that work for you. Your questions are an important part of that process.

A key moment in my personal journey to social justice investing was a question from one of my first financial planning clients who wanted to invest in alignment with their values. In one of our regular check-ins, they surprised me by saying:

> We don't want to financially support companies that profit from incarceration. How can we take private prison companies out of our investment portfolio?

I didn't have an immediate response. I took a deep breath and answered with the most honest and straightforward response possible, one that had served me as a teacher and as a financial counselor, many times before:

> This is a great question. I don't know the answer. I'll research this and get back to you.

Alan and Kim were among my first clients when I started my own financial planning practice. The Boston-based couple earn six figures together. With dual incomes, a home requiring much-needed repairs, and three children in grade school, they first contacted me for help organizing their finances. Their personal goals were saving enough for retirement, contributing regularly to education savings accounts for their children, and achieving financial security. When I first met them, Kim worked for a racial justice nonprofit and the family wanted to invest according to their values.

Their question energized me and I was determined to help Kim and Alan remove companies involved in the prison industry from their investment portfolio.

Unfortunately, my formal training as a Certified Financial Planner didn't automatically prepare me to support a client interested in investing according to their values. And at that time, impact investing was mostly led by environmentally focused investments. There were no investment products focused on divesting from, or advocating against, companies profiting from incarceration.

I turned to online research and tapped into the community of financial professionals for support. I joined a newsletter from Sonya Dreizler, a thought leader in sustainable investing. I met other advisors doing abolition work, within their firms and in their personal organizing work. I learned about the Racial Justice Investing coalition, a global group of financial professionals combatting structural racism through finance. I attended a presentation hosted by a local investment firm. The presentation was led by Worth Rises, a nonprofit organization dedicated to dismantling the prison industry. I also learned about the work of The American Friends Services Committee's Investigate project, and the importance of defining the problem and having the right research before attempting to divest from the prison industry in one's portfolio.

During my exploration, I also learned about publicly available investment screening tools, such as As You Sow's prison-free funds screener. Based on those tools, I was able to confirm that Kim and Alan did have investment positions in companies they didn't want to hold. Unfortunately, since their investments were held in their employer-sponsored 401(k)s, they were limited to choosing from the menu of investments offered by their employers.

I reviewed each investment option in their 401(k) investment menus but couldn't find immediate solutions. Although I had learned so much from the research I had done in response to their question, I was disappointed with the answer I had to deliver during my next call with them.

"I'm really sorry to share this. I looked through the menu of 401(k) options provided by your employers, but none offered a prison-free approach."

"Thank you very much for digging into this, Phuong. We appreciate your hard work."

Kim and Alan are still clients and I continue to support their goal to build a strong financial foundation for their family. While I wasn't able to meet their values-based objective in that initial research dive, their question primed me to keep an eye out for future options. Even while moving forward with their personal financial goals, I kept learning so I could support their impact goals. At every step, I asked questions to guide my learning:

> What tools exist to help investors sort through generic-sounding index funds? Are there investment products, either on or off Wall Street, that support a more just economy and world, or at least reduce harm to people and the planet? Why don't 401(k) accounts have more values-based investing options?

Having these questions in my mind informed my work moving forward. When Alan transitioned to a new company, I reviewed his new 401(k) fund menu and found options that did not include investments in prison-related companies.

Later, when they asked me if they held positions in weapons and fossil-fuel companies, we were able to screen for these industries much more quickly.

Kim and Alan launched me on a winding path to better understanding what it means to invest in a socially just way. Their initial question led me to asking deeper questions about my role as a financial advisor—and I found a community of advisors asking these questions too.

I met financial professionals and activists eager to collaborate so we could explore together how financial services perpetuate harm against people and the planet, and what we can do about it. That network led me to Adasina Social Capital, a social justice investing firm, where I worked to help build the first exchange-traded fund that offers everyday investors an investment product with rigorous and transparent community-led divestment standards.

I'm really fortunate to have had the opportunity to work on building a financial product that meets the divestment standards my clients asked me to put into action for them years ago. I'm grateful to my clients for continuously encouraging me to provide financial planning in line with my values and not holding back their meaningful and important questions.

Contributing Author Biography

Phuong Luong, CFP® (she/her) is an educator and financial planner at Just Wealth. Phuong understands the current and historical barriers to building financial wealth for so many communities in the United States. This knowledge comes from her experiences as a former teacher, nonprofit professional, and student of financial history and structural/systemic inequality, and from her own upbringing. Phuong is a member of the CFP board's Center for Financial Planning's Diversity Advisory Group to build pathways to attract and retain financial planners from diverse backgrounds into the financial planning profession, and recently served as chair of the CFP board's Council on Education, where she advised on the development of education standards and certification requirements for CFP professionals. Previously, she worked with Adasina Social Capital to develop their global social justice index and ETF. Phuong is also a facilitator for the Boston University Financial Planning Program and a contributor to Morningstar, where she writes about financial planning and sustainable investing for an advisor audience.

6.

Do I Need—and Can I Afford—a Financial Advisor?

Whether you're working through an employer-sponsored retirement plan like Tom, pursuing a DIY investment strategy like Angela, or working with a professional financial advisor like Nicole, you'll likely seek advice from time to time from a trusted partner. Your financial partner may be a human resources manager at work, a mobile app on your phone, or a financial advisor you pay to execute your financial vision. Perhaps you call a parent, friend, or sibling for financial guidance or investment tips.

Insider's Tip: No matter what, your significant other is most definitely a financial partner that you need to bring on this journey with you.

YOUR SIGNIFICANT OTHER IS YOUR MOST IMPORTANT FINANCIAL PARTNER

Most people forget their most important financial partner: their significant other. I've lost track of how many times a friend confided in me of their need to circle back to the beginning of their investment journey to onboard their spouse, partner, boyfriend, or girlfriend.

Amy March, in Greta Gerwig's 2019 adaptation of *Little Women*, hit the nail on the head when she described marriage as an economic proposition. While modern relationships are based in romance, love, and commitment, they are also financial partnerships.

While you don't have to agree on investment approaches, you do need to find a way to reconcile any differences into a workable arrangement. Perhaps that means you keep separate financial portfolios or 401(k) selections. Maybe you hire two separate financial advisors. If the stars align and you and your partner both identify as social justice investors, you may even design a joint account that finances the future you envision together.

Either way, if you have a significant other, they'll be one of your most important financial partners.

For advice on how to broach the subject with your partner, please refer to the conversation scripts for "The Talk" in chapter 8.

DO I NEED A PROFESSIONAL FINANCIAL ADVISOR?

A financial advisor (also known as a financial coach, money manager, wealth manager, investment advisor) is a trained professional who provides guidance in how to manage your money according to your financial situation, goals, and investment personality. In the United States, financial advisors must complete specific training and be registered with a regulatory body in order to provide advice.

Hiring a financial advisor can feel intimidating. Many people feel like they don't belong in the "investing class." Others have heard that financial advisors have a reputation for arrogance or pretentiousness. Still others worry that a financial advisor may judge them for how much or how little money they've saved or invested before now.

Your feelings are valid and I respect your experiences, yet I'm asking you to start fresh as a social justice investor. Whether you're examining your 401(k) options, putting aside a few dollars every month to create an investment portfolio, or considering how to tackle accumulated wealth, financial advisors can be a powerful ally to have in your corner. Plus, financial advisors now offer a wide range of pricing options to meet their clients' budgets.

Let's start by addressing a few common assumptions about hiring a financial advisor:

Yes, you can afford a financial advisor.
Yes, a financial advisor will be helpful in creating wealth for your family.
Yes, you can find an option that works for you and your family.

It's extraordinarily helpful to lean on someone who can help you manage your money according to your values and financial objectives. Someone who *makes it their job* to watch the market and look for opportunities that meet and exceed your expectations.

A financial advisor is trained to transform your vision into reality. Otherwise, your goals are more likely to remain daydreams.

COMMON TERMS DESCRIBING FINANCIAL ADVISORS

A financial advisor might have any of these certifications or titles, but you can think of them as shorthand for their type of education, experience, and specialization.

Certified Financial Planner (CFP): A CFP is an individual that has received a formal designation from the Certified Financial Planner Board of Standards, Inc. CFPs help individuals in a variety of areas in managing their finances, such as retirement, investing, education, insurance, and taxes. Becoming a CFP is a difficult and stringent process. It requires years of experience, successful completion of standardized exams, a demonstration of ethics, and a formal education.

Chartered Financial Analyst (CFA): A CFA charterholder is an individual who has received a formal designation from the CFA Institute. A CFA charterholder is an investment professional who provides investment guidance and portfolio management for individuals, businesses, and other organizations. CFA charterholders often work with corporate clients on the investment analysis side, whereas a CFP works with individual investors in building a financial plan.

Certified Public Accountant (CPA): A CPA is a designation provided to licensed accounting professionals. To become a CPA, you must pass a rigorous exam; meet education, work, and examination requirements; and complete 150 hours of education. Many people hire professionals with a CPA designation to help prepare and file their taxes.

Chartered SRI Counselor (CSRIC): The CSRIC program is a designation program for financial professionals offered by US SIF. This program provides experienced financial advisors and investment professionals with a foundation knowledge of the history, definition, trends, portfolio construction principles, fiduciary responsibilities, and best practices for sustainable, responsible, and impact (SRI) investments.

Financial Counselor: Financial counselors, sometimes called "money coaches," help people build financial skills and improve their overall financial health. Financial counselors often help families manage current expenses, build savings, and make plans to pay off debt. Financial counselors are often the most affordable type of financial advisor.

UNDERSTANDING THE COSTS

Financial advisors are commonly perceived as being too expensive for the everyday investor. We've been taught to believe that investors must bring hundreds of thousands of dollars to the table to be treated with respect as a potential client.

I have good news for you. Innovative disruptions in the traditional financial planning industry have spurred today's advisors to change their business plans and pricing policies in order to retain existing clients and attract new ones.

Today's financial advisors face intense competition from web-based platforms like online DIY investment accounts and AI-based financial planning tools.

These disruptive innovations have created a path for everyday investors to access financial planning services that were previously only accessible to the already-rich. In other cases, clients who've been conditioned to feel intimidated by financial advisors are flocking to alternative resources that don't come with emotional baggage.

To compete with automated investment opportunities, financial advisors now offer a wide range of pricing options, including affordable options for investors on a budget. For instance, a "fee-only" advisor charges a flat fee per hour of work, enabling the investor to negotiate a defined budget for a specific scope of work.

As more and more financial advisors offer approachable price ranges, new investors are discovering that partnering with a trained and motivated financial professional allows them to get serious about their investment goals.

For instance, employees seeking to better understand their 401(k) choices can ask for help from a financial coach (sometimes available through and paid for by their employers). Families blessed with accumulated wealth may hire a financial advisor to sort through their list of investments and design a strategy that better matches their values.

For DIY investors, the most affordable option is to forgo the help of human advisors entirely and instead use online trading platforms to invest their budget of investment dollars.

Either way, today's social justice investors can select from a wide range of pricing scenarios and corresponding levels of support from financial professionals, as described below.

Pricing scenario 1: Bypass the financial advisor and "do it yourself"

The rise of web-based platforms has enabled everyday investors to move their own money without paying fees or commissions to professional advisors. A DIY approach works well for people with both investment management skills and adequate time to use those skills.

On the flip side, a DIY approach also means that you forfeit the oversight and support of a trained professional who is paid to manage your portfolio on your behalf.

Today's DIY investors benefit from a plethora of online investment account platforms. You've probably heard of Schwab.com, Ellevest.com, Robinhood.com, and Fidelity.com, each with its own pricing structure. Given the multitude of platforms, many offer their clients benefits like commission-free trading and no account minimums.

The DIY approach is best for people who are confident in their abilities to manage their money without the assistance of a trained financial professional. Be careful, though. DIY investors will need to consistently carve out the time required to manage their portfolio's performance and stay up-to-date on social justice investment opportunities not always advertised on mainstream financial media.

Pricing scenario 2: Fee-only or hourly-rate financial advisor

The "hourly fee" pricing structure (also known as fee-only financial planning) has emerged as a new financial advisor subculture. It is designed for beginner investors with smaller portfolios looking to improve their financial health through guidance on budgeting, retirement planning, and tax considerations. Hourly fees democratized financial planning services for everyday people who don't yet have a financial portfolio measured in hundreds of thousands of dollars.

Even 401(k) investors, seeking help understanding their menu of investment options, may hire a fee-only financial advisor for a few hours using a limited budget. Because they charge on an hourly basis, financial advisors using this pricing structure can work with clients regardless of their wealth and aren't influenced by the size of their clients' portfolio. Families are also delighted to discover that these financial advisors don't just offer investment opportunities, but also offer guidance on everyday financial planning approaches like how to apply for a home mortgage, build an emergency fund, create a retirement savings plan, save for a child's college tuition, invest an unexpected financial windfall, or allocate investment assets based on your age.

A fee-only financial advisor charges their clients a flat fee for their work, which can range anywhere from $50 to $400 per hour. Investors working with fee-only financial advisors will need to be careful about managing the number of hours the financial advisor spends on their account. Be clear and determine upfront whether your budget and your expectations are aligned with the financial advisor's expertise and affordability.

Social justice investors should aim to find a financial advisor that has experience with or is willing to research investment options that reflect social justice values.

Pricing scenario 3: Percentage-based financial advisor

Percentage-based financial advisors are old-school money managers who charge a fee based on the dollar size of their clients' portfolio. Typical costs range from 0.5% to 1.25% of your total portfolio dollar size, though that annual fee is broken into monthly or quarterly payments. An advisor will typically charge a smaller percentage as the portfolio gets larger.

As a result, percentage-based financial advisors are best for investors with larger portfolios ($200,000 or more) who want an advisor to manage their portfolio for growth.

Consider the math. If you have $10,000 to invest, the pricing structure means an advisor would only earn $50 to $125 on your portfolio each year. It takes the same amount of time to create a diversified, well-performing $10,000 portfolio as it does a $200,000 portfolio. This pricing structure requires a significant volume of assets to offset the costs.

Even if your portfolio exceeds the threshold, social justice investors may find it challenging to work with percentage-based financial advisors, who are incentivized to grow their client's portfolio (and accompanying fees) through profit maximization. It's hard to establish and maintain a portfolio that generates social justice returns if you're consistently encouraged to accept profit-maximizing return opportunities.

Indeed, partnering with a percentage-based financial advisor means a series of hard conversations and the discipline to stay focused on social justice priorities.

HOW DO I DECIDE?

The good news is that you have lots of options to choose from. The bad news is that it can feel overwhelming to figure out where to start, much less finding the best fit.

Here's a decision tree to help you along your way.

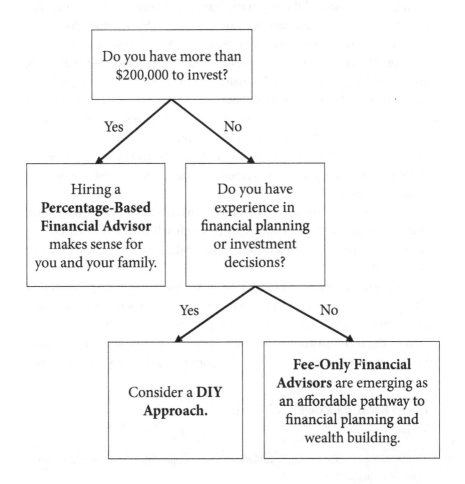

If you have more than $200,000 to invest, then your significant financial portfolio offsets the costs of traditional money management. Managing this volume of money requires time and skill, and hiring a **percentage-based financial advisor** makes sense for you and your family.

If your financial portfolio is less than the $200,000 threshold and you do not have experience in financial planning or investment decisions, you may want to consider working with a **fee-only financial advisor.** This subset of financial advisors is emerging as an affordable pathway to financial planning and wealth building. The next section will help you identify a planner that both fits in your budget and works to meet your financial goals.

If you do have experience in financial planning or investment decisions, then you may consider a **DIY approach**. Your experience means you may take advantage of online investment accounts, which enable you to reduce costs and manage your own portfolio based on your specific investment objectives. Of course, if you prefer a person to provide you with guidance and guardrails, consider working with a fee-only financial planner for additional guidance.

You are not restricted to a single course of action. It's perfectly acceptable (and fairly common) to split your financial assets into more than one portfolio.

Wealthy families often hire multiple percentage-based financial advisors to further diversify their portfolios and compare performances over time.

Other families keep their retirement savings plans separate from their wealth-building portfolios.

Or, if you want to try your hand at DIY investing, you can always open a small account and build your skills through self-directed research and trading while working with a fee-only financial advisor to manage the rest of your assets.

The variety of options means it's easier to customize the approach that makes you feel empowered to get the financial and social justice returns you want. No matter what route you've chosen, getting started can be intimidating.

Here's the secret to accomplishing a big goal: keep taking the next step. You can always refer back to the other options if you change your mind later.

Energy Boost: Date Night with Bob Iger

Leah Fremouw

To me, the perfect date night includes romance, laughter, and life-changing career decisions.

My husband and I schedule nights out to coincide with the Richmond Forum series at our local Altria Theater. We love listening to innovative leaders describe their secrets to success in business, politics, arts, and education.

This particular evening, Jacob and I had ventured out into freshly plowed streets to listen to Bob Iger, The Walt Disney Company's recently retired CEO, speak about all things Disney, tech, business, and leadership.

It isn't every day that Bob Iger speaks at a community theater in Richmond, Virginia. If he was going to brave Richmond airports and roads immediately following a snowstorm, then my butt would be in my seat, even if I had to climb across the row in my snow boots.

Twenty minutes after the theater's lights dimmed, Mr. Iger and his interviewer, Kara Swisher (tech journalist at the *New York Times*), got into the good stuff.

I was perched on the edge of my seat, fully engaged in the conversation. Ms. Swisher coaxed out Iger's sense of humor and their combined energy radiated out through the room.

When Mr. Iger began talking about the need to push boundaries at work, though, my laughter faded.

For months, or maybe even years, I had been resisting the urge to break away from my current career trajectory to carve out a new path for myself.

I had been with my current company, a financial institution focused on lending in Virginia's low-wealth communities, for over six years. I dearly loved (and still love!) my colleagues there, and I learned so much about working in finance and investment—from credit-underwriting policies (who should get a loan and for how much) to accounting technology to lending operations.

While each function is vital, I had discovered *my* joy in building relationships with the people and communities in which we invested money.

I love driving across Virginia to visit with people brimming with ideas about how to build their community, whether through small businesses on Main Street or creating affordable housing by repurposing a historic factory . . . if only they had access to capital.

As it was, the communities I visited felt locked out of the financing they needed to succeed. Sometimes even by community lenders like the one I worked for.

My job was to dig deeper, identify a solution, and forge a pathway connecting communities to affordable financing.

I found many pathways for the people and places I visited. Sometimes my solutions were approved by the company and financed spectacularly successful programs.

Other times, they were blocked at the outset.

The explanations for the rejections were always reasonable. Sometimes the pathways would have required substantial changes to operational infrastructure. Other times they would have required an exemption from board-approved credit-underwriting policies. Even for a loan fund committed to providing capital to underserved communities there seemed to be red tape I just couldn't cut.

I understand and respect my company's position. They had to answer to investors, funders, and regulators that wouldn't have understood why we were willing to change our time-tested underwriting approach to reach a particular community. If your investors capitalize your balance sheet with the explicit agreement that your underwriting policies cannot be changed with their written approval, I wouldn't want to make any unnecessary tweaks either.

Still, rejected pathways meant the people and communities already shut out of capital were still locked out of the financing they needed to reach their full potential.

So when Bob Iger spoke about pushing boundaries as a leader, the desires that I kept pushing down came bubbling up to the surface.

When Mr. Iger said he felt like he had finally arrived when he was given a role where he could push boundaries and break the mold, goosebumps prickled over my arms.

I had the skills and relationships. Friends had helped me get the funding. I actually had what I needed to make a difference for people who had been shut out from their full potential for so long.

What I lacked was the autonomy and flexibility to carve out more innovative financing pathways.

Goosebumps prickled because I was considering an opportunity to take a chance on pulling this off.

A group of funders wanted to break the mold of community lending and they were willing to put up the cash to do it. They wanted to create a lending organization that made loans without pulling credit scores and to build credit analyses through more comprehensive (and less biased) credit indicators.

They wanted to hire me as the new organization's CEO.

I was scared.

I was my family's main breadwinner. My career at my current company was stable, certain, and predictable. It came with great benefits.

But when Bob Iger described how every success emerged from the risk of breaking the mold, the hairs on the back of my neck stood up.

I gripped Jacob's hand. My husband knows me well enough to realize I was thinking about the job offer. He grinned at me and squeezed my hand.

"I believe in you. Do what you need to do." He was echoing his sentiments from every family discussion we'd had about me rocking the boat on my family's financial health.

I pulled out my phone before I lost my nerve. I hid my phone under my scarf and tapped out a quick message to my good friend and soon-to-be boss.

"I'm here at the Richmond Forum listening to Bob Iger. I'm ready to make a move. Let's talk tomorrow."

My phone buzzed a few moments later to reveal a thumbs up emoji.

About two weeks later, I accepted the job as president and CEO of Bridging Virginia, a nonprofit community lender with big dreams and a little bit of money.

Launching a startup hasn't exactly been a piece of cake. I'm convinced that formalizing credit policies and documenting operational practices cost me several years of my life.

Even with all the headaches, I love the ability to create new pathways for financing to flow to the people and places with whom I'd spent years building relationships. I love returning to communities with a "Yes, the solution you suggested is happening. The money is coming soon. Let's get to work!"

I'm proud of the collaborations I've pursued with colleagues from my previous company. As it turns out, working together means we can reach deeper into communities that previously heard "not today" or "not quite ready yet."

Now, however, my husband Jacob warns me that we can't go to the Richmond Forum for date nights if it means I'll be inspired to pick up a new business line.

We picked up pickleball instead.

Contributing Author Biography

Leah Fremouw's commitment to her community brings her out of the office and into on-the-ground community investing initiatives. Her current role as CEO of Bridging Virginia, a nonprofit community lender, enables her to form a bridge between Virginia's low-wealth communities and investors dedicated to inclusive growth. Leah is also board president of the Virginia CDFI Coalition and cohost of *Renegade Capital: The Activist's Podcast for Finance and Investments*.

7.

How to Hire a Financial Advisor

This chapter is designed for investors who are interested in hiring a professional financial advisor to support and help execute their investment goals. It provides step-by-step instructions for how to identify and hire either fee-only or percentage-based financial advisors, which are described in chapter 6.

HOW TO FIND A FEE-BASED FINANCIAL ADVISOR

Everyday investors generally find fee-only financial advisors through two methods: referral from a friend or a cold Google search.

First, ask your friends and family if they happen to work with a financial advisor. If your friend or family is happy with their financial advisor's performance, they will gladly recommend their services to a friend. You get the peace of mind that comes with knowing that someone else is satisfied with their performance. Here's a conversation starter:

> I'm looking to improve my family's financial position and need some help. Do you happen to know of any financial advisors that you would recommend? I'm specifically looking for guidance on budgeting and investment decisions.

If you do receive a positive recommendation, ask for the financial advisor's name and contact information.

If your friends and family don't currently work with a financial advisor or if you'd prefer to keep your search more private, then a cold Google search is an excellent way to find a fee-only financial advisor.

Enter "fee-only financial advisors near me" into the search bar and voilà: the World Wide Web delivers once again.

To try and narrow your search, you can include additional terms that might point you to an advisor that has experience with social justice investing, such as "ESG" or "socially responsible." While this won't turn up every advisor capable of helping you invest according to your goals, it can be comforting to know you are working with an advisor already experienced in creating values-aligned or impact-focused portfolios for their clients.

Conversation script for a prospective financial advisor

The next step is to contact the financial advisors on your list and ask for an introductory conversation. Nervous about making cold calls? Here's a sample conversation script to help you along your way:

> **You:** Hello, my friend Jane recommended you as a financial advisor. (Or: I found your contact information through a Google search.) I'm looking to improve my family's financial position and need some help. Are you currently accepting new clients?

> **Financial advisor:** So nice to meet you! Yes, I am accepting new clients. Could you please tell me about yourself and the type of financial planning services you are looking for?

> **You:** I am looking for a fee-only financial advisor who can help me get my finances together. I'm interested in learning more about your services regarding budgeting and wealth building.

> **Financial advisor:** Wonderful, I can absolutely help you with that. Let's schedule an introductory conversation with all the family decision-makers.

> **You:** Great. Here are a few times that work for us. Before we continue, can you please give me a sense of your hourly rate? My family is working on a budget and I want to make sure we're on the same page.

> **Financial advisor:** Absolutely, my hourly fee is $75. I appreciate my clients' budgets and will work with you to find the right balance. The

introductory conversation is free and we can nail down a budget and scope of work if we decide to work together.

You: That sounds fantastic, thank you.

Financial advisor: Great. I'm looking forward to our next phone call. Do you have any other questions before we hang up?

You: Yes. I'm very interested in aligning my money according to my values. Do you have any experience with social justice investing?

Pathway 1:

Financial advisor: More and more of my clients are interested in socially responsible investing and I have been researching options that work well for them. Let's discuss your objectives in greater detail during our upcoming call and see what might work best for you and your family.

You: Fantastic! Looking forward to connecting with you then.

Pathway 2:

Financial advisor: Unfortunately, I don't specialize in nontraditional investing.

You: I understand. Aligning my portfolio with my values is very important to me. Could you please point me in the direction of someone who might have this expertise?

Financial advisor: Yes, I recommend Jonelle Smith. I'll send you her telephone number.

You: Thank you!

Repeat this step until you identify the financial advisor that offers the services you need, works within your budget, and can deliver products that meet your social justice investing objectives.

Making the hire

Finding "The One" takes time to get right. Remember that your investment journey is a marathon, not a sprint. We're talking about finding the person who will manage your ability to build wealth and advance social justice. Spend the time you need to get it right, even if it means a handful of phone calls. Schedule time to make one of these 10-minute phone calls every day for a week. At the end of the week, you'll have conducted significant research and will feel more confident in your hiring decision.

Once you've interviewed several prospective financial advisors, you may be wondering how to select from among them for affordability, experience in the services you require, and ability to deliver social justice investment opportunities.

When evaluating financial advisors, I recommend finding someone with relevant credentials or professional training. For instance, the Certified Financial Planner (CFP) designation is the highest professional standard in the financial planning industry. CFP denotes that a financial planner has extensive training and knowledge, as there are rigorous education requirements and a lengthy certification exam to earn the certification.

As an added bonus, advisors can also earn the Chartered SRI Counselor (CSRIC) designation to denote their expertise in sustainable, responsible, and impact investments. A CSRIC designation is a very good sign that your financial advisor will understand how to integrate social justice investments into your financial planning goals.

You can also ask your financial advisor for references from existing clients. You can ask questions about the advisor's ability to stick to the budget, experience with social justice investments (or socially responsible investments if the other client is unfamiliar with the term), and customer service. You cannot ask personal questions about the client's financial position, but you can ask if the client is happy with the advisor's ability to help improve their financial position.

The final step is to sign an engagement agreement, or promise that you will pay for services rendered on an hourly basis, with your selected financial advisor.

Many financial advisors use a standard engagement agreement to formalize advisor–client relationships. This is a great opportunity to ask the financial advisor to walk through the agreement section by section, paying particular attention to hourly fees, commissions, and other pricing structures. You also want to review the scope of work to ensure that it meets your expectations of the type of services your financial advisor will provide. You can also ask that the advisor include a budget ceiling that needs to be renegotiated if the total fees exceed a certain dollar amount.

HOW TO HIRE A PERCENTAGE-BASED FINANCIAL ADVISOR

Hiring a percentage-based financial advisor is very similar to hiring a fee-only financial advisor.

Start by identifying a pool of prospective percentage-based financial advisors, sometimes called wealth managers, either through references from friends and family or through a Google search.

You'll likely encounter household names like Merrill Lynch, Charles Schwab, and Fidelity, or perhaps you'll get a reference for an independent wealth manager not connected to one of the major houses.

How to screen a percentage-based financial advisor

Once you've identified a list of prospective advisors, the next step is to screen your shortlist based on performance history, schedule of fees related to trading fees and commissions, and client references.

As described in the previous chapter, percentage-based financial advisors usually charge the investor a set percentage of an investor's portfolio value and are incentivized to grow their client's portfolio's total dollar amount as quickly as possible. The higher the value of your portfolio, the higher their take-home pay.

Percentage-based financial advisors typically demonstrate their value to prospective clients based on their performance history of growing their clients' wealth. Investors interested in working with percentage-based financial advisors should ask prospective advisors how their assets under management have grown over a given time period and what percentage fee they'll charge to manage and grow your portfolio of financial assets.

Evaluate their willingness to pursue social justice returns

The final step is to ask the financial advisor to describe their ability and willingness to pursue social justice investment opportunities

Percentage-based financial advisors are typically incentivized to prioritize the highest growth opportunities permissible in a given risk appetite. Social justice investment opportunities, which are not usually considered a high earnings opportunity, are often screened out of percentage-based portfolios seeking the highest financial return possible.

Social justice investors employing percentage-based financial advisors will require consistent discipline and dedication to insist on a portfolio characterized by positive social justice returns. This approach is very possible, but it does require your financial advisor to be a willing and cooperative participant.

Luckily, there are a growing number of financial advisors who specialize in impact investing, social justice investing, and other types of values-based investing. It's best to screen for this at the beginning of a relationship rather than struggling through a series of uncomfortable and frustrating conversations.

For tips on how to start "The Talk," please refer to chapter 7. Until then . . .

Make the hire

The final step is to sign an engagement agreement with your selected financial advisor. Most financial advisors use a standard engagement agreement to formalize advisor–client relationships. This is a great opportunity to ask the financial advisor to walk through the agreement section by section, paying particular attention to fees, commissions, and other costs.

DISRUPT THE PATTERN, HIRE DIVERSE

Repeat this fact until you can cite it in your sleep: 98.6% of people who manage wealth in the United States identify as both male and white.

Yep, wealth decisions in the United States are managed by people who almost exclusively identify as white males.

Think about all the butterfly effects of having a financial system controlled almost exclusively by people who identify as both white and male.

Take the time you need for a deep sigh.

Social justice investors disrupt this pattern by hiring from a diverse pool of financial advisors. We do our absolute best to hire an advisor who is either a person of color or identifies as female or outside the gender binary. Or both.

Will hiring diverse impact my portfolio's performance?

I can happily write that taking your first step toward embracing your role as a social justice investor has multiple benefits. In addition to supporting diversity in the financial industry, you will also enjoy a higher likelihood of exceptional financial performance.

A robust January 2019 study released by the Knight Foundation and Bella Research completed a deep dive of diverse-owned firms (i.e., women-owned firms and minority-owned firms) in the wealth management industry. The research waded knee-deep into the numbers and found that despite the obstacles and barriers inherent in the current investment industry, diverse-owned and diverse-managed wealth management firms are more likely to deliver top-tier performance than their nondiverse peers.

You understood me correctly—our financial earnings could be higher if we move our financial assets to women-owned and minority-owned firms.

There is real power (not to mention money) in intentionally shifting assets to financial advisors who identify as women, nonbinary, and/or people of color.

Just think of the ripple effects of creating a financial system in which money is controlled by people who look like and have similar experiences to the people and communities in which they invest.

Expanding the financial services talent pool is easier than you might think.

Financial advisors live and die by the happiness of their clients. The simple act of asking about the diversity makeup of your financial advisor's firm exercises your power as a social justice investor. Client questions about diversity send a serious signal to leadership to hire and promote more women and people of color.

Yes, you have that kind of power.

Even if you've been in the back seat of your investment journey until now, always remember: **it's your money**. You have every right to move into the driver's seat and embrace your authority.

Energy Boost: Build a Bigger Table

Sonya Dreizler

"I can do this. I am prepared and ready to say my piece." My silent pep-talks held my nerves from freefalling as my pre-stage nervousness kicked in like clockwork.

I peeked around, anxious that someone might see my knee nervously twitching.

Nope. Mistake. Looking around made it worse.

The other people seated around my table were focused on my friend and mentor George, who was addressing the crowd of 800 financial professionals from the main stage.

The main stage in this giant hotel ballroom full of people. Not just any people. MY people. My colleagues and mentors, my clients and prospects, industry gatekeepers.

My other knee started shaking.

I had been invited as a keynote speaker at the 2018 SRI Conference, renowned as a top-tier industry event for leaders in the socially responsible investment (SRI) industry. Finance and investment professionals attend this event for insights about how to move their clients' money into portfolios that better reflect their environmental, social, and governance (ESG) values. The leaders seated around this ballroom had collectively defied the expectations of traditional investors by insisting that returns are measured by more than just financial earnings. They had built an investment subculture by listening to their clients' desire to move money according to their values.

I have huge respect (and more than a little awe) for the people in that room.

And me? I was about to walk onto that stage, presumably to give a talk about my insights as a "next generation" impact-investing leader. But what I was actually going to use my 15 minutes for was to challenge the crowd's self-perception of race and privilege.

But the wired microphone taped up my neck kept slipping off the top of my ear.

"You can do this. It's only a 15-minute speech. You've given plenty of talks before. You're a pro!"

I knew why I was nervous.

Another deep breath. George was wrapping up the introduction. My introduction. I glanced down at my Fitbit.

Huh. Never seen my heart rate that high before.

Ok. Deep breath in. Deep breath out.

Deep breath in. Deep breath out.

I was out of time. George was wrapping up. ". . . happy to introduce my friend, Sonya Dreizler."

I had to consciously remind myself how to press down into my feet and straighten my knees before willing my torso to rise from the chair. I smiled and placed one foot in front of the other. Somehow, I made it onto that stage.

I leaned hard on my instincts and public speaking experience to launch into the speech. I had been sweating over every phrase and dramatic pause for weeks. I had even enlisted a few friends to help give feedback on the talk, something I don't typically do.

When I started speaking, I didn't recognize my voice. My heart was still racing and I couldn't catch my breath.

But I kept going.

After introducing myself, I quickly shifted to the uncomfortable topic at hand: convincing the audience that when it came to racial equity it was time to take a look in the mirror. If we want to address racial inequities and racial justice issues with portfolio companies, we needed to start by looking at our own industry, our own companies, and yes, even ESG and SRI companies.

I began gently, asking the audience to spend 20 seconds thinking about the very first time they were hired into a financial services job. After giving them a moment to collect their thoughts, I asked them to write down the top three factors that contributed to them being hired for that job.

Then I shared my own story of privilege—how I had climbed the corporate ladder, starting with a successful interview for an executive assistant position that ultimately led (many years later) to being CEO of a financial services firm.

While I got the job on my own and I did well on my own, I reminded the audience that the opportunity was due to my privilege. I landed the interview for the executive assistant role because my dad was kind enough to introduce me to the firm's CEO. The university listed on my resume was enough for my interviewer to overlook the fact that I had no experience working in financial services. My privilege allowed me to jump into the deep end without any prior experience.

I rounded out that story with a call to look internally about how "privilege grants you access without credentials."

Deep breath in.

Here comes the hard part. I'm about to talk about race to a room of—mostly white—finance and investment professionals.

"I want you to look around the room and look around your table. I want you to notice who is here. And who is not here. What I mean is: Why do we have so few Latinas in this room? So few Black women? Why are there hardly any Indigenous folks in our community? Why are there very few people of color in our community in relation to the American population?

"We're missing a big piece. And we need all of those perspectives at our table in order to solve the problems that we're working on.

"My generation wants equity, inclusion, and justice centered in all we do. We want your help.

"To make an inclusive community, there's no 'Easy' button. It requires action on everybody's part. One person at a time. One action at a time."

By now I was in the groove. My heart was no longer racing and I was enjoying being on stage. But also, like clockwork, my mouth had gone completely dry.

Water. Water would help. I made my way to the podium and took a sip.

Deep breath.

And back in.

"We need to turn the mirror on ourselves. Some of my colleagues and I have been collecting data from socially responsible investing companies about how diverse we actually are. We'll put out a paper on our findings, but I want to give you a little preview.

"We have a lot of work to do."

I steeled myself for the first call to action.

"I want you to expand your circle. And here, I'm mostly talking to the white folks in the room. If everybody you listen to, the people whose opinions you value, the people you talk to every day . . . are white, I'm asking you to intentionally expand your circle so you're getting more perspectives in your circle.

"When I'm talking about diversity, I'm not trying to take anything away from the white men in the room. I don't want to take away your seat at the table. What I want, and what my generation wants, is to build a bigger table. A table that welcomes everyone.

"My generation wants the firms that we work with and work for and the communities that we invest in to be reflective of the communities we serve and, more broadly, of the United States.

"I'm asking for your help. Let's build a bigger table together. Thank you."

Silence.

Phew. It was done. I believed everything I'd said and if there were negative career consequences, so be it. I told myself, *It's ok. Just put the presentation clicker down and go down the stairs.*

I almost dropped the clicker when the audience started clapping. I had to remind myself to stay on stage for a moment, accept the applause with grace, and take the moment in.

They kept going—clapping for what seemed like a very long time. I don't remember walking down the stairs, but I do remember the big bear hug from my dad. He had been in the audience and was likely the one clapping the loudest.

Today, I no longer work as a consultant in the ESG space. Instead, I'm proudly building that bigger table, working to lift the voices of women, nonbinary people, and people-of-color financial professionals on conference stages and in the media. In 2022, Liv Gagnon and I launched Choir, a diversity-tech platform that includes the Choir Certification™, the financial industry's first benchmark for conference diversity and representation. Our goal is to make conference stages across all sectors of finance representative of the US population.

We've been listening to the same voices for too long. No one is expected to give up their seat, but you may need to lend a hand in building a bigger table.

Contributing Author Biography

Sonya Dreizler is the cofounder of Choir, a financial services diversity-tech platform. She is also an author and speaker focused on fostering candid conversations about gender and race in financial services. She believes that financial services in the United States should be reflective of the population of the United States, from entry level to the board room, and all of her work advances that cause. Sonya has a 20-year history in the field, including as a broker dealer and Registered Investor Advisor (RIA) executive.

8.

Conversation Scripts for "The Talk"

Creating investment goals, especially as a social justice investor, often requires "tough conversations" with your financial partners, whether it be with your significant other, financial advisor, human resources manager, or financial coach.

For instance, if a client or new investor expresses a desire for *high* return investments while maintaining a *low* risk appetite, a financial advisor must explain that the only way to achieve high returns is by taking on a fair amount of risk. You can't expect high returns from low-risk investments.

These "rubber meets the road" conversations may seem boring and technical at first, but remember that they can have significant butterfly effects that ripple out through future investment decisions. These nitty-gritty conversations are the foundation of the financial and social justice returns we seek.

My first time having "The Talk"

My financial advisor, Becky, and I had a tense conversation about applying my social justice investment goals to my portfolio. Becky has decades of experience managing wealth and had been my advisor for several years before I approached her about layering in social justice investments.

Let me first state that I love my financial advisor. She provides excellent financial guidance and is my human guardrail for making wise investment decisions. She listens to my goals and incorporates my feedback along the way. I really appreciate that she's not afraid to express her hesitation about potential investments. I value her advice and I almost always agree with her pushback. Still, having "The Talk" was nerve wracking.

We initially butted heads on my request to incorporate social justice returns into my portfolio. Becky is an old-school traditional investor who manages her clients' money to maximize their wealth through smart, efficient trading. Becky built a large client book through her reputation of trading as infrequently as possible. Her clients appreciate her integrity and careful eye toward minimizing commission expenses.

Becky builds wealth for her clients by selecting the boring, low-fee, sustainable growth stocks and bonds.

Here I come along to ask for social justice investments, some of which have higher trading commissions than her preferred low-fee stocks and bonds. To add insult to injury, many of the investments I requested were flagged as "ineligible for trading" on her company's gatekeeper system.

I am not her easiest client.

During one frustrating call when her system denied purchase after purchase, Becky initiated our tensest and most productive conversation to date.

I knew I was in for a big conversation when I heard her sigh into the phone. "Andrea," she started, "I'm not sure if this is the best approach for your portfolio. My system doesn't let me purchase any of these investments, even when I try a manual override."

I paused, struck by a change in Becky's normally indefatigable nature. "Why aren't these positions going through? They're active positions that I've fully researched."

(Please note this conversation happened years before nonprofit groups like As You Sow and Invest for Better developed their easy-to-use research databases. At the time, I was relying on my formal training as a financial analyst to research social justice investments. Now I would just point Becky to a publicly available database for underlying product details.)

I heard tapping and clicking through the phone line. "I'm not sure. My system comes up with an error message that says they're over-leveraged."

Now I was confused. Over-leveraged means that the underlying company has taken on more debt than it can handle. I was asking Becky to purchase an exchange-traded fund (ETF), or a basket of stocks. The ETF structure I wanted to buy wasn't a fancy Wall Street product that bought the stocks on credit. It was a plain vanilla, relatively simple structure.

Again, I was using formal training as a financial analyst to puzzle this out. Today, you'd have research products at your fingertips and could point your financial advisor to publicly available research for any details.

Leaning back, I frowned. "Becky, that can't be right. It's structurally impossible for this type of investment to be over-leveraged."

Silence on the line. "You're right. But my gatekeepers won't let it through." We both paused, unsure of how to proceed. Becky continued with a slight edge to her voice, "You know, if you really want to purchase these securities, you may have to go through a self-directed (DIY) brokerage account."

My shoulders slumped. I maintain a full-time job and do my best to be a good mom to my three young children. This wasn't a good time for me to take on another responsibility. I hired Becky because I need someone to keep an eye on my portfolio on my behalf.

Our tense conversation evolved into a discussion of my investment objectives. I explained that while I wasn't married to these particular investments, I *did* want a portfolio that reflects my social justice values. Becky, ever the pro, relaxed into the conversation that I call "The Talk," or the tough conversation where investors explain precisely what I mean by social justice investing.

Social justice investing does not guarantee a straight path. Like me, you might find yourself up against red-tape that feels like it doesn't make sense. This is when having established, crystal-clear investment objectives is especially critical. In those moments, instead of being tempted to give up, you'll feel empowered to return to your core needs and values and reevaluate your next move.

"The Talk" crystallizes your social justice goals into your overall investment strategy.

BREAKING DOWN THE "THE TALK"

The first step is simple, straightforward, and catalytic: call your financial partner.

Phone calls are hard. I know. But some conversations won't work via email. And let's be real—this discussion deserves voice time. Pick up the phone and dial.

(A prop is necessary for the next step. Take a moment to grab a glass of water.)

After greeting and catching up with your financial partner, be deliberate in clearly communicating the reason for your conversation. Telepathy is not an effective communication strategy. You must express your intention clearly:

> Thank you for making time to speak with me today. I would like your advice in my goals to apply a social justice lens to my investment portfolio. Specifically, I'd like to revisit my portfolio to ensure that my return objectives are comprehensive and include a directive to fulfill social justice return goals.

Immediately stop and take a sip of water. Then take a deep breath and get a bigger sip.

We have a cultural and psychological block from asking for what we want. Pausing to sip water keeps you from jumping in to immediately downplay the importance of your request. It also gives your counterpart a moment to process your direct request.

The hardest step is to stand your ground and respond definitively.

Your financial partner will likely respond by asking for more clarity. Here are a few talking points to consider:

Financial partner: I see. What do you mean by "sustainable financial earnings?" What are your financial return expectations?

You: My return expectation is sustainable financial earnings coupled with social justice returns. I want my financial returns to be enough to cover my expected expenses as well as form a reasonable financial cushion for unexpected life events. At the same time, it is important to me to prioritize positive social justice returns as a core return objective.

Financial partner: What do you mean by social justice returns?

You: I'd like to align my investment portfolio with my social justice objectives. Racial justice is important to me and I would like my money to promote organizations that provide products and services that close the racial equity gap.

This script can be modified or expanded to consider the social justice concern you specifically wish to address. Other examples may include:

Climate justice: "I don't want entire populations to be left out of the green economy because they don't have affordable pathways to integrate energy efficiency products. I want my investments to flow to companies that offer environmentally friendly goods and services for low-wealth communities."

Social justice for people with disabilities: "I want my money to support people with disabilities. Could you please point me to companies that demonstrate a commitment to equality for people with disabilities?"

Social justice for Indigenous people: "I want to support Indigenous communities. What are some options for investing in small businesses owned by Indigenous Americans?"

Social justice for rural communities: "I want my portfolio to support investments in rural areas. Do you have any investment options that create quality healthcare in rural communities?"

Financial partner: Can you please provide an example of a social justice investment?

You: I'd like to divest of any investments in private prison operators and invest in companies that create affordable housing in Black and brown communities.

Congratulations. By clearly expressing your goals and desires to your financial partner, you've set the wheels in motion to create a social justice investment portfolio that you'll be proud to call your own.

FOLLOWING THROUGH WITH THE "FINANCIAL EARNINGS" TALK

As you'll recall from earlier chapters, social justice investors target *sustainable* financial earnings coupled with social justice returns.

Your financial partner will likely express concern that you may be giving up financial earnings in order to generate social justice returns.

Please keep in mind that your financial partner is doing their job by pressing you on your comfort with this balanced approach.

In fact, if your partner is a paid advisor, it is a financial advisor's fiduciary duty to ensure you are absolutely 100% aware that by targeting social justice returns, you will likely be turning away from many opportunities to earn higher, profit-maximizing financial earnings.

The tradeoff between social justice returns and financial earnings is a balancing decision that will be different for every person or family. It's a fair question for a financial partner to ask. It's also a balancing act that they can help you navigate.

At this point, social justice investors and their financial partners experience a persistent question that keeps floating up to the surface:

> Social justice returns are critical, but I also need to build wealth to cover my family's financial needs. How will I pay my children's tuition or establish my retirement account if I'm limiting my financial return?

Remember, that's where *sustainable* financial earnings come into play.

There is no hard-and-fast equation for the balance between financial earnings and social justice returns. It differs for each person, based on their own definition of "sustainable." Even more precise, each investor has specific financial objectives that will "sustain" their own particular lifestyle.

Every investor, every person, has unique and distinct life circumstances that affect the financial earnings required to sustain their way of life. Sustainable financial earnings for Melinda Gates are different than that of the average American family. While the everyday American family may need a 7% average return to build sufficient wealth for a housing down payment in 4 years, college tuition in 10 years, and retirement in 30 years, Melinda Gates will likely require a far lower growth rate to cover her financial needs over time.

Despite their vastly different financial return requirements, both Melinda Gates and our hypothetical family are committed to investing in the potential of people. (I do not know Melinda Gates or her financial situation. I'm using her as a familiar household name that everyday people associate with extreme wealth.)

Conversation script for creating sustainable financial earnings

Here is a sample script that you can follow when inviting your financial partner into a conversation to discuss your understanding of sustainable financial earnings. This is a continuation of the conversation script for "The Talk" we started a few pages ago.

> **You:** Thank you for taking time to speak with me today. I'd like to discuss my return objectives with you.
>
> **Financial partner:** Alright. Please tell me more.
>
> **You:** I am interested in pursuing a sustainable financial earnings return coupled with a social justice return.
>
> **Financial partner:** Ok. Let's research some investment options that may meet our social justice return objectives. What type of financial return are you targeting now that you are also targeting social justice returns?
>
> **You:** I would like to identify a financial earnings return target that will enable me to sustain what I consider to be a comfortable quality of life. Let's figure out what the return target would look like.

That simple script will initiate the conversation that will move you and your financial partner's intentions into reality. Now that you've established a clear understanding of your goals, you can work together to create an investment strategy focused on sustainable financial earnings coupled with a social justice returns.

Energy Boost: We Are One Community

Ebony Perkins

If I had selected the breakfast rush rather than the lunchtime assignment, maybe I would have preserved my carefully curated perception of reality for a few years longer.

But it was summer break and, unlike most 16-year-olds, I was an early riser and always doing something in the summer. My mom did not allow me or my brother Raymond to, in her words, "sit around and do nothing." In fact, my parents always encouraged us to find ways to build up the community that surrounded us.

I dressed quickly and tried to remember whether I had signed up through school or through church. Maybe I would know one of my fellow volunteers and we could chat through the afternoon.

"Ebony, where are you off to this morning?" My mom asked as she pulled out a water bottle from the cabinet and filled it at the sink.

I grabbed my keys from the hook by the door and thanked Mom for the water. "I'm going to volunteer at the food bank. Today we're passing out lunches at the park."

Mom nodded. "I'm so glad you're volunteering this summer. You know, we are one community. We are called to love all our neighbors," Mom started.

My brother Raymond chose this moment to roll into the kitchen. He caught my eye and we both looked away before our grins turned into a fit of laughter.

"I see you! I see your faces," my mom chided.

She could never play angry. Her smile was too quick, even when she tried to hide it behind her coffee cup.

"I know, Mom," I said quickly. "We lift as we climb."

Raymond stuck his head out of the pantry. "Did you happen to buy any more Pop-Tarts? I don't see any of the brown sugar cinnamon ones I like."

Seizing her momentary distraction, I grabbed my sunglasses off the counter and waved goodbye.

"Be back around four!" I called. "I'm stopping at Chick-fil-A for breakfast!"

Sadly, I didn't know any of the other volunteers. I accepted a roll of aluminum foil and started rolling cans of soda and bottles of water. It was a hot summer day in South Carolina and, even in the shade, you needed a cold beverage to manage the heat.

Today the mobile food bank was parked under the shade of a local park's magnolia trees.

Churches and school administrators organized and communicated the food bank's locations well in advance. Mondays, Wednesdays, and Fridays at the local park. Tuesdays, Thursdays, and Saturdays in the middle-school parking lot. Sundays were at the church.

After the drink station was fully stocked and the meals were packaged, three volunteers spread out behind two folding tables. We each formed the front of a line to serve meals to people in our community who couldn't afford groceries.

I handed out hot dogs, potato chips, apples, and chocolate chip cookies to many people that day. I added a few extra cookies and apples for moms and dads with a kid in tow. I pointed out the drink station and encouraged folks to stay hydrated.

I was reaching into my stash of extra cookies when I saw Stephen* walk into the picnic shelter. (*Name has been changed to protect privacy.)

He nodded to a group of men chatting over their potato chips and smiled at a mom who asked if she could take a few extra water bottles to keep her little ones cool for the walk home.

When his eyes met mine, his smile froze.

Oh, shit, I thought frantically.

I dropped my eyes quickly, but not before his silently bored into mine. "Chill. Let's just handle the situation as best we can," his gaze seemed to communicate.

While I was completely out of my depth, I got the feeling he had experience navigating situations far more precarious than this one.

I decided to follow his lead.

The little girl in front of me touched my elbow. "You okay?"

"Yeah . . . Yes," I stammered as I fished out a few cookies for her. "Here you go."

My ears buzzed as memories whipped through my mind. Stephen and I went to school together. He was a year ahead of me and entering his senior year. We weren't really friends, but I knew him well enough to exchange head nods in the hallway. We knew all the same people. We were part of the same community.

My mind couldn't get the pieces to fit together.

Stephen was here. To get lunch? From the mobile food bank?

But I *knew* him. In the great equalizer of high-school social scenes, he was just another guy.

Then something happened that changed the course of my life forever.

In that moment, the perspective my parents had carefully built around me evaporated. Now, I could make out the thriftiness of his outfit and recall how he was always busy when our friends went out to the movies.

He was part of my community, but also distinctly separated from the reality I lived.

When I glanced back at Stephen, he had entered the line furthest from mine. I couldn't help but notice his squared shoulders and set jaw. His mind was obviously racing too, but he knew how to stay centered.

How could we be one community if I'd never had to face down a school-mate's judgment to get food for the day?

I'd never been more grateful to be ignored. On that blustery day, Stephen pretended not to know me and I pretended not to know him. We muddled through as best we could. After he scooped up a bottle of water, several people invited him to sit with them for lunch. He waved off their invitations, opting instead for the quick exit I craved.

Even 20 years later, I'm still shaken by the maturity Stephen possessed that day. I don't think I'll ever reach that level of sure-footedness under pressure that he had mastered by the time he was 17.

He certainly didn't have the privilege to wait until he was 16 years old to feel reality's cold punch, as I had. Since that day, I have continued to remind myself to look in the mirror and recognize all the good and abundance I enjoy every day. If I had volunteered for the breakfast rush rather than the lunchtime crowd, maybe I would have been able to hang onto my simpler understanding of how the world worked.

Then again, maybe it was time for those walls to evaporate.

That day also taught me that communities are complex. We all live in our own reality and do our best to support each other. Some of us have more than others and will feel guilty about that no matter how much others tell us to chill.

I channel guilt into work that makes a difference for people living reali-ties that are a lot tougher than mine. As much as I thought I was building up the people around me, my community lifted me far higher than the volunteer hours I contributed.

It took me some time to come full circle, but now I can see why my parents spent so much energy reinforcing core values about community. They knew it would always keep us grounded, no matter how complex the situation.

"We are one community. We are called to love all our neighbors. Even as we rise to tackle new challenges, we lift up the people around us. Always stay grounded in love and respect."

The most humbling experience is when you realize that, as much as you thought you were supporting your community, they were the ones lifting you into bigger and better opportunities the whole time.

Contributing Author Biography

Ebony Perkins is a dedicated, solution-oriented social entrepreneur whose heart beats to community investing. As a champion for giving, she has demonstrated an ability to lead teams and work with investors and philanthropists to help them make smart and strategic decisions. Ebony is currently the director of impact investments at a Fortune 500 company and cohost of *Renegade Capital: The Activist's Podcast for Finance and Investments.*

9.

Getting Started as a 401(k) Investor

EMPLOYER-SPONSORED RETIREMENT PLANS

An employer-sponsored retirement plan is a workforce benefit offered by some companies to provide workers with income in retirement. If you're fortunate enough to work for an employer offering retirement benefits, retirement savings plans like a 401(k), 403(b), individual retirement account (IRA), or pension are highly effective investment vehicles to build wealth.

Fun fact: the names 401(k) and 403(b) originate from the section of the US Internal Revenue Code in which they are described.

My blessing to you, reader: may you never have to dig through federal tax codes in your professional or personal endeavors.

In all seriousness, employer-sponsored retirement savings plans (colloquially referred to as 401(k)s throughout this book) are considered "employee benefits" because they offer tax advantages while helping you plan for your financial future.

With a 401(k), an employee sets a percentage of their income to be automatically taken out of each paycheck and invested in their account. You can choose how to allocate your funds among the choices in a menu of investment options offered by your employer.

Tax benefits

Traditional 401(k)s are funded with an employee's pretax dollars. Because your contributions are withdrawn from your paycheck before you've paid any taxes, your taxable income will be lower. However, when you withdraw from your account in retirement, your withdrawals and investment earnings are generally fully taxable.

A Roth 401(k) works in reverse. You make contributions with after-tax dollars, but you pay fewer taxes when you withdraw the funds in retirement.

How does a 401(k) work?

In either case, 401(k)s are employer-sponsored investment vehicles that offer a disciplined approach for employees seeking to save money for retirement. Many employers will match an employee's contribution to their respective 401(k) account. The most common approach is a 3% match: when the employee contributes 3% of their salary into a 401(k), the employer will match the amount (3% of the employee's salary) and contribute it into the same 401(k) account. Over time, the contributions combine and, when invested, compound into the employee's retirement fund.

401(k) accounts are a great option for people who prefer to "set it and forget it." As an employee, you can select your investment approach through a menu of options, determine what percentage of your salary you'd like to contribute each pay period, and monitor the account's performance over time. This approach also forces discipline on investment habits, as the cash is automatically deducted from your paycheck and siphoned into your retirement account.

Also, because your employer sponsors this plan, they usually handle the logistics, from hiring financial advisors and plan administrators to curating a menu of investment options for employees. Your job as an employee is to select your specific investment approach from a drop-down list of options and then monitor performance over time. You may also choose to increase or decrease your contributions over time.

401(k) investment menu

401(k) investors select products from the employer-provided preset list of investment options known as the 401(k) investment menu. The employee selects which investment option best meets their needs to fund appropriate retirement plans. In most cases, companies are required to offer at least three investments that are diversified and have materially different risk-and-return characteristics. On average, companies offer 19 investment options to employees through the investment menu. Employees can select multiple investment options, indicating what percentage of their contributions should be allocated to which investment options.

While 401(k) accounts are effective retirement savings plans, the preset list of options available on the 401(k) investment menu is quite limited compared to the universe of investment products available for purchase in private and public markets.

What if I have an IRA?

If you ever leave your employer, you can roll over the 401(k) to a new company or to an independently managed, tax-advantaged retirement account (usually an individual retirement account or IRA). If you roll your 401(k) into an IRA, you'll avoid immediate taxes and your retirement savings will continue to grow tax-deferred. An IRA can also offer you more investment choices than most company 401(k) plans.

More and more companies, especially small businesses, offer payroll deduction programs to fund employees' IRAs as an easy way for businesses to give employees an opportunity to save for retirement. Employees can select between a Traditional IRA and a Roth IRA. With a Roth IRA, you contribute after-tax dollars, your money grows tax-free, and you can generally make tax- and penalty-free withdrawals after age 59½. With a Traditional IRA, you contribute pre- or after-tax dollars, your money grows tax-deferred, and withdrawals are taxed as current income after age 59½. In other words, you choose whether your upfront contributions or your retirement withdrawals are taxed.

STARTING A NEW JOB AS A 401(K) INVESTOR

Sitting in the HR offices on their first day of work, many people feel overwhelmed by the sheer volume of paperwork to review and sign. By the time we're presented with a list of investment options to select among for our 401(k) investments, most of us are more than a little drained. We're certainly not in an ideal mindset to sift through dozens of different investment products characterized by unfamiliar words like "large cap," "growth," "balanced," "expense ratio," or "fixed income."

Please take a deep breath when you start reviewing the retirement options. Ask your new human resources manager if you have time to review the investment options for a few days before making a decision. Request a deadline. Give yourself space to think. It's a reasonable ask, especially when you're establishing your primary investment account.

In fact, your human resources manager is often a wealth of knowledge and tips for how to maximize your employee benefits. Ask for insights on whether the company hires a financial advisor for their employees and what type of education the company offers about retirement savings plans. Glean information and advice available through the company before hiring a financial advisor to coach your investment decisions.

Asking for time will give you some cushion to assess your options, apply a social justice filter, and make the best decision for you and your family.

ALIGNING YOUR SOCIAL JUSTICE VALUES WITH YOUR 401(K) CHOICES

Today's social justice investors have more tools and solutions than ever before to improve their investment options to better match their personal values while saving for their retirement goals, including within their employer-sponsored retirement plans.

Let's pick up Tom's story from chapter 2, where he was first introduced as one of our three fictional social justice investors.

Tom, who recently started a new job in Cincinnati, plans to sign up for a 401(k). To maximize his savings, he agrees to have a percentage of each paycheck paid directly into the 401(k) investment account. His employer will match his contribution up to 3% of his salary. Tom gets to choose from 15 different investment options on the company's predetermined 401(k) investment menu.

When we last left Tom, he had paused, unsure of how to proceed.

He was drawn to the target-date index fund that matched his projected retirement age. He figured that he could pick the fund, contribute as much money as he could into that fund, and trust that a team of financial analysts would manage the money on his behalf until he was ready to retire at the specified target date. He liked it because he could set it and forget it.

However, it had been a long first day of work already and he was hitting a mental wall. Rather than selecting a random series of options from the preset investment menu, Tom looks to his HR manager for advice.

"Tammi," he asks, "do I need to complete my 401(k) paperwork today? Or do I have a few days to decide? I'd like to spend some time researching the options before nailing anything down."

Tammi smiled and nodded her head. "No problem, Tom. Employees have thirty days to select their investment choices. However, if you don't submit this form in that time frame, you'll be automatically enrolled in the default fund."

Tom's shoulders immediately relaxed as he dropped his pen into his shirt pocket. "Great. I'd like to take my time with this."

Watching as her newest employee carefully placed the 401(k) paperwork into his backpack, Tammi offered some advice.

"You know, Tom. As an employee here, you're entitled to meet with an investment consultant the company hires to manage the 401(k) portfolios. In addition to selecting the investments, our consultant is also available to advise employees on the options in the investment menu and how they may support your retirement goals."

Tom zipped his backpack and settled back into his chair. "Thank you, Tammi! I'd appreciate his contact information if you have it. I'll take whatever advice is available! I'll also bring these home and do a bit of background research in the meantime."

Tom left the office feeling confident that he had all the tools necessary to select investment options that met his retirement goals.

Energy Boost: Rewriting the Rules

Lakota Vogel

"Hey Mom?" I called into the kitchen. "Do you know what this word means?"

I heard a spray of water followed by the light *clink* of a dinner plate hitting the drying rack.

"Lakota," my mother responded in a soft voice I strained to catch. "If you want to ask me a question, please come into the kitchen and talk to me. Do not yell at me from the living room."

I rolled my eyes at my cousin, Allison, who I had invited over to watch TV and eat dinner. We had cheese pizza and Kool-Aid and were playing Monopoly until Allison's mom arrived to take her home.

I trooped across the living room and poked my head around the corner.

"Sorry, Mom," I said as I held up the Monopoly card I had drawn. "Do you know what the word 'mortgage' means?"

Mom dried her hands on a towel and took the small playing card from my eager hands.

"I don't know," she said, handing the card back to me. "Now go play with Allison while I call her mom. It's getting late and the weather is starting to turn."

Whether she truly didn't know—or just didn't want to explain it to a nine-year-old, it was clear in the tone of her voice that the concept of a mortgage was inconsequential to our family's reality.

The immediate fix was easy—we decided to remove all the mortgage references from the game.

Now, as I reflect on these moments in hindsight, I'm consistently amazed by the life lessons I learned while playing that classic board game.

My name is Lakota Vogel and I'm an enrolled member of the Cheyenne River Sioux Tribe, born and raised on a ranch in South Dakota. I am also the executive director of Four Bands Community Fund, a 22-year-old rural community lender that started by serving all residents of the Cheyenne River Sioux Reservation in north central South Dakota and expanded in 2013 to serve Native entrepreneurs across the entire state.

Our collective goal is to overcome the economic inequities that Native American individuals, families, and entrepreneurs face on the Cheyenne River Reservation and throughout the state of South Dakota. About three-quarters of our clients are low-, very low-, and extremely low-income, and more than 90% are of Native American descent. In addition, the majority of our clients are female heads of household (64%) or business owners (57%).

Our clients are *local* and our team is deeply entrenched in the communities we serve. We run into our clients in the grocery store. We sit on the daycare board of directors, desperately trying to keep these vital programs running. We know what our communities need because we *are* the communities we serve.

One of the lessons Four Bands has learned time and time again is that "how you perceive is how you proceed." Even while traditional financial providers see deep risk in lending to Native American communities, we perceive opportunity. We are confident that our success as nation builders is intricately woven into the success of our neighbor. We proceed accordingly, making loans that mainstream financial institutions won't touch.

Our success has been consistent and expansive. In 2021, a time marked by severe economic and health insecurity, Four Bands broke its personal record with an annual loan deployment of $5.5 million while maintaining a 1% delinquency rate within our portfolio. We made more investments to Native communities in the era of Covid-related cash flow disruptions and made sure that only 1% of our loans went unpaid.

That means 99% of our loans were fully performing. Even though we're consistently written off by mainstream finance.

How?

We reject the misperception and overvaluation of rugged individualism as a key economic driver. Instead, we see how a community strengthened by funding a small restaurant in a town of 400 people. We invest in *relationships* and are rewriting the narrative on risk.

We underwrite to the success of our communities and have been rewarded by a well-performing loan portfolio.

Despite our success in breaking down barriers to effective financing, today's Native communities are still stuck on the Monopoly board.

Many of us have played Monopoly at one time or another in our lives. I'm sure it was during a blizzard or some other catastrophic event . . . like Thanksgiving, when you're forced to spend time with your relatives.

It's a game in which you embrace your inner capitalist and develop a thirst for heartlessly bankrupting your family members.

What's not to love?

So now imagine you arrive late to Thanksgiving and all your cousins have already started play without you. As you scan the board to see what properties are left, you discover all the prime properties are bought up.

The monopolized board is exactly where modern-day Native economies started from. All our economic infrastructure was wiped off the board during this country's era of colonization.

A few centuries later, we were finally invited to play. Of course, by that point, all the cards had been dealt, the rules had been written, and the best properties were already purchased.

After lengthy negotiations, they eventually gave us back Baltic Avenue, that tiny little property on the corner that doesn't amount to much.

It's not enough.

That's why my work is to invest money into the Baltic Avenues of South Dakota and all the individuals who step onto this monopolized board with courage.

The team at Four Bands realizes that capital will never solve poverty.

But rewriting the rules *will*.

So we'll continue examining our perception of risk while ignoring the naysayers.

Because no one got anywhere by believing the cynics.

So go ahead. Step onto the board with courage. We'll high-five as we go around the board together.

Contributing Author Biography

Lakota Vogel is the executive director at Four Bands. In this role, Lakota provides leadership for the community loan fund, establishes new and fosters existing partnerships, and leads and manages efforts to reach organizational goals. Prior to becoming the executive director, Lakota served as the assistant director at Four Bands for five years. She graduated from the University of Notre Dame with a Bachelor of Arts degree in sociology. Upon graduation, she joined Teach for America and taught on the Rosebud Sioux Reservation at Todd County High School. Lakota obtained her master's in social work from Washington University in St. Louis with the Kathryn M. Buder Center for American Indian Studies. Lakota individualized her course of study to concentrate in economic security and social development through the life course of American Indians.

Lakota is excited to be back home on Cheyenne River and to be able to spend time with her family, especially her nieces and nephews, to whom she teaches the finer points of Monopoly-based mortgage strategies.

10.

First Steps for the DIY Investor

WHAT IS A DIY ACCOUNT?

A DIY account is a financial account through which investors buy and sell investment products like stocks, bonds, ETFs, and mutual funds. DIY accounts can be structured as brokerage accounts (no limits on contributions, but no tax benefits) or an individual retirement account (tax benefits, but limits on contributions).

Today's investors can open accounts on easy-to-use internet platforms through companies like Fidelity, eTrade, JPMorgan Chase, Ellevest, Robinhood, and Charles Schwab, just to name a few. Some platforms even offer financial incentives like up-front cash bonuses, commission-free trading, and complimentary advice from financial advisors.

This section provides step-by-step instructions for social justice investors who want to start building their portfolios as DIY investors.

FIVE REASONS INVESTORS OPEN A DIY ACCOUNT

You lack access to a 401(k) account or your employer doesn't provide a retirement plan.

You plan to set aside regular contributions and need a way to convert your savings into investments.

You don't want or don't need to pay a financial advisor to coach you through investment decisions.

You want to try your hand at managing money like an investor rather than a saver.

You're frustrated by the lack of social justice investment opportunities available through your 401(k) and want to move money to a wider universe of investment options.

HOW TO OPEN YOUR OWN DIY ACCOUNT

Should I open an IRA or a brokerage account?

The first step is to determine which type of investment account works best for you. The two main options for beginner DIY investors are an individual retirement account (IRA) or a brokerage account.

Investors can open both types of accounts through online investment platforms. In fact, you can open several accounts at once. The key difference between the two types of accounts are their tax advantages, contribution limits, and ability to withdraw cash.

IRAs are designed to help investors save for retirement. Similar to employer-sponsored retirement plans, IRAs offer tax advantages for investors on capital gains, interest, and dividends, which help you save for retirement by reducing your tax expenses. However, investors cannot pour unlimited financial resources into tax-advantaged IRAs. In 2023, the IRA contribution limits are $6,500 for those under age 50 and $7,500 for those age 50 or older. In other words, you can only contribute $6,500 to $7,500 per year into an IRA. At the same time, investors cannot withdraw any funds until age 59½, a proxy for reasonable retirement age.

Brokerage accounts, on the other hand, allow more freedom while offering almost no tax advantages. Indeed, there are very few rules for brokerage accounts. You can withdraw your money at any time, for any reason, and invest as much as you'd like every year.

	Brokerage account	IRA
Taxes	May incur capital gains tax on investment income; investments sold one year or less after buying are subject to ordinary income tax.	Typically no tax on capital gains. Offers tax-deferred or tax-free growth.

Contributions	Unlimited.	Caps on annual contributions.
Withdrawals	No limits or penalties.	Penalties for withdrawing before a certain age, unless exceptions are met.
Bottom line	Stock trading for investors who need or want access to their money before retirement. Or, additional long-term investments after maxing out IRA accounts.	Long-term growth, retirement savings.

There are pros and cons to either type of account, depending on your strategy and cash needs. If you're saving for retirement, an IRA is a smart, tax-effective type of account because you won't need to withdraw any cash until you reach retirement age. However, if you're growing investments to someday purchase a house, then you'll need to consider a brokerage account to ensure you can withdraw cash when you need to fund a down payment.

Alternatively, you can establish an account of each type and contribute funds accordingly. For instance, if you're saving for retirement and your annual contribution exceeds the $6,500 to $7,500 limit, you can always max out your IRA before contributing excess funds to a brokerage account.

DIY accounts allow you the freedom and flexibility to design a portfolio that is customized to your financial needs.

Research pricing

Once you determine the type of account you want to open, it's time to compare costs and incentives of the various online trading platforms available to you.

Online trading platforms are competing for your business and offer varying costs and incentives. For instance, many online accounts offer commission-free trading (i.e., they don't charge you a flat fee every time you purchase or sell a stock or bond) and enable you to open an account with a $0 minimum. Many online trading platforms will even offer cash bonuses as incentives for you to open an account, which in many cases can cover your first investment purchases. Do your research to find the account that will boost your long-term success.

In addition to pricing, it's also worth considering different services and conveniences offered by the various trading platforms. While the platform itself is necessary to purchase or sell a security, you'll also need access to the tools required to make a well-informed investment decision. For instance, online trading platforms may offer free access to investment research and stock options, fractional shares (a terrific benefit if you don't have enough cash to purchase an entire share of your favorite company), mobile apps, human interaction, and the ability to connect your bank account to your investment account.

With so many trading platforms offering reduced costs and extra incentives to attract business, it's a good time to experiment with some extra cash (or that nice upfront cash deposit) to start or expand your investment trajectory.

Forms are "the other 'F' word" in finance

When opening an online investment account, you'll need to complete a few forms. Be prepared with some identifying information like your social security number and driver's license. If you decide to pursue more complex financial transactions more frequently used by Wall Street professionals, you may be required to complete additional forms and submit information about your net worth, employment status, and investable assets.

Deposit cash in your newly opened account

Once your account is opened, it's time to move that cash money!!

In all seriousness, the investment platform will probably give you a few different options to move cash into your shiny new account, including electronic funds transfers, wire transfers, check deposits, or asset transfer. Any choice will successfully move your cash from your bank account to your investment account, but please note that some cash transfers are more expensive than others. Always check the accompanying fee to find the most affordable option.

ANGELA DISCOVERS DIY INVESTING

Consider how Angela, one of the three fictional characters introduced in chapter 2, finds her way to DIY investing.

Angela recently left her job as a third-grade teacher to manage her full-time workload as a 40-year-old mother of her five-year-old twin girls and two-year-old son. One of her biggest anxieties about leaving her job was walking away from yearly contributions to her pension. Determined to have the best of both worlds, Angela resolved to find an alternative path to financial freedom.

First, Angela had to determine whether she could afford to make regular financial contributions into an investment account. Where would she find the money?

Angela sat at her kitchen table, notebook in front of her. After several years of trying to balance a full-time job with family responsibilities, Angela and her husband, Roy, decided to shift from being a dual-income to a single-income family. Roy had recently been promoted to a position with a substantial raise, but also significant travel requirements.

After a few months of trying to make it work, Angela had approached Roy with some back-of-the-envelope calculations.

Angela recalled her hesitation in proposing a change to their family dynamics. "Hey, Roy," she had said, tentatively. "Do you have some time to think through an idea I'm wrestling with?"

Roy had stood and reached for her hand. She loved how he had sensed her hesitation and was immediately focused on calming her. "Yes, of course I do. What's up? You seem upset."

Angela pulled him to the couch and took a deep breath. "I've been thinking about how hard it's been to juggle everything and how expensive it's been to hire extra childcare since you've started your new job. I'm so proud of you and support you, but I don't think what we've been doing is sustainable. I feel like I'm burning the candle at both ends trying to manage my work schedule while spending more and more time solo parenting. Even with the extra help from our babysitter, I feel like I'm failing on both fronts."

Angela paused and looked at Roy. His right hand had never left hers, but his left elbow was on his knee and his forehead was planted in his palm. "I'm so sorry, sweetheart. I feel so guilty for traveling so much and leaving the lion's share of the house and family responsibilities with you."

Angela wrapped her arms around Roy's shoulders. "Hey, love. It's okay. We'll figure this out. We're partners in this relationship. We knew the travel would be hard. I'm asking that we make our own changes to accommodate your new job responsibilities."

Roy nodded slowly and asked, "What did you have in mind?"

Angela took a deep breath and proposed, "I think we should consider me leaving my job to focus on the family and the house. We could let our baby-sitter go and save that expense. I mean, three-quarters of my paycheck goes to our babysitter anyway. I'd rather spend the time with the kids rather than sitting at my desk if the money nets out that close to zero anyway. Plus, your raise offsets that last quarter of my paycheck."

Angela paused and looked at Roy. "What do you think?"

Roy stared at Angela for a long moment before answering. "Your proposal makes sense. No surprises there—you've always managed our family's finan-cial and day-to-day decisions. However, your career is important, too. I worry you'll resent me for making you give up your job."

Tears threatened Angela's composure. "Yeah. I've been struggling with this idea for months now. I love my teaching job. I love my kids. But I'm falling apart inside trying to be a good mom and a good employee. But at the end of the day, my highest priority is my family. Full stop. And it's not like I can't find another job teaching in the future. It's not like the teacher shortage is going away anytime soon."

Roy nodded. "All that is true, but it's an incredibly large change in our family." Then he paused to lock eyes with Angela. "I want you to be happy. Will you be happy if you leave your job? Our family and your happiness are most important to me. It's a full stop for me, too."

By the end of the evening, Angela and Roy were both crying in the living room as they mapped out their new life together. They thought through all the consequences and implications of Angela leaving her professional job to focus on her other full-time job: shaping and nurturing three tiny humans.

Now, several months later, she sat at her kitchen table, staring at a blank notebook.

After she resigned her position, one concern remained. Angela would no longer receive contributions to her teacher pension. It was a modest sum, to be sure, but it was her only source of financial wealth and she grieved having to give it up.

That grief had been gnawing at her subconscious. She wanted to have her cake and eat it, too, gosh darn it. Cake is delicious!

But today, a new idea had materialized while Angela was walking the dog. What if she created her *own* investment account and made contributions to it on a regular basis? It wouldn't be as convenient as the teacher pension, but then again, the state government wouldn't be tempted to dip into it when financial emergency loomed.

Twirling her pen between her fingers, Angela considered where she could find the money to make regular contributions. Their family budget was manageable, but lean. There weren't any dollars left to squeeze from her regular expenses like utilities, gas, or grocery runs. If anything, their grocery bill got more expensive every time she went to the store. Her kids could eat!

She didn't want to give up her gym membership; she had only just gotten into the habit of going to run three times a week. Nor did she want to pull her kids out of any after-school activities; that wasn't fair to them.

She finally turned to the idea her brain kept pushing away. Angela grumbled her favorite curse word while writing "use your Starbucks money" on her blank white paper.

How much could she be spending on Starbucks anyway? When they went through their budget together, Roy insisted that Angela keep a line item for Starbucks.

"You love your coffee, my dear. Don't give that up," Roy had insisted, and proposed that Angela spend $15 every week on whatever seasonal latte was promoted at her local store.

Angela sighed and groaned. If she wanted to create wealth, she would have to make sacrifices. Now she felt petulant and silly. She was bemoaning giving up her twice-weekly latte. And sometimes croissant. "Let's not make this more dramatic than it is. It's absolutely worth it. I'll use that $15 every week to build a pension replacement."

Then Angela smiled to herself and joked to her dog, "I'll get to have my cake and eat it, too. But I'll have to wash it down with home-brewed coffee." Her dog stared back at her. "You know," Angela told her dog, "You reacted with as much appreciation for that joke as Roy would have."

After talking it over with Roy, who readily agreed, Angela reallocated her $15 per week away from her Starbucks runs to an investment account she planned to grow into a plump nest egg over time.

Goodbye, seasonal lattes. Hello, financial security.

Based on some back-of-the-envelope calculations, Angela figures she can invest $60 every month, eventually growing into about $750 by the end of the year.

Angela begins by researching costs and incentives offered by web-based investment platforms and is delighted to discover one offers a $3,000 cash deposit upon account opening. Suddenly, her initial $60 catapulted into $3,060.

Eyes opened, she sips her home-brewed coffee with renewed vigor.

Energy Boost: Living My Father's Mantra

John Holdsclaw IV

If I have one regret in my life, it's that my son, Braden, didn't really get a chance to know my father. Sadly, my dad passed away when my son was only three years old.

My dad was one of those people who took the time to form a genuine relationship with a complete stranger in a random encounter. He was quick to extend his hand and introduce himself as "John Holdsclaw the third. Pleasure to meet you."

I'm proud to follow his legacy as John Holdsclaw. The fourth.

More than anything, I hope I'm honoring my dad by living the same mantra he explained to me, in his own way, many years ago.

One moment remains crystallized in my memory as especially formative.

Newspapers lay scattered across the faded green sofa in the middle of my home's living room. Even in high school, I was an avid news junkie and soaked up every word of the *Statesville Record & Landmark* in the afternoons before football practice.

Today, however, my eyes ran across a familiar name—my own! Well, John Holdsclaw III anyway. My father had won the prestigious Jefferson Citizenship Award for his contributions and services to the community. My pride overflowed into a wide grin as I read how my father's peers had recognized and appreciated my father's devotion to the people in our town.

Reading through the descriptions of the ceremony that celebrated this year's round of prize winners, confusion and a sliver of hurt crept into my boisterous pride. Why hadn't my father told me about this award? He hadn't mentioned it to me once and he certainly hadn't attended the ceremony.

Why wouldn't he have shared this news with me?

My grin dissolved as I carefully folded the newspaper sections and arranged them into a neat stack beside my father's favorite chair. I left the section with his announcement on the top of the pile.

Then I sat, waiting for him to return from work.

Funny, I thought to myself. *Usually, the situation is reversed and my father is waiting for me to return home after practice or spending time with friends.*

Still, I waited. I couldn't understand why he had kept this from me.

Right on time, my dad walked through the front door and toed off his dress shoes. He knew something was wrong the moment he saw my face.

"Hi, son," he greeted me calmly. "What's going on? Don't you have practice tonight?"

Silently, I stood, strode over to my father, and slid the paper into his hands. He looked down, read the announcement, and cocked his head to one side.

"What's all this about?" he probed again.

Finally, my unease broke through the surface. "I didn't know you won this award! Why didn't you tell me? Why didn't you go to the ceremony last week? This is a big deal!"

My father sat down in his beloved armchair—another antique that once belonged to his grandmother—and read the paper I had placed in his hands a moment before.

"Nah," he said, returning the newspaper to me. "It just wasn't important to me."

I stared, incredulous. "What do you mean it wasn't important? The mayor was there! Didn't you want to shake his hand and get a picture?"

My father leaned back in his seat and waited for my eyes to connect with his.

I'll never forget his response. His mantra, really. It was the moment I adopted his life mantra as my own.

"In the end," he explained, "all I want is to help people."

Then he stood, patted me on the shoulder, and walked to the kitchen to prepare dinner.

"Now get on to practice. You don't want to be late."

I wasn't late, but I did have a new lease on life.

I started recognizing all the ways, both large and small, my dad would go out of his way to connect with and help the people around him. Sometimes it was helping a neighbor find a new job. Or how we always seemed to have an extra guest for dinner on nights when their groceries were running low. Or how he always seemed to know which one of my friends needed an extra "Hey there. You okay?"

What I never appreciated until much, much later was my father's approach to raising children. What I can see now that I'm raising my own child is how he never *told* me how to live; he *showed* me.

I wish I'd had more time with him. To ask the questions I never realized I'd crave his guidance for. For my son to observe and absorb the content of his grandfather's character, firsthand.

Instead, I do my best to honor my dad's legacy by living the mantra he taught me all those years ago. For me, that means finding ways to care for people through my choice of profession: community development finance. I honor my dad every time my company finances a grocery store in a food desert, or lends long-term, low-cost money to a Head Start classroom in an under-resourced community.

While my professional purpose is to create equitable access to capital, it's grounded in my and my father's guiding principle: in the end, I just want to help people.

I'm finding my own ways to show my son how to live a life characterized by integrity, hustle, and kindness. Recently, I brought my son to a professional gathering of the African-American Credit Union Coalition. We're a group of professionals who have dedicated our careers to creating a financial system in which no one is left out.

I brought my son so he could better understand why I've poured so much of myself into my career. I wanted him to know the people I associate with, to understand what it means to put food on the table, and why I devoted my career to community lending.

One of the most gratifying moments as a father was hearing my son explain to a friend why he was okay with my frequent travels. "Nah, it's okay," my son explained. "He's putting good money in communities. He's helping people."

I'm incredibly proud of my son and the man he's becoming. He knows there's a bigger world out there. And that while he doesn't have to adopt my line of work, he does have a responsibility to help others.

I believe my father would recognize his own spirit in my son.

My father may have passed away more than 13 years ago, but I believe my son has learned many of the same lessons I did.

Because when my son spends time with me, he's spending time with my dad, too.

Contributing Author Biography

John Holdsclaw IV currently serves as president and CEO of Rochdale Capital, a newly formed, national nonprofit community development loan fund that provides financing and technical assistance to cooperative enterprises and other community-based organizations. Rochdale Capital focuses on making financial services accessible to under-resourced communities, specifically to women and/or minority-owned small and growing businesses. John currently serves on the board of directors of Global Communities, Groundswell, Partners for Common Good, and American Bankers Association (ABA) Stonier Graduate School of Banking. In addition, John is the immediate past president of the Community Development Financial Institution Coalition (CDFI Coalition), and immediate past chair of ABA's Diversity, Equity, and Inclusion Advisory Group.

11.

Capital Markets—Booths on the Marketplace

Financial markets that bring buyers and sellers together to trade stocks, bonds, and other financial assets are called capital markets, which are sometimes colloquially referred to as the stock market. For example, the New York Stock Exchange (NYSE) is a well-known capital market where buyers and sellers trade stocks, bonds, and other publicly traded financial assets.

Increasingly, capital markets throughout the world are building more robust investment marketplaces for investors interested in selecting products that reflect their values. In many ways, European markets like Germany's Börse and the London Stock Exchange are blazing the trail for US markets to follow.

Fortunately for us, capital markets have evolved to meet the needs and preferences of investors who want to build investment portfolios that satisfy their financial and nonfinancial return objectives.

But what are capital markets?

For all their pomp and circumstance, capital markets operate in much the same way as your local farmer's market. Sellers (often called "issuers" in capital markets) display and market their goods to buyers. Instead of peaches and corn, buyers consider purchasing stocks and bonds.

While the depth of products available on today's capital markets can be quite robust, everyday investors can usually keep it straightforward with the "plain vanilla" versions. We'll leave the more complex iterations to Wall Street professionals with more nuanced needs.

In all seriousness, "plain vanilla" is actual (and frequently used) terminology for financial professionals. Plain vanilla is the most basic or standard version of a financial product. "Exotic" products, on the other hand, alter the components of a basic financial structure, resulting in a more complex investment product.

For example, an everyday example of a "plain vanilla" financial product is a 30-year fixed-rate mortgage. It's the most basic and standard version of mortgage products available to everyday people. The product allows homeowners to repay their housing-related debt over a longer time period, which means lower cash payments month over month.

While most people think of mortgages as 30-year products, your mortgage broker likely has several other options on their menu list. For instance, you could probably get a quote for a 15-year fixed-rate mortgage, which allows homeowners to repay their debt more quickly with a higher monthly payment. A shorter payment period also means the interest rate may be lower than the 30-year option, which means more of your monthly payment goes toward principal repayment rather than interest expenses. Another "exotic feature" may be an adjustable rate mortgage (ARM), where the interest rate periodically adjusts to reflect prevailing market rates.

Exotic features enable investors to tailor their financial products to precisely match their individual needs. However, be aware that intricacy comes hand-in-hand with complexity, which must be managed with care.

Many will remember that the financial crisis of 2008 was fueled in part by homeowners' inability to pay their increasingly expensive ARMs. Borrowers could be enticed into an initially affordable mortgage in which payments would skyrocket in three, five, or seven years with built-in "exotic features" like teaser rates (special low rates that would last for the first year or two of a mortgage).

I share this cautionary tale not because all "exotic features" are inherently duplicitous, but to remind us to stay alert and circumspect when considering different financial products. As a rule, social justice investors stick with "plain vanilla" structures and let social justice returns serve as our "exotic feature."

As you grow more confident in your knowledge and experience, you can structure portfolios with more intricate designs. For now, though, we'll keep it simple. Simple and straightforward gets the job done without the extra headache of maintaining complex layers.

To keep us grounded, this chapter will explain "plain vanilla" investment staples like fixed income, equities, exchange-traded funds (ETFs), and mutual funds as if they were fruits and vegetables available for sale at your local farmer's market. After all, social justice investors visit the capital market to buy and sell the financial products they need to stock their investment portfolios.

A NEW KIND OF FARMER'S MARKET

The first thing you'll notice upon entering the SJI Farmer's Market is the wide center aisle that separates the left side of the market from the right side. Walls on either side are lined with vendor booths showcasing summer squash, peaches, corn, tomatoes, cheese, eggs, yogurt, meat, and milk. While the products are similar, the presentation and method of purchase are strikingly different. Much like the produce at a farmer's market might have "organic" or "locally sourced" designations, capital markets also offer designated products based on underlying criteria.

The left side offers the neat efficiency of a well-organized exchange. A large sign designates these booths as being the "Publicly traded" market and describes how the left side's significant standardization requirements promote transparency and streamlined efficiency. Every product is identified through its QR code, which includes information about the item's name, price, farm of origin, nutritional values, and recommended pairings. The vendors submit QR code information for their products at the beginning of the season and are only permitted to sell items with approved QR codes. The buyers can research the products prior to arriving and can shop with the list of available products.

The market's right side is dominated by signs that read "Privately traded market: Products and prices depend on season's availability. Vendors are available for special requests."

The shopping pace is markedly slower than publicly traded transactions as buyers stop at each booth to ask questions of the vendor and sample the available products. While every item on the left side is prepackaged and stamped with a QR code, items on the privately traded side are available for the buyer to touch, smell, and sample. Buyers visit each booth to discover which products are available for sale this week. Sometimes buyers are disappointed to have missed the last of the fresh peaches, but are delighted by the surprise of early cherries. Buyers can inquire whether the vendor will sell half a watermelon (easier to carry home) or if they'll demonstrate how to peel brussels sprouts off the stalk. Prices are more likely to be negotiated and vendors can recommend how this week's peaches would pair well with the pork chops from the butcher in the next booth, marinated with bourbon and brown sugar.

Either way, you have every opportunity to fill your shopping bag with the goods and products you'll need for the dinner party you're throwing for your neighbors. Buyers can cross the aisle to purchase whatever product combination works best for their needs. You can purchase green beans from the left side and eggs from the right. You might fall in love with zucchini on both sides and take them home to compare in your homemade batter for fried squash. You do you.

Similarly, your investment portfolio can be filled with your ideal mixture of products from either market, depending on the resources you have available, your financial needs, and your social justice values. Some people may only shop from the publicly traded market right now because they feel short on time; it feels overwhelming to wade through so many options in the privately traded market. Others may prefer the ability to highly customize their purchases on the privately traded side and decide to prioritize building relationships with local farmers. Which market you shop in, and how much you buy from each, might also change over time, and that's okay too. Both markets provide opportunities for the everyday person to create a portfolio aligned with their social justice values.

A BALANCED DIET

When choosing investments, you will likely need to maintain a diversified portfolio spread across several different types of products. Similar to how a trip to the farmer's market will include a balanced mix of fruits, vegetables, and other goods, a diversified portfolio will include a mix of fixed income, equities, and maybe even a few exchange-traded funds (ETFs).

For the sake of simplicity, let's start by covering the basics of each of these investment "food groups." Later, we will discuss how to choose specific investments from each asset class that strike the right balance between our financial and social justice return objectives.

Product type 1: Fixed income

Fixed income investments, which are commonly referred to as debt securities, bonds, notes, or even certificates of deposit (CDs), offer investors *predictable* financial earnings based on the instrument's interest rate, which is "fixed" and cannot change over time.

When a company or government issues debt securities, it is contractually obligated to repay the amount to its borrowers (i.e., the principal or face value of the debt) at a specified future date. The cost of using these funds is called interest, which the company or government is contractually obligated to pay until the debt matures or is retired. For example, if you purchase a three-year, 5% interest bond for its face value of $100, then you would receive $5 at the end of year one and year two. On the third anniversary of your purchase, you'd receive $5 in interest plus the principal repayment of $100.

Everyday investors typically purchase fixed income positions as part of a "conservative risk" investment strategy. In financial terms, investments are chosen based on a strategy that exists on a risk spectrum from "conservative" to "aggressive." Whereas a conservative strategy is designed to deliver predictable, consistent financial earnings, an aggressive strategy is preferred by investors willing to take on more risk for the possibility of higher financial earnings.

Since fixed income investments are on the conservative, predictable end of the spectrum, they often take up a higher percentage of an individual's investment portfolio as he or she nears retirement age. Fixed income payments can replace the consistent cash flow you previously received from regular paychecks. They tend to be less volatile and more conservative than equity investments (which we'll discuss next), but also have lower expected returns.

For our "plain vanilla" purposes, we can assume that bonds and notes guarantee a fixed interest rate, which means a fixed percentage return on money invested. Please note, however, that more complex iterations can include rates that float with the market's evolving interest rate environment or can be modified based on market conditions.

When considering fixed income investments, investors should understand their key features. Here are a few terms you should know:

Issuer: Company, organization, or entity that is responsible for generating the financial earnings associated with the interest payments. For instance, General Motors may issue debt securities to expand product lines or finance current operations. Many governments issue bonds to raise capital to pay down debts or fund infrastructure improvements.

Maturity: Refers to the date when the issuer is obligated to repay the outstanding principal amount.

Principal: Dollar amount the issuer agrees to repay the bondholders on the maturity date. Also known as a bond's "par value."

Interest rate: Financial payment the issuer agrees to pay the investor for lending funds. Interest rates are expressed as a percentage of the total loan amount.

Frequency: The number of times per year the bond makes interest payments.

How to purchase fixed income investments

Social justice investors can purchase both publicly traded and privately traded fixed income bonds to meet their portfolio objectives. Going back to our farmer's market example, you can purchase from either side of the aisle, or both, to meet your needs.

For instance, you may consider the sustainability bond issued by Alphabet (Google's parent company) in August 2020 through the publicly traded capital markets. As part of a $10 billion debt offering, Alphabet issued $5.75 billion in sustainability bonds and dedicated the proceeds to support investments in both environmental and social issues, including affordable housing, commitment to racial equity, and support for small businesses.

Investors who want to curate their portfolio to address a more precise issue might consider tailoring their portfolio through privately traded bonds. For instance, social justice investors may consider reaching out to their local community lender to inquire whether they accept debt investments from individual investors. You and the community lender can negotiate key terms (principal amount, maturity, interest rate, frequency, etc.), and you might direct the community lender to lend the proceeds into small businesses in low-wealth neighborhoods in their geographic footprint.

While the private investment requires significantly more time to execute, the investor has more control over the use of proceeds. On the other hand, investors can purchase Alphabet's sustainability bond with relative ease through the public capital market's standardized trading mechanisms and be confident that their contribution is funding loans to small businesses across the country. However, the investor has no control over which neighborhoods will ultimately receive the bond's proceeds.

At the end of the day, both debt instruments finance small businesses in low-wealth communities. Buyers can select fixed income investments from whichever side of the aisle works best.

Product type 2: Equities

Equity investments represent an ownership position in the underlying company or organization. When you buy stock in Netflix, you own a small percentage of, or share of, the company's net assets (assets remaining after the company's liabilities are subtracted out). Equities create wealth for their shareholders through both price appreciation and dividend payments. For instance, your ownership stake entitles you to a proportional *share* of dividends Netflix makes to its *shareholders*, where *dividends* are regular payments by a company to its shareholders out of its profits.

Unlike fixed income investments, equities do not offer predictable cash flows, but instead deliver dividends that reflect profits earned in the specified time period. Equity investments are significantly more volatile than fixed income positions and depend entirely on the company's ability to generate profit.

Equity investments generate financial wealth through both the price appreciation (or growth) of the stock's value as well as recurring dividends. For instance, assume you bought a single share of Netflix stock when it was trading for $100. You received quarterly dividend payments of $3, $3.50, $2.25, and $4.75 (total annual dividends of $13.50) in the first year. One year after your initial purchase, you sold your share at the market price of $120. Your share had appreciated in value by $20, thereby generating $20 of wealth for your portfolio. When added to your financial earnings generated through dividend payments, you earned $33.50 in financial wealth.

However, if the company's performance deteriorated in the first year, you could have lost money in the exchange. For instance, if Netflix's earnings declined, your shares may have only paid out a total of $1 in dividends each of the four quarters (total annual dividend earnings of $4). With its softer performance trajectory, the stock price in this hypothetical scenario could have declined to $80 at the time you needed to sell your position. Rather than building financial wealth, selling at a 20% price depreciation means that you would have lost $16 over the investment period ($20 in price depreciation mitigated by the $4 in dividend payments).

In broad strokes, equities sit on the aggressive end of the investment spectrum. They are the high-risk, high-return foil to fixed income's low-risk, low-return nature.

While more volatile than debt securities, investors seek the higher growth potential of equity investments to grow the total value of their portfolio over time. When given enough time and patience to mature, equity investments' price appreciation can be a significant driver of wealth for everyday investors. Younger investors' portfolios tend to be more heavily weighted toward equity than debt securities because they have more time for those investments to increase in value. As investors draw closer to retirement age, they begin to sell equity positions and use the proceeds to invest in less volatile fixed income positions that are more apt to deliver consistent cash flows for the post-paycheck era of their lives.

When considering equity investments, investors should understand their core characteristics. Here are a few terms you should know:

Share: Unit of ownership in a corporation. An investor who owns shares of a corporation is a "shareholder."

Dividend: Sum of money paid regularly (typically quarterly) by a company to its shareholders out of its profits or reserves.

Initial public offering (IPO): When a private company first sells shares of stock to the public, this process is known as an IPO. An IPO means that a company's ownership is transitioning from private ownership to public ownership. Having "gone public," the company is now considered publicly traded.

Stock price: Price at which the company's stock is trading.

Market value: Total dollar value of a company's equity. Also referred to as market capitalization. This measure of a company's value is calculated by multiplying the current stock price by the total number of outstanding shares.

Frequency: The number of times per year the shareholder will receive dividends.

Unlike a fixed income investment, when a company issues equity investments, it is not contractually obligated to repay the money it receives from shareholders.

If you purchase shares for $200, the company is not obligated to repay you the $200, nor is it contractually obligated to make periodic payments to shareholders for the use of their funds. In other words, there is no guarantee of dividend payments.

Instead, shareholders have a claim on the company's net assets (what's left of the company's assets after all liabilities have been paid). Because of this claim, equity shareholders are fractional owners of the company.

Investors who purchase equity securities seek wealth through a company's ability to generate and share profit (through price appreciation as well as dividend income), whereas investors who make fixed income investments seek consistent, predictable cash flows (through interest income and principal repayment).

Publicly traded equities versus privately traded equities

Most everyday investors will purchase equity securities through publicly traded platforms like the New York Stock Exchange (NYSE) and the Nasdaq stock exchange. The ease and convenience of trading for most people significantly outweigh the potential upside of privately traded stock positions. The transparency and standardization required by public exchanges are especially helpful for investors without specialized knowledge of due diligence and valuation. Like in our farmer's market, it is comforting to know that even if you don't understand the nuances of tomato growing, you can purchase a tomato that has met standards required to obtain a QR code.

Alternatively, companies not available via publicly traded platforms are available through the privately traded market, often primarily owned by friends, family, and early-stage private equity investors. Much like the privately traded farmers' market, these investments are based on relationships and an abundance of resources. This is why private equity is usually the playground of wealthier investors who can hire financial analysts with the experience and expertise necessary to make well-informed investment decisions about privately held companies. Substantial levels of wealth are required to play the numbers game, and private equity investors finance many prospects in hopes that one will be the windfall that covers the money lost on the failed ventures. Private equity's rule of thumb is that for every 20 investments, only one will be a big winner. You keep your fingers crossed that the winner's profit wipes out the losses of the other 19.

Topics like private equity due diligence, analysis, and valuation are too advanced for this book and the reasonable skill sets of everyday investors. If you're interested in private equity plays for social justice investing purposes, I strongly advise you to seek the guidance of trained professionals with the relevant specialized expertise.

Product type 3: Exchange-traded funds (ETF)

An exchange-traded fund (more commonly referred to as an "ETF") is a prepackaged basket of equity stocks and/or fixed income bonds traded as a single investment product. ETFs usually follow a predetermined list of stocks, but they can also include a list of fixed income securities.

Returning to our farmers' market analogy, imagine a vendor spending most of his Friday evening creating prepackaged fruit baskets to sell at Saturday's market. He sets out 100 woven baskets and then systematically distributes equal amounts of different fruit selections into each of the baskets. First he places a peach in each of the baskets. Checking his list, he hauls over a large container of apples and carefully distributes a single apple in each basket. Our farmer continues this process for pears, nectarines, and plums. Afterwards he stamps each basket with a QR code that links to information about "Robert's Fruit Salad."

The transaction is convenient and effective. The buyer can buy a basket of goods for a single price without having to track down every item on the list. ETFs can also have a democratizing effect on capital markets, as they create a path for buyers who want to make a fruit salad (i.e., portfolio diversified of multiple stocks) but cannot afford to buy a quart of each fruit (i.e., entire stock share) when they only need one of each (i.e., slice of a share available through ETF ownership).

For investors who want to build a diversified portfolio, buying hundreds of individual stocks or bonds can be too expensive for their budget. Purchasing an ETF gives an investor exposure to small slices of individual stocks without buying each one outright.

Typically, ETFs track a predetermined list of individual stocks. ETFs can track a particular index, sector, commodity, or other asset. Our farmer's market ETF tracked medium-sized fall fruits (peaches, apples, pears, nectarines, and plums). Capital ETFs might track the S&P 500 (giving the investor exposure to the largest 500 companies rated by S&P). Another might track stocks in a single sector (e.g., the ETF contains shares of technology companies).

If you only have $50 and want to invest in equities, you can either select a handful of individual stocks or can buy a single share of an ETF that tracks several hundred companies. Diversification across this many companies is an effective risk management strategy. If one company fails, you have several hundred others to buoy your overall wealth. If you had only selected four stocks and one tanks, your average returns would be pulled down by the one bad pick. Instead, ETFs track the weighted performance of all the stocks in the basket and smooth out earnings volatility by spreading exposure risk across multiple stocks.

ETFs can be extremely appealing to social justice investors as a way of targeting social justice issues. Many are packaged to address a particular industry, or in this case social justice cause. Terms like ESG are often used to designate ETFs that are created using a broad consideration for environmental, social, and governance (ESG) issues. Others might be labeled "sustainability ETFs" for investors who are interested in investing in climate solutions. This allows social justice investors to choose a single ETF that covers a broad range of issues or several ETFs to target very specific causes.

Product type 4: Mutual funds

A mutual fund is another type of prepacked investment which includes equity stocks as well as bonds and other securities. However, instead of a set "fruit salad" recipe like ETFs, mutual funds are similar to a community-supported agriculture box you might buy from a local farm. You know that you will receive a box of fruits, vegetables, and other products, but the exact ingredients might change depending on the season. Similarly, mutual funds are actively managed by an investment firm, which means that the specific investments in your mutual fund will change over time.

Mutual funds are similar in structure to ETFs (both are baskets of securities), but differ in management style, costs, and tax costs. Let's dig a bit more into how those approaches work:

Management style: Whereas ETFs *passively* track a list of predetermined stocks, mutual funds are *actively* managed. Active management means that as market conditions evolve, fund managers proactively substitute in different securities that more closely match the mutual fund's stated return objectives. Fund managers might sell underperforming securities and substitute in higher-performing securities. Fund managers are professionally trained financial analysts who closely follow market conditions and the performance of relevant securities. (*Passive management* follows a "buy and hold" strategy, where managers stick to the original plan with exceptions for significant market movements. Passive management is a "hands-off" approach to investing.)

Costs: Mutual funds are generally considered more expensive than ETFs. Active management costs money that passive management avoids. Actively managed mutual funds must hire financial analysts to assess the performance of the portfolio and its underlying securities. Active trading of underlying securities may require fees that add up over time. Passively managed ETFs avoid trading fees (also called trading commissions) and employ fewer money managers. There are exceptions to these general rules, and investors should always examine the relative costs of ETFs and mutual funds that track the same index lists.

Tax costs: ETFs tend to be more tax efficient (i.e., incur fewer taxes) than actively managed mutual funds. Every time you sell a security, you incur a capital gains tax on the profit. Actively managed mutual funds are defined by the buying and selling of underlying securities to maximize financial performance. Every profitable sale incurs a capital gains tax to be paid by the investor. ETFs, on the other hand, implement a buy-and-hold strategy that generates fewer capital gains taxes for investors.

Mutual funds are effective structures for investors who are looking for a fund that could potentially beat the market. They are ideal for investors who can absorb the tax expenses to afford high-touch investment management.

For social justice investors who target *sustainable* financial earnings and evidence of social justice advances, mutual funds are generally not worth the expenses incurred through active management. If we're not interested in profit maximization, we avoid the associated costs.

However, 401(k) investors may have access to a balanced approach, as mutual funds are often options in their employer-sponsored retirement plans. Employers generally have more capacity to absorb tax expenses and see mutual funds as an effective means to a professionally managed portfolio of equities, bonds, and other securities. After all, while mutual funds are expensive relative to ETFs, they are less expensive than hiring a dedicated team of financial analysts and money managers. 401(k) investors can benefit from layering mutual-fund financial earnings with social justice returns from other products.

FARMERS' MARKET TO CAPITAL MARKETS

Just like our farmer's market, investors can select countless variations of products from multiple vendors. With time and practice, social justice investors learn which stalls offer their favorite goods that best fit their needs. In time, you'll start noticing which stall offers the pristine summer squash and be able to taste the difference between a yellow squash and a green zucchini.

After a few trips to the market, you'll get a better sense of whether you prefer the convenience of the public markets or the more personal but time-intensive experience offered by private markets. The market will also change over time. Some vendors will exit, others will grow to multiple stalls, while still others will enter as fresh-faced issuers.

You don't need to be a capital markets expert to consider yourself a successful social justice investor. You don't need to visit every stall or memorize the differences between a peach and a nectarine. You can listen to other people's experience and consider costs based on your personal budget. You may even decide to send a financial advisor on your behalf with a shopping list or a general objective to buy ingredients for a summer picnic.

The important piece is to know what you want to cook and to be familiar enough with the market to know how to get the products you need.

Energy Boost: Blazing a New Trail

Bill Bynum

When I moved to Jackson, Mississippi, in the early 1990s, most Black neighborhoods were banking deserts. When friends and family were unable to lend a hand, many were forced to call upon the predators of the financial system: payday lenders, pawn shops, and check-cashing outlets that charged exorbitant rates and imposed impossible repayment terms.

A bill for car repairs could wipe out a year's worth of savings. A trip to the hospital could burden an entire family for generations. Securing reasonable financing to purchase a house or launch a small business was all but impossible.

Having spent years building community development loan funds and credit unions, I was all too familiar with the vicious cycle of debt traps leading to financial ruin.

Still, despite my professional experience, I didn't anticipate the question that would change the trajectory of my life's work.

You see, relocating to Jackson also meant finding a new church home. Luckily, I found Anderson United Methodist Church, which welcomed my family and me with open arms.

Open arms and a call to ministry.

"Tell me about yourself," Pastor Stallworth eased our conversation forward. "What brings you to Jackson?"

When I shared that some of my most rewarding experience was time spent supporting minority credit unions in their efforts to fill financing gaps across North Carolina, Pastor Stallworth's face lit up and he leaned forward in his chair.

"I've wanted to organize a credit union in this community for years. There are no banks here and our families have to pay an arm and a leg for any type of financing."

I nodded, thinking that he was describing the very conditions that drew me to Jackson, and that fueled my professional endeavors to drive affordable capital to low-wealth communities in the Delta.

Pastor Stallworth rubbed his chin and thumped his knuckles against the arm of his chair. "I've got to say, this feels like divine intervention."

I rocked back, somewhat uneasy. My goal in meeting with Pastor Stallworth had been to join a church. Not to build a financial institution from scratch.

I sat pinned to the back of my chair. My chest rose and fell as Pastor Stallworth's eyes pierced through to my soul. "We've been wanting to organize a credit union for some time," he said. "And here you are, sitting in my office with the skills and network we need to pull off this ministry."

I stared back, silent, still trying to process it all.

Pastor Stallworth waited a beat, then continued, as if he hadn't just detonated a spiritual depth charge.

"Well," he said. "Will you do this? Will you create a credit union for our community?"

In that moment, two paths materialized under my feet. One led toward the career I had been planning for and working toward: leading a team of professionals focused on helping businesses generate good jobs for Delta residents. The other path stretched deep into the unknown: organizing a volunteer credit union in a Jackson, Mississippi, banking desert.

I must have said yes, because moments later I found myself holding Pastor Stallworth's hands as we prayed for a successful ministry.

I would later come to understand that forces beyond my comprehension were in control as, over time, what I thought were divergent paths would merge into a powerful force for good in communities across the Deep South.

Credit union organizing means months and months of tedious, taxing, uncertain work. We needed to marshal volunteers to oversee financial management, deposit raising, operations, compliance, product design, marketing, and myriad other tasks required to meet the needs of our local community.

Mississippi hadn't approved a single credit union in the previous eight years. Across the country, new credit union charters were on the decline.

Still, we moved forward. Church members stepped up to navigate the grueling process of applying for a credit union charter. We collected commitments for deposits after worship and transformed the church's tithing room into our first branch.

Slowly but surely, we worked through the mountain of paperwork, regulations, fundraising, and policies required to establish a credit union. A small group of volunteers blazed a trail toward affordable finance in North Jackson. We enlisted the head of the state credit union association for guidance and assistance. We rallied the community around the common goal of everyone deserving access to responsible, affordable financial services.

Many hours, regulatory forms, and prayers later, we succeeded.

Mississippi's secretary of state delivered the charter from the pulpit at a celebration emceed by a beloved local news anchor. The event spilled into the parking lot, where balloons streamed from tables overflowing with soul food and dessert. Children screamed with laughter as they jumped in rainbow-colored bounce houses. It was a remarkable day of triumph and fellowship that I'll never forget.

In that moment, I was surrounded by friends, colleagues, regulators, and volunteers who shared a common goal of helping their community and neighbors. It reinforced what I had seen many times over the years, that dedicated people, working together, can slog through the toughest of barriers.

Hope Community Credit Union (now Hope Federal Credit Union, and better known by our community as HOPE) was organized in 1995 by the members of Anderson United Methodist Church as Mississippi's only church-sponsored credit union. It would be another 20 years before Mississippi approved another credit union.

HOPE became a beacon for our community and has grown far beyond a handshake promise in the pastor's office. In 2002, the paths of my day job and my ministry officially converged, when Hope Enterprise Corporation became the sponsor of Hope Credit Union. In 2005, we were recognized as the fastest-growing credit union in the nation for building its deposit base. A 2007 survey ranked Hope Credit Union fifth in the nation for the largest increase in membership growth during 2005 and 2006.

Now, nearly 28 years after its founding, HOPE has generated nearly $4 billion in financing that has benefitted more than 2.6 million people throughout Alabama, Arkansas, Louisiana, Mississippi, and Tennessee, all while shaping policies and practices that have improved conditions in opportunity-starved communities nationwide. In 2022 alone, more than 110,000 people lived in households served by HOPE. Nearly half of all HOPE members did not have a banking relationship, or relied on predatory lenders before joining the credit union. Today, HOPE is one of the nation's largest Black- and women-owned financial institutions.

My colleagues and I remain rooted in the communities we serve. We lead by listening to our member-owners and responding to their needs.

One of my favorite examples is a mortgage borrower, Tellisha Crawford. Tellisha was a recruiter for Goodwill who has always dreamed of owning a home. She and her husband wanted to create a loving environment for their two adopted children. Mounting medical bills, other debts, and a low credit score, however, prevented her from securing a mortgage. After learning about Hope Credit Union from a success coach at Goodwill, she met with Hope's team in Biloxi, Mississippi. A close look at her finances revealed that she could lower her monthly debt payments by refinancing her auto loan. Before long, she had improved her credit enough to qualify for the mortgage. In her words, "I believe in giving a hand up and not a handout. . . . Hope lifts its members up."

While Hope Credit Union began as a project in a Jackson church, the ministry has extended far beyond the tithing closet walls, empowering people throughout the Mississippi Delta, the Alabama Black Belt, and in towns and cities across one of the most economically distressed regions in the country. It's a testament to what is possible when people come together to help their neighbor.

Contributing Author Biography

Today, Bill Bynum leads the family of HOPE organizations (Hope Enterprise Corporation, Hope Credit Union, and Hope Policy Institute), which provides financial services, leverages private and public resources, engages in advocacy, and otherwise acts as a catalyst to fulfill its mission of strengthening communities, building assets, and improving lives throughout the Deep South, and mitigating the extent to which factors such as race, gender, birthplace, and wealth limit one's ability to prosper.

12.

Align Your Cash with Your Values

Unless it's stuffed under your mattress or hidden in a Gringotts vault, your cash is working on your behalf and in your name. Social justice investors put that cash to work for good.

Cash is the most liquid asset a person or organization can possess. Unlike bonds or stock, which can take a few days to sell, cash is immediately available for withdrawal, for any purpose. Most people keep their cash invested in savings, checking, or money market accounts at banks and credit unions, which dutifully offer modest interest rates.

Your choice of bank or credit union is one of the most socially and environmentally impactful decisions you can make with your money. Your deposits will fund the financial institution's investment strategy, whether it's financing Main Street businesses or Wall Street financial instruments, solar farms or fossil fuel extractions, mortgages for veterans or investments in private prisons and gun companies.

Social justice investors align their cash deposits with banks and credit unions whose investment strategies are aligned with their own personal values. This chapter will guide you through your cash options and explain how to research your financial institutions to determine their effectiveness in executing your social justice investment goals.

What's the difference between a bank and a credit union?

While both are depository institutions (i.e., legally permitted to accept cash deposits from customers), the main difference between banks and credit unions is their profit status. Banks are organized as for-profit companies, meaning they are either privately owned or publicly traded, while credit unions are nonprofit organizations. The difference in profit status creates many differences between the products and services each type of financial institution offers.

A credit union is owned by its members and is almost always set up as a cooperative. Credit unions typically open membership to individuals who share a common interest or bond. For instance, some credit unions offer membership to people employed in the same industry, the community they live in, their faith group, or membership in another organization.

As nonprofit organizations, credit unions are focused not on profit maximization, but rather on providing members with the best terms the unions can afford for their financial products.

Banks, on the other hand, are focused on making a profit for their shareholders while also creating financial products and services for their account holders. On average, banks charge more fees, and at a higher rate, than credit unions do.

Is my cash safe?

As long as your cash deposits sit in an FDIC-insured bank or NCUA-insured credit union, the federal government will cover your cash deposits up to $250,000 per depositor, per financial institution. Megabanks receive the same government insurance protection as your local community credit union.

If you decide to move your cash to another institution, be sure to confirm that the new institution has either FDIC or NCUA insurance. If it does, then your protection remains intact.

FDIC insurance covers all deposit accounts at insured banks up to the insurance limit of $250,000 per depositor, per FDIC-insured bank. Insured accounts include checking, savings, money market deposit accounts, and certificates of deposit (CDs).

Cash deposited in a federally insured credit union benefits from the same insurance amount (up to $250,000) and is administered through the FDIC's lesser-known sister organization, the NCUA, which is a federal insurance fund backstopped by the US government.

How does my financial institution use my cash?

Though we may be tempted to believe the money deposited in our savings accounts is stored in heavily guarded vaults miles below ground, there's a very strong likelihood that your cash is actively being used to create profit for your bank or credit union.

Today's financial institutions sweep your deposits into pools of money from which they make loans and investments to other people and organizations. That's how banks make their money: by using your cash deposits to make more money. All while ensuring you have access to your cash any time you need it, for whatever reason, immediately.

Financial institutions use your cash to make any number of different investments, and each bank has a different investment strategy. Their options range from making consumer and small business loans to government bonds to publicly traded investments to real-estate transactions, among countless other strategies.

It's all perfectly legal and mostly ethical. As long as your deposits are within the $250,000 insurance threshold, your cash is safely insured by the US government.

How to research banks and credit unions

Researching the investment strategies of banks and credit unions has never been easier. Organizations like Mighty Deposits, Bank for Good, and Global Alliance for Banking on Values, have done all the heavy lifting and organized their results into easily searchable online databases available for free.

I prefer MightyDeposits.com because, while it's the most comprehensive US source of information about where banks and credit unions invest money, it also organizes its findings into a user-friendly, searchable database. Simply type the name of your financial institution into the website's search feature. Users will be able to see what percentage of their money is invested in Main Street investments (referred to as community investments) versus Wall Street investments; the breakdown of community investments across small businesses, housing, public works, and farms; and how much money stays in your local area (versus being exported to lucrative opportunities in other communities).

When I first researched my financial institution, I was shocked that my FDIC-insured bank used only 8% of my dollars toward community investments. A whopping 92% financed Wall Street strategies that likely weren't aligned with my values.

If you face similar results, it's time to weigh your options and consider moving your cash toward strategies that fund the change you want to see in the world.

Finding a financial institution that works for you

With today's publicly available resources, social justice investors can find banks and credit unions that work for them with relative ease.

Sticking with Mighty Deposits as our primary tool, social justice investors can begin by using the "Find Banks" or "Find Credit Unions" tool available on the organization's website. Within either tool, start by completing the following sentence:

> "I want a [select bank or credit union] located in [enter city, state, or zip code] that is [select social justice priority from dropdown list]."
> Next, select "Find Banks" or "Find Credit Unions" based on your preference.

You'll be presented with a list of financial institutions, with every listing including information on what percentage of your deposits will be used for community investing plus an analysis of how the financial institution performs against the national average. Beyond the summary list, users may click through to more detailed information about each bank or credit union.

From this summary list, select three to five banks or credit unions that align with your values. This is now your shortlist, from which you'll select a new banking partner.

Now that you've confirmed that the financial institutions on your shortlist both operate in your local area and match your social justice values, the next step is checking whether they offer modern conveniences you may rely on for your daily financial habits.

This research requires some internet sleuthing or phone calls to your shortlisted banks and/or credit unions. You're trying to determine whether the financial institutions on your shortlist offer conveniences and benefits like a local branch in your area, a network of ATMs, mobile apps, electronic statements, online portals, mobile check deposits, automatic bill payment, and other services important to you.

Online sleuthing and phone calls will also help you determine the friendliness and helpfulness of their customer service team, which will be critical as you complete the bank transfer process.

Once you've landed on your bank or credit union of choice, you're ready to move forward in rewiring your financial ecosystem.

PAUSE FIRST BEFORE REWIRING YOUR FINANCIAL ECOSYSTEM

Changing your primary banking account means rewiring your everyday financial habits. As your financial life has evolved, you've likely set up your checking account to receive direct payments like salaries, expense reimbursements, tax returns, and government benefits. Even more complex is the web of payments like your mortgage, rent, car loan, credit card bills, insurance, utilities, student loans, and childcare expenses that are pulled from that same checking account.

This web of payments, both incoming and outgoing, will take time and energy to unwind from your old account and then reestablish using your new account. You'll need to dedicate hours to updating banking information across your entire financial ecosystem. Not to mention the vigilant watch of both bank accounts to avoid any late payments or overdrawn accounts.

Before you move forward, make sure you're in the patient, diligent mindset required to rewire your financial ecosystem. Choose the time that's right for you.

What if I can't change my primary account right now?

If you decide that unwinding your existing banking practices is impractical at this time, you still have options for leveraging your cash for social justice purposes.

Perhaps you advocate that your existing bank or credit union do better. Write a letter to the CEO of your bank asking for a greater percentage of cash deposits to be used toward community investments.

Or perhaps you maintain separate bank accounts for your emergency funds or rainy-day savings. These nonprimary accounts exist outside your checking account and are not set up for recurring inbound or outbound payments. These accounts are less likely to be connected to your web of incoming and outgoing payments and be operationally easier to transfer to a financial institution aligned with your values. You can preserve your existing checking account while moving these separate accounts to a bank or credit union aligned with your values, all while maintaining your financial habits.

There are many banks and credit unions that will make opening an account as easy for you as possible. Consider Hope Credit Union (HOPE), which created a product called "Transformational Deposits" for individual investors who want to expand HOPE's lending into low-wealth communities in the Mississippi Delta, one of the nation's most impoverished regions. The minimum size of Transformational Deposits is $1,000, and the product is available through a share certificate (credit union equivalent of a bank CD) or a money market account (hybrid checking and savings account). Either product is federally insured up to $250,000 per depositor.

Social justice investors play an instrumental role for financial institutions like Hope Credit Union. Moving your cash to organizations that know how to convert it into loans for minority-owned small businesses and affordable housing for low-wealth individuals creates substantial advances for social justice.

How to open your new checking account

First, determine how much money you want to hold in cash. Your cash accounts might be spread across checking and savings accounts as well as CDs or money market deposits. Next, consider whether you want to move your money in stages or all at once.

Once you've selected a new financial institution using the process outlined above, it's time to open a new account there. Many depository accounts (i.e., checking, savings, money market) can be opened online using your social security number and a few forms of identification.

Once opened, inquire with the customer relations team about the process used to fund the new account. If possible, be careful to start with a deposit that's large enough to eliminate any monthly fees. You'll also want to order your checks, debit card, and ATM card, which can take a week or two to arrive.

If your salary is paid through direct deposits, ask the financial institution's customer relations team for a direct deposit authorization form, which should include your new account information. You can give this document to your employer and any organization that makes direct deposits to your account. Your human resources manager may also ask for a voided check from your new account. The payment switch may require two or three payment cycles to take effect. Watch for the incoming payment before making any outgoing payments from your new account.

Once your direct deposits are being sent to your new account, it's time to update your automatic bill-payment systems. The trick is to unwind any bills that are automatically pulled from your old account and reconnect them to your new account. Start by making a list of any companies that automatically debit your account for their bill payments. Think about your biggest expenses (i.e., rent or mortgage, childcare expenses, credit card payments, student loans, small business financings, car payments, insurance bills, etc.) and work your way down to smaller expenses (i.e., utility bills, tuition savings plans, Netflix subscription, etc.). You can also go back through your bank statements to catch any automatic payments you may have missed. Use this opportunity to do financial "housecleaning," eliminating any recurring services you no longer need or want.

If necessary, transfer more funds to your new account to be sure there is sufficient money to cover the payments. Leave enough money in your old account to cover checks that haven't cleared or automatic payments that may still be made.

Even after you've switched over all your recurring transactions from your old account, it's best to leave the old account open another three months just in case any unexpected payments occur. You'll also want to confirm that any outstanding checks have cleared. During this time, leave sufficient funds to avoid penalty fees for low balance.

During this waiting period, download PDFs of any financial statements you may need. Keep in mind the IRS may need records for tax purposes. You can check their website to verify how long you should be saving those records. Additionally, if you're applying for a loan, the financing company may require several months of statements.

After this waiting period has ended, transfer the remaining cash balance from your old account to your new account.

Now it's time to close your old account by following your bank or credit union's prescribed procedures. Do not assume your account has been closed just because there is no money left in it. To avoid any low balance fees or penalties, close it out formally by going through the official procedures.

Whew! It takes some work to reconfigure your daily financial habits. Take a moment to breathe in your accomplishment. Now your cash is working to advance social justice.

Energy Boost: A Person of Many Firsts

Dr. Riordan Ledgerwood

Pacing around the living room of my apartment, I read the same text message for the umpteenth time in the past two minutes. This single text was absorbing every ounce of my energy and concentration. This text could dissolve over a decade of study and work in 200 characters or less.

The thought of losing my future life as a medical doctor before it had really even started made my toes flex and stretch into the carpet. This unconscious movement reminded my feet to keep moving, beating another 10 feet of carpet. I looked around the small room, reliving every sacrifice over the past four years of med school. I thought about the countless hours poring over textbooks and memorizing countless concepts and diagnoses. My mind flashed to my class-mates and the extreme emotional swings that catapulted us from nervous breakdowns to relief-fueled celebrations within a single week.

With this one text, I was about to risk all of it. After working so hard to hang on. To make it just one more day. Day after day, year after year.

Another lap around the coffee table.

Our last celebration had been a big one. Three weeks ago, I had celebrated my graduation from medical school and my journey to the East Coast, where I was starting a residency program at Walter Reed National Military Medical Center. A captain in the US Army, I followed strict military protocols. My path would eventually lead to deployment in an unknown destination, the sole physician to an armored combat unit.

Before deployment, however, I had to successfully complete residency, which is a daunting, grueling climb for any doctor in training.

Earning a spot in my specialty of choice (pediatrics) within the army was surreal. Watching the stars align to accept a position surrounded by military and civilian doctors focused on pediatric medicine almost made me believe in fate. Was I really going to risk it all through a text? One of the deans at my med school had advised me against everything I was doing in this text, as it would risk my position at the residency program.

My toes flexed again, propelling me into the kitchen. I found a pint of ice cream in the freezer and pressed it against my forehead, anything to distract my runaway mind.

My heart pounded in my ears and my breathing grew shallower.

This single text could define my entire life and the rest of my career.

I could either continue living the image I'd projected in my initial application or I could step into the person I truly was, openly. Either way, I had to make a decision before entering residency.

My phone buzzed in my hand. Words of encouragement from a friend. She knew my plan to text the program director of the residency program. She knew how scared I was to lose my place and everything I had worked for.

I have good friends.

Her encouragement calmed my anxiety. I was going to be me. My authentic self. A new chapter called for a new, authentic beginning.

One last time, I steeled myself to reread the text that could end it all. I gasped a shallow breath before sending a vulnerable text to the program director of the medical residency to which I had been accepted. He was a lieutenant in the US Army.

"Hello, Sir. This is Ri. Happy to be part of Walter Reed Pediatrics and looking forward to beginning residency soon. For your situational awareness, Sir, I'm genderqueer and I use they/them pronouns."

When my thumb brushed "Send," I felt my future swing from firmly secure to a cascading freefall over a cliff.

My mind went blank and my ears began to ring, high pitched. I shook my head to try and clear it.

I placed the phone on the coffee table, walked back to the kitchen, and sat at the table.

"What have I done? Did I just throw everything away?"

I stood and let my feet carry me around the room again. On the second loop around my coffee table, I stopped, put my hands on my knees, and gulped huge breaths of air. After a moment, I sank lower to lean against the couch. I spotted the boxes I had yet to unpack after my move across the country. This new living room was going to experience its first nervous breakdown, as I held my head in my hands, my anxiety threatening to overtake me.

Living my authentic self might cost me the chance to be a doctor. How was I going to repay all that debt if the army kicked me out?

A few choice four-letter words crawled through my head.

I closed my eyes and reminded myself it would all be okay.

It will all be okay.

It will all be okay.

My phone buzzed. My heart skipped a beat.

My phone buzzed again. I almost threw it across the room, just to delay for one more moment, and exist in this world where nothing was wrong.

Instead, I somehow found the grace to calmly lift it from the coffee table and unlock the home screen.

The program director had responded to my text, less than five minutes after I had sent what was quickly feeling like the most reckless missive of my life.

Program director: "Hey Ri. Let's have a sit-down meeting to talk about this."

Program director: "I'll loop in some other people—Major Roach and Dr. Olsen—to join us."

Ri: "Okay, thank you, Sir. Talk then."

Meanwhile, still in my apartment, a few more four-letter words ran through my mind. Even after my feet settled, my mind continued churning with fear and anxiety. By the time I walked into the Walter Reed National Military Medical Center four days later for the meeting, I was eagerly anticipating resolution of any kind.

I had spent all four of those days on a pendulum between reminding myself it was right and good to live my authentic self and the other extreme of psyching myself out for the worst. My motto had always been that if you expect the worst, you'll always be prepared, though I hardly felt like it.

At Walter Reed, I sat in one of the small meeting rooms scattered throughout the pediatrics department. I chose a seat on one side of the long conference table. All three chairs on the left side of the table had been pulled away from the table to make room for the white board and projection screen. I looked around, desperate to find a distraction from the severe mental anguish I was enduring while waiting for the program director to arrive. My eyes landed on the map of the area and the fire safety plan. I read every word, forcing my brain to focus on something, *anything* other than the cold dread digging into my spine.

Footsteps echoed through the hall. I tore my eyes away from my escapist reading material to sit straighter, reminding myself that, regardless of the outcome, I was ready to openly step into the person I knew myself to be.

My heart kept beating to the approaching footsteps. I forced my lungs to fill with air.

I stood and accepted handshakes from the program director, Major Roach, and Dr. Olsen. I had met all three doctors during my medical student audition rotation last year and was grateful for the familiar faces. I sent up a final, desperate prayer to keep my spot in the program.

"Please sit down," the program director invited me.

I sat and refilled my lungs.

"Ri, I'll cut to the chase. . .," he began.

Please don't kick me out, I thought desperately while keeping my face as expressionless as I could manage.

". . . I want to thank you. Thank you for sharing. We're so glad you're joining this program. You're going to make us so much better."

Time stopped. Shock prickled along my neck.

I leaned forward, pressing my toes into the ground.

My eyes blinked closed and I let reality crash into me. I was sitting in a military medical facility. Doctors who I respected and admired were welcoming me as my true self into their community.

I blinked again, rapidly pushing away the wave of emotions threatening to ruin my carefully crafted professionalism.

I would get to live my best life as my true self: a captain and doctor in the US Army who was genderqueer with they/them pronouns.

Shock collapsed into relief. I blinked furiously and cleared my throat.

Somehow, I kept it together.

I left that room with my shoulders held higher, my chin up, and a ready smile for anyone I passed.

When I next returned to Walter Reed, I don't think my feet hit the floor. My soaring heart guided me through the hospital instead.

My new apartment and the carpet I had paced so frantically would soon bear witness to a new series of pendulum swings. Some nights my poor feet couldn't make it to my bedroom and I fell asleep before my head hit the couch cushions. My coffee table was quickly buried under textbooks and notebooks.

My apartment also hosted many celebrations throughout residency, like the impromptu dance party when Harvard Medical School invited me to discuss my experience integrating sexual and gender minority health into medical education.

I entered the University of Louisville medical school in 2014, the year it became the pilot site for coursework and training in LGBTQ+ health issues based on guidelines from the Association of American Medical Colleges.

Talk about being in the right place at the right time.

At Louisville, LGBTQ+ healthcare topics are woven into the curriculum in classes that explore issues such as gender-affirming hormone therapy, taught along with more traditional coursework.

I remember classmates who felt it didn't apply to them or their future practices. It went against their beliefs and they didn't feel like they should be wasting their time on this subject.

Louisville now serves as a model for other medical schools.

I'm proud of the investment I made in myself to live my authentic self. The returns quickly stretched beyond personal fulfillment. My patients and my colleagues' patients have access to comprehensive sexual- and gender-relevant healthcare. More pediatric patients feel comfortable discussing their health-care needs with medical professionals.

I may never quantify the full impact of stepping into my true self, but I know it's made a difference for my patients. Risking it all was a small price to pay for the healthfulness and happiness of the patients who walked out with soaring hearts.

Contributing Author Biography

Captain Riordan Ledgerwood, MD, is a person of many firsts. They were the first openly trans medical student at the University of Louisville School of Medicine. They were the first openly trans resident at Walter Reed National Military Medical Center. And they became the first openly trans military pediatrician in the United States when they outed themself in a single text back in 2018. Currently they are serving in a dual role as an army pediatrician and a physician for an armored combat unit.

13.

Design Your Roadmap

Investors define and document their objectives and constraints in a governance document called an investment policy statement (IPS). An IPS, also known as your investor roadmap, is the reference tool that helps you stay on course when making investment decisions, so it's important to spend the time getting it right from the outset of your journey.

Policies are powerful agents of change

In his book *How to Be an Anti-Racist*, Dr. Kendi describes an activist as a person who makes change. More specifically, a person must change *policy* in order to consider themself a true activist. Initially reading this passage, I questioned how I could ever create policy change to advance social justice.

But then I realized:

I have power over my financial portfolio, which is filled with my money. I own my portfolio and exercise full decision-making authority over the *policies* that govern its direction.

I may not be able to knock on senators' doors to ask for legislative change, but I do have control over my own actions and my own assets.

Dr. Kendi reminds us that we all have power. In the investment world, we certainly have the power to update the policies that govern our investment decisions.

The change is simple: expand your investment objectives to reflect your personal values in addition to your financial needs. A simple bullet point that defines returns in terms of both financial earnings in addition to social justice advances creates a butterfly effect across all subsequent investment decisions.

Plus, since you added this bullet point to your personal IPS, which is an investment *policy* statement, you will have successfully created a policy change. By Dr. Kendi's definition, you can now consider yourself an activist.

Don't roll your eyes! We all start where we can and do our part to create the world in which we want to live. Adding a bullet point may seem minor at first blush, but it creates powerful butterfly effects through every subsequent investment decision. This bullet point forces you or your financial partner to always consider new investment purchases through the lens of "How will this advance social justice?" as well as "Will this investment achieve my financial goals?" Your commitment to social justice cannot be forgotten or deprioritized when it is a defining tenet of your investment objectives.

Expanding your investment returns to include social justice advances is a truly significant milestone for any social justice investor. Celebrate this accomplishment for the win that it is.

Financial term: Liquidity

The term "liquidity" describes how quickly or easily an asset or investment product can be converted into cash. Highly liquid investments like publicly traded stocks, bonds, and ETFs can convert to cash in two to three days. Less liquid investments like real estate or a rare book collection take significant time (i.e., weeks to months and sometimes even years) to identify a buyer, complete due diligence, and negotiate legal documents.

For example, when Nicole needed to withdraw money from her investment portfolio to cover the down payment on her condo, she was surprised that her cash wouldn't be available for five days. Her advisor explained that it would take a few days to sell stocks from her portfolio. The stocks would be sold for cash at the current market value. The sale would take three to five days to clear the various financial systems before it was delivered as cash to Nicole's account.

HOW TO CREATE AN IPS

Whether you're working with a financial advisor, navigating options within a preset 401(k) investment menu, or designing your own DIY investment portfolio, writing an IPS is the chance to create a document that clearly states your investment objectives (returns and risk you feel comfortable targeting), as well as any constraints (liquidity needs, legal and timing considerations, tax implications, any unique circumstances).

Social justice investors can create an IPS by answering the questions in the righthand column of the below grid with answers that resonate with their own financial situation.

Investment Policy Statement—Template	
Objectives	
Return	What level of *financial earnings* do you or your family need to satisfy future cash needs for financial events? What *social justice advances* do you prioritize?
Risk	How much volatility are you willing to withstand to meet your financial goals?
Constraints	
Liquidity	Describe any cash needs you foresee in the immediate, medium-term, and long-term future. Examples may include college tuition payments, down payments for homeownership, or healthcare-related needs.
Legal	Describe any legal parameters that impact your financial decisions. Examples include spousal or child support requirements, inability to hold certain investments due to job-related conflicts of interest, etc.
Timing	Describe when you expect any cash events, including cash withdrawals described in the "Liquidity" section. State your retirement timing goals.
Taxes	Describe any unusual tax circumstances that impact your financial decisions. Examples include inheritance taxes, ownership stakes in small businesses, significant ownership stakes in privately owned corporations, self-employed status, etc.
Unique Circumstances	Describe anything not covered above. Examples include sentimental value of specific investment positions, stakes in family-owned businesses that cannot be sold, or desire to focus on specific industries like healthcare or technology companies. For traditional investors, describe any values-based investment goals like environmental or social designations.

Creating an IPS for Angela

An IPS is one of those things that's easier to understand if you can walk through a real-life application, so let's create an IPS for Angela, one of our recurring characters introduced in chapter 2, as an example.

Angela creates an IPS that documents her desire for moderate risk, moderate return investments. Angela is the 40-year-old married woman who recently left an outside-the-home profession to raise her three young children. She designs an IPS for her DIY investment portfolio, which complements her family's other investment portfolios (i.e., three tuition savings accounts, her husband's 401(k) retirement account, and the pension she built during her 15 years as a schoolteacher).

Angela's Investment Policy Statement	
Objectives	
Return	Moderate. Angela targets a 7% financial return. Angela equally values the generation of social justice returns, which are measured through evidence of social change. Specifically, Angela targets returns that support Black and brown communities across the United States.
Risk	Moderate.
Constraints	
Liquidity	None—Angela's goal is long-term wealth creation, so she does not need any "liquid" investments (i.e., investments that can easily and quickly be withdrawn in cash). Instead, Angela's family relies on an emergency cash fund they keep in a bank account to cover any unforeseen financial events.
Legal	None—Angela does not have any legal considerations (e.g., alimony, child support, lawsuits, contractual obligations, etc.).
Timing	Thirty-year time horizon. Angela hopes to build an investment portfolio to use later in life when her husband joins her in retirement. She does not plan to withdraw any investments until that time.
Taxes	Unlike her teacher pension or her husband's 401(k), Angela's self-directed investment account offers no tax advantages.
Unique Circumstances	None.

TAKE THE TIME YOU NEED TO GET IT RIGHT

An IPS is a living, breathing document that will change as your financial conditions evolve. Wise investors will take their time in establishing an IPS that meets their objectives while conforming to their investment constraints.

Even after you've written a beautiful investor roadmap, social justice investors should also carve out time at least once every year to review and update their IPS with their financial partners to ensure their investments will grow and mature to deliver enough cash at key points in their lives.

Since your IPS will serve as your roadmap for all subsequent investment decisions, many investors, even those pursuing a DIY approach, may find it valuable to consult a financial advisor during this crucial step. Financial advisors are uniquely positioned (and professionally trained) to help you find the right balance between financial earnings and social justice advances.

Energy Boost: Laying Cash Tracks

Christina Travers

Even in the moment, a meeting with Michael was surreal. He was a "master of the universe" type on Wall Street, meaning that he believed his opinion was the authority for finance and investment decisions on the biggest stage in the world.

One day, he and his team showed up at my office to discuss how Wall Street could finance community development in the United States. To be honest, I didn't believe they would really show up until I watched as he leaned his elbow and forearm on our reception desk.

We had submitted a proposal to Michael's firm to finance our lending operations through a fixed income bond traded through Wall Street. Michael had come to our offices to respond to our request that his team facilitate the bond's issuance.

As a senior leader at one of the biggest household names on Wall Street, Michael was a proud representative of traditional investing. The influence his firm held over the US capital markets was powerful. The firm's stamp of approval could overcome some of the arbitrary barriers that keep low-wealth communities from access to basic financial products.

If he said yes.

My team represented the Treasury and Capital Strategies Division of one of the largest social justice investment shops in the United States: Local Initiatives Support Corporation (better known by our acronym, LISC). Our job was to bring money in so our loan officer colleagues could lend it out.

Our loan officers were incredible at their jobs. They underwrote historically marginalized and/or low-income borrowers who had been overlooked by mainstream financial sources. They worked with borrowers to create a loan agreement and servicing plan that worked for the borrowers, their communities, and LISC.

My job was to (a) raise the capital needed to make these loans and (b) make sure we repaid our investors the principal and interest as it came due.

My job got a lot harder after the 2008 financial crisis. Even though the organization performed very well throughout that period of economic upheaval, bias against our client base only got worse. Mainstream investors had bought into the opinion that low-wealth communities, particularly those with Black and brown borrowers, were uncreditworthy, meaning that LISC, which almost exclusively served these communities, was inherently "high risk."

No amount of audited financials, cash reserves, or other data-based evidence could convince them otherwise. After all, logic is not an effective means of combating bias.

I felt painted into a corner.

Our capital sources had dried up. After the financial crisis, money-centered organizations like banks and insurance companies had added layers of risk mitigation to prevent future losses. Despite our strong performance, LISC was hamstrung by shorter terms and restrictive conditions that kept us from reaching our borrowers in these underserved communities.

Managing a loan fund's financial capital is like laying tracks ahead of a moving train. A train of loan officers is hurtling forward, driving capital and loans to the people and communities we serve. My team built the cash tracks, making sure we always had cash in the bank to wire money out to our approved borrowers. The train couldn't take its cars of capital anywhere if there weren't tracks to get them there. To do so, I was constantly raising capital in some type of financial product (usually a loan or a grant) from financial organizations like Michael's. Then the loan officers would deploy that capital to our borrowers to use for projects like small businesses, childcare facilities, and affordable housing. Sometimes it felt like we were building the track just ahead of the moving train to keep it on schedule. It was constantly surging forward. Money in, money out.

In the early 2010s, the capital was slow and restricted. The individual tracks were shrinking to smaller pieces; I had to work faster to lay the same length. Market conditions meant that I had to knock louder and longer at doors to buy more track. Some doors stopped opening. Others offered shorter and shorter lengths of track.

The train was in danger of slowing to a crawl, trapped in its own circular route. Something had to give. We had to try something new, even if it meant taking a few hits.

That meant that, despite my instinctual pessimism about why Michael was in our office right now, I found myself hoping this wouldn't be one of those hits.

"That idea is never going to work."

I felt my flickering hope die.

Michael launched into a lengthy diatribe and I steeled myself for a very familiar resolution. My team had already encountered a steady stream of politely hesitant responses from investment bankers up and down Wall Street—or worse, exuberant positive reception from sales representatives who provided terms too optimistic to believe for a first-time bond.

Michael's speech was cresting, finally reaching the point:

> "No investor will buy a bond from a community lender at these prices and terms. Plus, the issuance is entirely too small. The market will reject anything less than a $500 million offering."

It was finally time to cut in.

I adjusted my watch and met his eyes. "I appreciate your points. We believe there's a market of investors who are interested in a financial product that offers a modest financial return and a rich social impact return. Is there a scenario in which you would consider underwriting us and selling our product to new investors?"

It didn't work out with Michael.

Fortunately, I wasn't the only person looking for ways to build more train tracks.

Serendipity would bring me a critical tool for our tool box. Worlds collided when a former classmate named Gerard (not his real name) and I were asked to speak on the same panel at a financial services conference. Our careers had never intersected and I was glad to reconnect with Gerard, who was now a senior leader at S&P Ratings, one of the "Big Three" investment ratings agencies.

Before that panel, I had believed that community loan funds had no pathway to apply for an investment rating from S&P Ratings. Without a rating, LISC wouldn't be able to effectively raise capital from the public capital markets. Public capital markets were the wide, well-lubricated tracks to the smaller tracks of private capital markets. At the time, we were forced to stick to these small tracks from private capital markets, knocking on one door at a time for terms and pricing that worked for the investor at the expense of our borrowers.

Luckily for me, Gerard was creating a new pathway for community lenders to pursue an S&P rating.

All I could see were train tracks. Long-term, low-cost train tracks that stretched to the horizon. And a bigger, faster train.

Public capital markets meant that we could knock on thousands of doors at the same time, asking for tracks of long-term, low-cost capital.

LISC's strong performance, as well as its financial strength, would propel us toward an investment-grade rating from S&P Ratings. That rating would be the key that unlocked the door to the public capital markets.

In fact, our initial offering was five times oversubscribed: we had $500 million of interest in the initial $100 million product. And we weren't the only community loan funds trying to crack the code. Within five years, community loan funds had raised over $2 billion through S&P-rated bond issuances in the public capital markets, at terms and pricing designed for positive community impact.

Access to the public capital markets has transformed how community loan funds are able to raise capital. We were delighted to affirm our position that investors are interested in an investment product that creates significant positive social impact returns while generating sustainable financial earnings.

Thanks to Gerard, we had the confidence to persevere, despite hitting walls and receiving negative feedback. Since that time, my team has facilitated hundreds of millions of dollars into low-wealth communities through community lenders like LISC.

That's a lot of train tracks.

Contributing Author Biography

Christina Travers is executive vice president and CFO of Local Initiatives Support Corporation (LISC), one of the largest community-development financial institutions in the United States. Prior to joining LISC, Christina was the CFO of Working Solutions CDFI, a San Francisco Bay Area micro-lender. Christina also spent over two years at the Low Income Investment Fund (LIIF) as vice president for finance and capital strategies. Before LIIF, she spent 10 years at LISC as senior vice president for finance and capital strategies. Christina has moved billions of dollars into low-wealth communities across the country.

14.

Redefining Risk

Risk is the possibility that an investment's *actual* gains will differ from the *expected* return.

Every single investment carries at least a nugget of risk. Stocks, bonds, exchange-traded funds, and mutual funds can lose value, even all of their value, if market conditions deteriorate. Even "safe" investments like US Treasury bonds backed by the US government come with inflation risk if they do not earn enough over time to keep pace with inflation, or the increasing cost of living.

WHY WOULD I KNOWINGLY ACCEPT RISK?

Investors must accept risk to generate return.

The world of investments is defined by the fact that risk and return are directly related. The greater the amount of risk an investor is willing to take, the greater the potential return. The smaller the risk an investor is willing to take, the smaller the potential return the investment will provide.

Then again, the higher the risk, the more uncertain the return.

How do investors manage risk?

While risk is inherent to investment, we *can* manage and mitigate investment risk.

Investors mitigate uncertainty through risk management strategies. For example, diversification is a risk management strategy that reduces uncertainty by mixing a wide variety of investments into a portfolio. An ETF may contain hundreds of individual stock positions, limiting your exposure to the potential volatility of any individual security. The rationale is that a portfolio constructed of different securities will, on average, yield higher longer-term returns and lower the risk of any individual security.

Imagine you're back at the farmer's market. You love fruit and have decided that this is the year you're finally going to try every peach recipe in the cookbook. You'd already decided that 90% of your budget was going to peaches this summer, so you sign up for a three-month subscription to peaches for the season. One month in, you learn there has been a blight on peaches and your subscription can only send half of the expected fruit in each scheduled delivery. All of a sudden, you don't have the resources you need to fulfill your recipes' needs.

Diversifying your investment portfolio across different products (strawberries, apples, and peaches) and even asset classes (zucchini, tomatoes, and corn) means that you will still have a balanced diet even in the face of an unexpected disaster that negatively affects one of the products you selected.

Now you're asking: but what if there's a drought that negatively impacts *all* my products?

That's called market risk. When overarching market conditions change, it can impact all your investments, all at once. If a war breaks out on the opposite side of the globe and it impacts the price of gas, prices rise across all economic sectors. The resulting inflation drives up expenses for every organization that relies on gas for any segment of their supply chain. This market risk means your investment portfolio may drop in value very quickly.

Successful investors manage this market risk by maintaining a long-term investment approach. In other words, keep calm and hold onto your investments in an economic downturn. As time passes, new market conditions emerge and eventually investment values return and surpass their previous values. Based on historical data, holding a broad portfolio of stocks and bonds over an extended period of time significantly reduces your chances of losing your money.

As covered in later chapters, investors can mitigate risk by researching prospective investments, investing in products that reflect the risk profile prescribed by your investor roadmap, and consistently monitoring their portfolio's performance.

SOCIAL JUSTICE INVESTORS REJECT BIAS-BASED RISK

Social justice investors think about risk both similarly to and in a radically different way than their conventional counterparts. Just like traditional investors, we consider risk as the possibility that our investments may not yield the financial earnings we expected. We apply similar asset allocation and diversification risk management strategies to mitigate the risk of financial losses that negatively impact our ability to meet both expected and unexpected life events. We bite our fingernails as we wait for improving market conditions to rescue our portfolio's current dollar value.

At the same time, we consider risk through a radically different lens than our conventional counterparts. Knowing that traditional finance is rife with racism and sexism, social justice investors challenge assumptions about *what* (or who) is an investment risk and *why* we consider it (or them) an investment risk.

How do we know traditional finance is rife with racism and sexism?

Rather than examine a laundry list of evidence that will be waved away by traditional investors as exceptions or special circumstances, we can instead point to the historical impacts of rampant exclusionary financial beliefs.

As the common saying goes, the proof is in the pudding:

> For instance, there is a reason that the median white family has 13 times more wealth than the median Black family in America. It's because traditional finance has institutionalized the bias that investing in dark-colored skin is riskier than investing in light-colored skin.

Even before the United States declared independence from Great Britain in 1776, the colonial financial system expanded and thrived in financing the slave-based economy; it even went so far as to pioneer asset-backed securities collateralized by enslaved people in the same way that today's banks issue mortgages backed by houses as collateral. If the enslaver did not repay a loan, the lender would take the enslaved person(s) listed as collateral to recover a portion of the unpaid principal balance. The market for enslaved people was very liquid, in that enslaved humans could be sold for cash at a local auction block.

Slavery created the foundation of modern American capitalism. Its effects can be traced through American financial history to explain why the racial wealth gap continues to widen generation after generation.

Another notable example of institutionalized biases in investment practices was the explicit integration of racial biases in government-approved underwriting policies from 1934 through the 1970s.

To restore faith in US credit markets following the Great Depression, the federal government hired Homer Hoyt, a respected economist at the University of Chicago, to develop the first national set of underwriting criteria—who is a good credit and who is not—for the new Federal Housing Administration in 1934.

The year before, Hoyt had published a list of racial groups, ranking them from having a "positive" to a "negative" influence on property values:

1. English, Scots, Irish, Scandinavians
2. North Italians
3. Bohemians or Czechs
4. Poles
5. Lithuanians
6. Greeks
7. Russians, Jews
8. South Italians
9. Negroes
10. Mexicans

The federal government's establishment of systematic underwriting policies and lending infrastructure helped save the collapsing housing market, but it largely excluded Black and brown neighborhoods from government-insured loans. Those neighborhoods were deemed financially "hazardous" and colored red on maps, a practice that came to be known as redlining.

Loan approval policies dictated that loans within redlined neighborhoods would be rejected, leading to a severe shortage of credit in geographic footprints with high percentages of Black and brown communities.

We still see the impacts of exclusionary financing policies in the pricing of housing owned by Black and brown families in the twenty-first century. In 2022, a Black family in Maryland sued a real-estate appraiser and online mortgage provider for discrimination. The lawsuit alleges the couple was discriminated against when their Baltimore home was undervalued due to their race. The proof? The home was appraised twice: When the Black family showed their home to the appraiser, the home value was reported as $472,000. When they removed any indication that a Black family lived in a house and asked a white colleague to stand in for a second appraisal, the same real-estate appraisal company valued the house at $750,000.

Research conducted by the Brookings Institute notes the misvaluation of houses owned by Black and brown families resulted in an average loss of $48,000 in value.

Proof, meet pudding.

Social justice investors go into the ring to fight everyday against the racist, sexist, and exclusive norms established by traditional financial and capital systems.

Traditional finance, and those that work within it, often hold deeply embedded assumptions and biases about what makes a particular security or investment risky. These biases permeate across all types of investment decisions, and as you might have guessed, they usually result in underinvested people and communities being even further removed from economic opportunities.

Social justice investors recognize that biases are not facts; we refuse to make investments that accept biases as universal truths.

Challenging assumptions that have been miscategorized by traditional finance as universal truths requires courage. You *will* get pushback. You *will* be told you're being ridiculous.

You must press on. You must uphold your values. If you don't, you'll be perpetuating a racist, sexist, and exclusionary financial system.

Time for a deep breath.

Really, close your eyes and feel the air expanding your ribcage. Hold it for a beat or two. Then release slowly.

When you open your eyes again, remember:

Your investments will finance change.

When social justice investors interrogate risk assumptions and question ideas that feel inappropriate or deeply flawed, it changes the flow of financing. When enough investors ask questions about biased assumptions, management starts to rethink investment decisions to avoid embarrassing questions.

Our collective work will change the flow of financing.

HOW DO SOCIAL JUSTICE INVESTORS CHALLENGE BIASED ASSUMPTIONS TODAY?

Social justice investors can challenge biased assumptions in today's investment culture by questioning how risk is assessed.

An answer you will often hear is that risk is determined by research and data, the leading risk mitigation strategy in the financial industry.

Today's mainstream financial system is built on data. In fact, in the United States, some of the largest banks consider themselves technology companies rather than financial institutions.

Data has tremendous influence and power over investment decisions. Financial institutions gather and store tremendous amounts of data on purchases, consumer habits, and borrower information. Economists and financial engineers then create financial models through which they pour the data to predict investment outcomes.

If an investment pitch cannot be backed with data, it is significantly less likely to be approved or even considered.

Invoking "data" is often used as a technique to shut down further questions. We're meant to accept the authority of this unseen data and its ability to predict important risk factors.

At some point, mainstream financial leaders convinced themselves that data cannot lie.

Data can lie.

Data must be gathered, cleaned, stored, extracted, and analyzed by human beings, each of whom has their own biases and misperceptions. A dirty little secret of finance is that data models absorb the personalities and philosophies of the human beings who create them.

That's not to say you shouldn't use data in your financial decisions. Rather, social justice investors dig a little deeper to understand how the data is prepared and whether the data methodology aligns with your values. You have to trust the human beings who handle the data rather than trust the data in and of itself.

Let's consider a modern example. Be warned—this one hits close to home.

FICO® scores can reflect biases

Because almost all risk is defined and managed through data, traditional investors rely heavily on easily accessible data like FICO® scores (also known as credit scores) to predict and mitigate risk.

Have you ever applied for a loan? If you have, then you'll remember that one of the first steps—even before you complete the loan application—is to check your credit score. Most people use FICO® scores, which grade a borrower's projected ability to repay a loan on a scale of 0 to 850. The higher the score, the more appealing the borrower is to the loan officer. This single assessment is used as a primary driver of credit decisions by 90% of America's top lenders. It is the most widely used broad-based score and plays a critical role in billions of lending decisions every year (Rob Kaufmann, "The History of the FICO Score," myFICO.com, August 21, 2018).

A key facet of American society is that almost everyone holds debt, and your credit score determines how much debt you will be able to take on. A FICO® score can determine if a person is able to get a mortgage to purchase a house, a student loan to attend school, or a loan from a hospital to affordably repay healthcare bills. I personally have a mortgage, student loans, a credit card line of credit, and a car loan. I watch my credit score meticulously and am pinged every time it changes—positively or negatively—because I know it is critical to my financial security.

FICO® scores lubricate our entire financial system, not to mention your ability to pay for your way of life.

The idea is that these credit scores can objectively determine someone's risk as a borrower. But have you ever considered how FICO® scores are actually calculated? What is included and what is left out?

A FICO® score is a bit of a black box, determined by a specific algorithm that is monitored and updated by a privately held company. While we do not know the proprietary algorithm, we do know some of the components that comprise your score. They include payment history, amounts owed, length of credit history, new credit, and credit mix ("What's in My FICO Scores?" myFICO.com).

Let's consider payment history, which is benchmarked to account for 35% of one's FICO® score. I say "benchmarked" because the actual percentage varies from person to person based on the corporation's proprietary algorithm.

Payment history assesses whether you've paid past credit accounts on time and is a strong indicator of your capacity and willingness to repay future debts on schedule. It's undeniably one of the most important drivers of credit prediction.

But let's dig in deeper. What types of accounts are considered in FICO®'s credit payment history assessment?

FICO® considers credit cards (Visa, MasterCard, American Express, Discover, etc.), retail accounts (credit from stores where you shop, e.g., department store credit cards), installment loans (loans where you make regular payments, e.g., car loans), finance company accounts, and mortgage loans.

Do you notice what's missing?

Recurring payments like rent, utilities, and cell-phone bills, which demonstrate an individual's ability and willingness to make regular cash payments over a prolonged period of time.

FICO® scores do not include fundamental drivers of credit for low-wealth communities. They don't include savings accumulation rates, history of making rent payments, or history of making cell-phone payments. FICO® scores, used by 90% of mainstream banks as the primary driver of credit decisions, do not include fundamental factors that predict the ability of low-wealth people to repay their debt. FICO® scores and mainstream banks reinforce a vicious credit cycle.

You can also begin to imagine how these FICO® score criteria begin to compound. Low-wealth people are unable to "qualify" for a loan from a mainstream bank because they do not have a FICO® score, but are unable to earn a FICO® score because they cannot repay a loan to a mainstream bank. Even after being excellent credit stewards—never missing a rent payment, always paying their cell-phone bills, setting aside a portion of their paychecks to savings—their efforts do not translate into FICO® wealth. Particularly when a key component of your FICO® score—length of credit history—suffers, the longer someone is kept from accessing credit. When life happens—as it does to all of us—they aren't able to translate their excellent track record into an affordable loan. Still rejected by mainstream banks, they turn to their only alternative—payday lenders—and sink further into an even more vicious credit cycle of predatory lending, forever excluding them from earning a good FICO® score and effectively shutting them out from America's financial systems.

While use of these credit metrics works for those already in the mainstream financial system, FICO® scores reinforce a vicious credit cycle where low scores keep certain communities from successfully applying for the mainstream loans whose successful repayment would improve their scores.

To create a financial system in which no one is left out, social justice investors must acknowledge and intentionally counter the industry's role in shutting out people of color and low-wealth communities from basic financial resources and investment products. Social justice investors understand how people who have been living outside the economic mainstream are not uncreditworthy, but have credit profiles that can be accurately assessed through alternative lenses that account for historical lack of mainstream financial resources.

So why is it important for you to know the history of the FICO® score and the role it plays in perpetuating a vicious credit cycle?

Because social justice investors question assumptions around data and risk. We think critically and ask questions about what assumptions may be impacting your investment decisions.

You will catch resistance from people who implicitly trust in traditional data, data models, and FICO® scores. Challenging the status quo means being brave. Don't let others rush you with the false reassurance of "it's always been done this way." The more you start to recognize the biases and systems in place that you hope to challenge, the more confident you will be in making unconventional decisions.

Social justice investors do not blindly accept the narrative presented by traditional investors, but instead ask questions and listen to the people and communities into which we are investing. We break down risk based on those conversations and create risk mitigants based on that assessment.

We need to know our history so we can recognize its patterns and refuse to repeat it.

HOW DO SOCIAL JUSTICE INVESTORS ASSESS RISK?

As a social justice investor, you will have to get comfortable about thinking for yourself and questioning what heralded financial leaders insist is correct.

Rather than accepting conventional wisdom as reality, we look to the fundamentals of risk (i.e., the potential for volatility) both in the short term and the long term. We consider whether the financial earnings and social justice returns are potentially volatile in the short run and also examine how an investment would impact the long-term volatility of the economy and society.

You brought your crystal ball, right?

In all seriousness, social justice investors lean on trusted partners and professionals for help in assessing the risk of any investment or portfolio of investments. Please know that there really aren't any foolproof mechanisms to assess risk. Investors of all stripes get it wrong all the time. But sometimes just asking questions about the way risk is determined, and who determines it, is enough to get started.

Luckily, there are resources available to guide you. From professional financial advisors to publicly available, justice-minded risk assessments, there are many tools to help you get your footing. We'll cover those tools later in this book.

In the meantime, start your mental preparations to push back, ask questions, and reject face-value interpretations of risk. If all else fails, follow your instincts and ask people you trust for a gut check.

You'd be surprised how frequently traditional investors fail to check their assumptions beyond face value. Your ability to recognize that oversight is your advantage.

Energy Boost: When It's Not Your Lottery Ticket

Catherine Berman

Economic opportunity often feels like a lottery system for many people living in America. Who gets access to economic opportunity and networks for career advancement feels like a game of chance. If you were born in a certain zip code, to a certain family, looking a certain way—you may feel like you won the lottery. Economic, social, and other opportunities flow your way and doors open magically with benefit of the doubt abound.

But if you didn't get that ticket, you'll find yourself in a different America. One where you are constantly trying to tear down misperceptions. Myths about who you are, your competencies, and even your potential. You constantly face down misconceived notions about what you can actually achieve if you're finally given the opportunity.

My mother and *abuelos* (grandparents) got a taste of the American lottery game. They fled Argentina during a time of government persecution in their search for a new life of opportunity in the United States. Like many immigrants they arrived with no possessions, showing up with thick Spanish accents, a different culture, and zero job prospects. There was no "friend of a friend" to help them get their first job. There was no "rich uncle" to pay the bills until they got on their feet. My grandparents and mother landed in Los Angeles to find themselves sleeping in a broken-down apartment infested with termites and struggling to figure out how to make it here when the lottery ticket isn't yours.

My Abuelo was a smart man. He spoke five languages, read feverishly, and worked hard. Unfortunately, due to a childhood trauma accident, he lost much of his hearing and struggled to learn English. This limited his job prospects and his community-building. Abuela was a fabulous and fierce partner—strong, kind, and with a "can-do" attitude. She was also incredibly lovable and made friends wherever she went. Together they stumbled through myriad jobs upon arrival—from factory jobs that meant 5 a.m. shifts and three-bus commutes for Abuela to door-to-door sales jobs that left Abuelo rejected and penniless.

For my *abuelos*, the ticket to opportunity did not arrive from birth or connections; it arrived from entrepreneurship. Taking what little money they had saved and adding a modest community loan, my *abuelos* opened their first *bodega* (little convenience store) next to a butcher's shop on the east side of Los Angeles.

It was exciting for my grandparents to finally feel in control of what could be an exciting financial future. Abuelo managed the front counter, eager to greet customers and remain watchful of theft, a constant peril of owning a corner *bodega*. My Abuela wandered the aisles to chat with customers, managed the store's inventory, and kept the *bodega* immaculate.

But the excitement unfortunately did not last long. Within the year, they noticed the butcher that shared the space with them was proactively discriminating against them. He would loudly tell his customers not to "trust those foreigners" and shared lies about my grandparents to dissuade his customers for buying from the *bodega*. To no one's surprise, the *bodega* failed.

But once my Abuelo got a taste of entrepreneurship, he never looked back. He sold that *bodega* and launched several more until he finally found the right corner and the right community. I'm delighted to say that the last convenience store made my *abuelos* happy and successful. They had secured financial freedom for themselves and my mother. My Abuelo never forgot the chance that community lender took on him to help him realize a dream of business ownership.

From business ownership came homeownership and, when my Mom was in her twenties, my *abuelos* were able to buy their first home in North Hollywood, California. I can still remember the insanely fragrant roses my Abuela was able to grow in her backyard. To date, I've never smelled anything like it. Their home was a happy one, filled with the scent of *mate* (Argentine tea), *dulce de leche*, and other treats brought home from the *bodega*.

Visiting my *abuelos* in North Hollywood, I never thought about their struggle before I arrived. I only knew the successful *bodega* that brought smiles and loyal customers—not the snarky comments and jibes that they experienced early on. But as I grew up, I learned about my family's path to financial security and came to appreciate the true opportunity that comes with entrepreneurship and homeownership—two of the strongest pillars of wealth creation—and what it can mean for generations to come.

My Abuelo passed on my birthday several years ago. But I think if he saw me today, he would smile. I, too, have chosen a path of entrepreneurship. One that supports entrepreneurs like him across the country from all backgrounds, from all cultures—and without that precious lottery ticket. I cofounded a company, CNote, whose mission is to expand economic opportunity for all so that our fate is not sealed with a Spanish accent, the color of our skin, or any other way society tries to limit us through perception rather than potential.

At our company we use entrepreneurship, homeownership, and grit as our lottery ticket. We are challenging the odds and creating economic opportunity in all corners of the United States. As a mother, I am raising two beautiful children to understand the importance of economic justice and racial justice, and am encouraging them to do their part to build a more equitable society.

No one in my family was born with that economic opportunity lottery ticket—and perhaps no one in yours was either. But together we can change the game on who gets access to capital, opportunity, and economic mobility—and that's a true win for all.

Contributing Author Biography

Catherine Berman is a three-time entrepreneur with experience launching and building scalable businesses. In 2016, she cofounded CNote, a women-led impact platform that uses technology to unlock diversified community investments to increase economic mobility and financial inclusion. Under

Catherine's leadership CNote has become a leader in the field, making it easier for everyday investors to invest in their communities. Before launching CNote, Catherine served as managing director of Charles Schwab, where she led a strategy division focused on the future of finance incorporating behavioral economics and predictive analytics. Her previous company, Global Brigades, is now the world's largest student development firm operating in five countries. Over the last two decades, Catherine has also held senior roles in both management consulting and venture capital.

15.

Create an Investment Budget through Asset Allocation

Just like you monitor cash available to cover your rent, utilities, and groceries, investors monitor their portfolio's ability to cover future financial expenses like retirement, the down payment for a house, or their children's college tuition.

Investors use asset allocation as a tool to move their money into the asset types (i.e., equity, fixed income, and cash) that best match their expected financial needs.

WHAT IS AN ASSET ALLOCATION BUDGET?

Your goal is to budget your investments into the three main asset types (equity, fixed income, and cash), each of which has its own strengths and challenges. Your job is to budget your investments into the right mix of asset classes required to successfully execute your investor roadmap.

By the end of this budgeting process, you'll have assigned what percentage of your portfolio should be in equities, fixed income, and cash. ETFs and mutual funds should be included in either equities or fixed income depending on the composition of the underlying securities. When combined, equities plus fixed income plus cash should equal 100% of your portfolio amount.

For instance, if you're hoping to retire in the next 10 years, you'll likely move more and more of your money into fixed income bonds that deliver consistent, predictable cash flows. You'll need those cash flows to replace the paycheck you previously received from your place of employment. In this case, you might allocate 70% of your assets to fixed income instruments and leave the remaining 30% in moderate return equity stocks with the hope that they continue to grow and can be converted into fixed income investments under optimal timing conditions.

Alternatively, if you are 30 years old and do not expect to retire until you're 70 years old, then you would likely allocate a high percentage of your assets into equity stocks, which are expected to grow your initial contribution into much larger sums as time passes. These "capital gains" sometimes require years of patient growth to realize their full potential. Still, if you keep all of your assets in equity stocks, it is challenging to withdraw cash in the case of a financial emergency due to timing constraints and tax implications. Instead, 30-year-old you may keep 30% of your portfolio in fixed income bonds in case you need quick access to cash and don't want to sell your equity stock.

Investors should also remember that they'll need to consistently monitor their asset allocation budget to make sure investments stay within their prescribed percentages. Investments are not static, but grow and shrink over time. You should assess your asset allocation mix at least once a year to make any adjustments necessary to stay within your budget.

Asset allocation rule of thumb

While professional Wall Street investors can design breathtakingly complex asset allocation strategies, most people start with a simple rule of thumb:

> To calculate an appropriate amount of equity, or stocks, in your portfolio, subtract your age from 100. For example, if you're 30 years old, you should keep 70% (100 minus 30) of your portfolio in stocks. If you're 60 years old, you should keep 40% (100 minus 60) of your portfolio in stocks.

The balance of your investment portfolio should be in fixed income securities.

How should I think about cash?

Cash should sit in your checking and savings accounts, not your investment portfolio.

Any cash sitting in your portfolio should be there only if it's waiting to purchase new investments or waiting to be withdrawn in the immediate future.

Instead, investors should maintain enough cash in their checking and savings accounts to fund their day-to-day expenses, with an emergency cash fund stretching out to cover at least three to six months of living expenses.

How you manage your day-to-day budget is up to you. However, the more money you save, the more money you can contribute to your investment portfolio to fund your future financial goals.

HOW DO ANGELA, TOM, AND NICOLE CREATE ASSET ALLOCATION BUDGETS?

Consider Angela, our DIY Investor. At 40 years old, Angela has time to adopt a long-time horizon for equities to grow into considerable wealth. Plus, Angela's family has several other investment portfolios (like her pension, her husband's 401(k), and tuition savings plans for her children) that enable her to take extra risk in her DIY portfolio. Taking advantage of her long lead time as well as the added financial security from the other portfolios, Angela starts by allocating 85% of her portfolio toward high-growth stocks, while keeping the remaining 15% in fixed income bonds in case she needs access to cash for an unexpected financial event.

Nicole, on the other hand, is 55 years old and is beginning to think about retirement. She begins to shift her portfolio to fixed income bonds, the interest from which she hopes will replace a portion of her full-time salary. Nicole decides to allocate 55% of her portfolio to fixed income bonds and the remaining 45% to equity stocks and ETFs. After all, she's not retiring immediately and wants her wealth to continue growing in the meantime.

Tom, our 401(k) investor, is presented with a different approach altogether: target date funds, which mix several different types of stocks, bonds, and other investments to help investors take more risks when they're young, and gradually get more conservative in their investment strategy over time. The "target date" is the expected date of retirement. As you get closer and closer to the target date, the mix of investments will transition from mostly stocks (more aggressive) to mostly bonds (more conservative). Tom is very interested in the target date fund, since it solves most of his concerns about creating and updating an asset allocation budget that works for him.

Energy Boost: Faith, Hope, and Investments

Dr. Andrea Abrams

Two more girls zoomed past while I dialed the phone. Their braids bounced across their T-shirts as they ran to join their classmates down the hall. These two newest students didn't even have registration papers to hand in; they just wandered in with their friends from school.

I sighed and rubbed my eyes, stealing the moment to rest my head against my hand.

The receiver clicked. Finally.

"Mom," I jumped in. "You *have* to close down the registration for this program. There are too many kids here as it is. We can't possibly add more."

"Andrea . . .," my mom began, her tone irritatingly patient.

"No, Mom."

I was determined to stop her before she could begin the "You are strong and capable" speech.

"We are bursting at the seams and our teachers are absolutely overrun by sheer volume. We cannot handle any more students in our classes. We just can't."

"Honey, it will all be okay. Each of those little ones needs a place to be a kid after school. We'll get it figured out. After all, we have you."

My sigh was so guttural that the girls down the hall stopped to stare. I coughed and dug my fingers into my forehead. My mother is a bright light in this world, but sometimes I need her to meet me in the chaos.

My parents had applied for a Bush Administration grant to run an after-school program through our local church in Wiggins, Mississippi.

In rather serendipitous timing, I had returned home to attend graduate school at Emory University. While I loved being close to my family, I was irritated to find myself volunteered to organize an after-school program that my parents had launched. Not only was I responsible for building the curriculum and managing the program's operations, but I was also educating congregation members and neighborhood parents in how to be after-school teachers.

I was overcommitted and under-resourced.

News of the program spread like wildfire through our local community. New faces showed up daily. Our teachers, already facing a steep learning curve, were visibly overwhelmed by the sheer number of children, volume of joyful shrieks, and noisy complaints about the snack selection.

I closed my eyes and let another sigh—silent this time—expand my ribs.

"That's all well and good, Mom. But we've reached capacity. We *have* to close the registration until we get our feet under us."

My mother cleared her throat.

My heart sank even as my mind held onto a thread of hope that she might agree.

"Andi, sweetheart. I know you're tired. You're juggling so many balls right now. And you're handling it beautifully. But we're not closing the registration to those kids. God said 'Let the little children come.' We're letting them come."

Silence filled the call. Her pen scratched against her notepad at home.

I knew better than to push back against a Jesus-based argument with my mother.

Dang it, I hate it when she pokes me in my faith.

The seconds floated past as I mastered my patience and prayed for grace.

"I need more teachers. This week. I'm not kidding. There are too many kids to manage as it is. It's not safe."

I could hear the smile in her voice. "Of course, dear. I've got two interviews this afternoon. Now I've got to run or I'll be late."

My eye twitched.

"Oh, and Andi. I love you and appreciate the energy you are pouring into these kids and this community. See you for dinner tomorrow! Your father is making his spaghetti sauce."

I heard the receiver click off and watched three more girls join their friends, all perched on the purple couch that the pastor's sister had dropped off last week. A girl in a pink T-shirt flicked her braid over her shoulder before delivering the punch line to whatever story she'd been weaving throughout the duration of my phone call. A current of giggles followed, infectious to anyone in earshot. Other heads turned to smile at the group of girls who were doubled over in glee.

Despite the exhaustion and the pressure to manage a fledgling nonprofit, the corners of my mouth tugged upward when their laughter pealed down the hall. It's hard not to soak in the joy from a gaggle of first-grade girls enjoying friends, jokes, and popsicles.

That year was tough. I was constantly training new teachers, negotiating with nine-year-olds about sufficient time for snacks, and reminding my parents that Jesus never had to submit grant reports to the US federal government.

I walked home each night feeling every moment in my legs, back, and feet. I fell onto my bed those nights asleep before my head hit the pillow.

Even then, when I thought my brain had permanently fried and I was desperate for half an hour of silence, I knew my contribution, however small it was, was making a difference.

Never before had I been part of something so deeply good. Never before had I been so confident that I was helping to make things better.

I was surprised to discover my reluctance to vacate my post when my mother hired a permanent administrator. I was relieved to step into my role as a full-time student, but sad to walk away from the joy of watching the returns from my investment of time and energy.

I had introduced the purple couch first-graders to some of my favorite stories through early reader books. By that spring, they had pulled me into their reading circle and were sharing their favorite stories from chapter books. Their eyes sparkled when they presented me with their school projects and report cards.

Their mothers hugged me and cried when they learned I was leaving. My eyes may have prickled, too. It is incredibly rare to be part of a community that surrounds you with love and support. I still treasure my time with those students, their families, and the incredible teachers whose learning curves were as steep as mine.

All the people in that community taught me an incredible lesson that continues to grow along my own path as a scholar and a teacher.

Faith in others is an investment.

My mother had faith in me that returned not only the beginnings of a successful after-school program, but also my growth as a person. I earned the soul-fulfilling satisfaction of working hard on something that matters.

The community had faith in the new teachers and their students. Their faith was returned with improved test scores, happier children, and community pride that overflowed into the surrounding neighborhoods.

The lesson stays with me today. I invest my faith in others and watch the returns flow through my community in unexpected ways.

I think my mother would be proud. She'd also remind me there's so much more work to be done.

Contributing Author Biography

Dr. Andrea Abrams is an American anthropologist, associate professor, president of the Association of Black Anthropologists, and author of *God and*

Blackness: Race, Gender and Identity in a Middle Class Afrocentric Church. Andrea is currently an associate professor of anthropology, gender studies, and African American studies at Centre College in Danville, Kentucky. In 2018, Centre College promoted Dr. Abrams to vice president for diversity, inclusion, and equity, recognizing "the momentous work that Andrea has led at Centre and the importance of our chief diversity officer as a senior leader in the College's administration."

16.

Budgeting Your Social Justice Priorities

This chapter will describe how to weave your social justice priorities, however you define them, into the asset allocation budget we created in the previous chapter.

Today's investors have the flexibility to work across a spectrum of approaches for allocating their social justice priorities. Some investors will decide that 100% of their portfolio will be allocated to social justice investments, while others will require time to transition a traditional portfolio into a social justice portfolio. Still others may carve out a percentage of their portfolio dedicated to social justice returns while preserving a large portion of their preexisting portfolio of traditional investments.

I want to stress that your fellow social justice investors offer no judgment on whatever percentage you assign to a traditional investment portfolio versus a social justice investment portfolio. Nor will we pass judgment on which social justice initiatives you prioritize within your portfolio. We all recognize that every person has different life circumstances. Just as we are all in different phases of our careers, caregiving paths, and life journeys. Many of us have started with a 100% social justice investment portfolio only to circle back to a 50/50 approach when we encountered an unexpected detour. Do what works for you and know that when life happens, you can adapt your portfolio accordingly.

HOW TO CREATE AN ASSET ALLOCATION BUDGET FOR SOCIAL JUSTICE PRIORITIES

For the sake of simplicity, this chapter presents the two most common approaches for a social justice asset allocation budget: micro asset allocation, which enables the investor to create a highly tailored division of social justice priorities, and macro asset allocation, which widens out the lens to more generic social justice opportunities.

Micro asset allocation

Social justice investors seeking highly tailored social justice returns may prefer a micro asset allocation approach, where delineation across asset classes is very precise.

This micro asset allocation strategy is like a custom order pizza: half of the pizza is green peppers, sausage, and pepperoni and the other half is ham and pineapple. In a nonmetaphorical example, you may wish to invest 25% of investments to Black-owned businesses, another 25% to affordable housing in Indigenous communities, 25% to Latino-owned businesses, and the final 25% to rural healthcare initiatives.

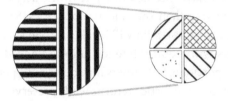

Micro Asset Allocation

≡ Traditional Investments

‖‖ Social Justice Investments

⠂ Black-Owned Businesses

⁄⁄ Affordable Housing in Indigenous Communities

▦ Latino-Owned Businesses

⧵ Rural Healthcare

For an enlarged version of this chart, please visit the author's website at TheSocialJusticeInvestor.com.

A micro asset allocation approach is generally better for people who prefer going "all in" with their investment decisions or sculpting precise advances in social justice based on their personal values. A tailored approach enables an investor to create a complex asset allocation configuration designed to address a robust set of goals. A micro asset allocation approach is ideal for social justice investors with the capacity and willingness to research how individual investments may meet their precise roadmap objectives.

Macro asset allocation

Alternatively, other social justice investors may widen out their lens to a more generalist view on social justice returns. Many investors prefer to split their investment portfolio into two macro buckets: one bucket for investments that seek traditional, profit-maximizing return goals and another bucket for social justice investments (i.e., sustainable financial earnings coupled with social justice returns).

In this case, you may allocate one portion of your portfolio to deliver social justice investor returns and another portion of your portfolio to deliver traditional returns. It's like when you can't decide on pizza toppings and order a half-pepperoni, half-cheese pie. This is a great approach for people who want to practice with a smaller portion of their portfolio before applying a social justice lens to their entire pool of financial assets.

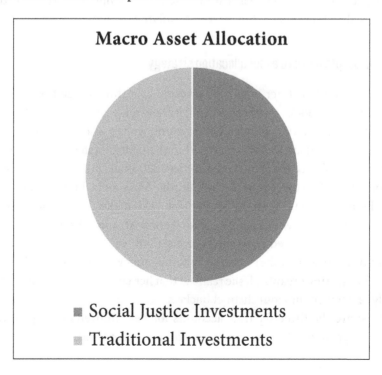

Applying a macro asset allocation approach is generally better for people who prefer adopting a gradual introduction to social justice investing and want to take one step at a time. Or perhaps you wish to execute a generalist approach to social justice investing and do not want to be overly prescriptive in their asset allocation strategy.

Managing your asset allocation budget

No matter your preferred asset allocation strategy, its implementation must be monitored and maintained to ensure it continues to align with your investment strategy over time. Monitoring can be as simple as scheduling time once a year to compare your asset allocation performance against the budget you planned.

As investments change in value over time, you may need to adjust your portfolio to remain within your budget parameters. Or, more realistically, you'll be able to fill your asset allocation buckets with investments that aren't yet available. For instance, if initially you couldn't find investments that satisfied your goal to invest in companies that address LGBTQ+ discrimination, you can check back in a year to search for new opportunities. You'd be surprised by how quickly the market is evolving.

Angela adopts a macro asset allocation strategy

Angela recently left her long-time position as a third-grade teacher at an elementary school in northern Virginia. Determined to set aside $15 every week to build wealth through a DIY account, Angela also feels a strong pull to support social justice initiatives within the United States. Her perception of the world shifted in spring and summer 2020 as she processed coverage of George Floyd's and Breonna Taylor's deaths. She watched the mass protests and found herself wishing she could do more to make change. She hosted a book club for Dr. Kendi's *How to Be an Antiracist*, and is listening to voices of those who have lived experiences of social injustice.

In Angela's words, she's ready to "put my money where my mouth is."

While getting organized, she realized that her family's portfolio is organically segmented into four distinct buckets.

First are the three separate accounts for her children's college tuition support. Second is her husband's employer-sponsored 401(k) account that receives regular contributions from her husband as well as an employer match. Third is her teacher pension, which stopped receiving contributions when she left her job.

Angela is hesitant to modify her children's education fund since she worked with a financial coach to create the funds when they were born. She trusts the work she created and doesn't want to tackle more than she can handle all at once.

Angela is also loath to make changes to her pension for fear of entering into any paperwork required by the state government.

She's encouraging her husband, Roy, to revisit the investments he selected in his 401(k), but otherwise leaving the account to his management.

Instead, Angela decides to isolate her social justice lens to a new wealth-building account she's creating through a DIY investment platform. She has the most freedom in this segment of her portfolio to orchestrate her personal vision for investment success. For Angela, this means pushing past her otherwise low-risk appetite to be more aggressive in pursuing investments with higher returns, including evidence of social justice advances. Since she feels secure that her family's baseline financial needs are met, she can flex other investor muscles in a separate account.

Angela knows she is not an expert in propelling social justice, but she knows she wants to invest in people with her dollars. So she decides that any and all investments in her DIY wealth-building account will apply a social justice framework targeting returns that support Black and brown communities across the United States.

Angela does not have a precise geographic footprint and is not focused on a specific subset of social justice advancements. Instead, she focuses on generalist social justice investments targeting organizations that deliver products and services designed to advance Black and brown people's ability to reach their full potential.

Utilizing a macro asset allocation approach enables Angela to isolate her social justice investment framework to the segment of her portfolio in which she has the most freedom to align her objectives with her values.

Nicole teases out a micro asset allocation strategy

Nicole, our New York–based marketing executive, decides to apply her commitment to social justice to her investment portfolio with scalpel-like precision. For Nicole, this means increasing access to affordable capital in low-wealth communities and supporting companies that promote gender equality.

With this level of detail—and the help of a trained financial advisor—Nicole applies a tailored asset allocation approach to her investment portfolio.

Nicole begins by transferring $5,000 from an emergency fund sitting in her primary banking account to a savings account at Hope Credit Union, a minority-owned credit union based in Mississippi that drives affordable capital to low-wealth communities in the American South. This supports her goal to increase access to affordable capital in low-wealth communities.

To fulfill her goal to invest in companies that promote gender equality, Nicole directs her financial advisor to use her next financial contribution to purchase an exchange-traded fund (ETF) comprised of stocks in companies with demonstrated commitment to gender equity through equal compensation and gender balance in leadership.

Tom opts for a hybrid approach

Tom, who recently began a new job at a manufacturing company in Cincinnati, decides to pursue his investment policy statement through two avenues. While one half of his 401(k) will be allocated toward the traditional, profit-first approach, the second half will be allocated toward investments defined by their commitment to social justice returns. The first half will satisfy his financial earnings requirements, while the second half supports his goal to create the world in which he wants to live.

Happy to arrive at a clear strategy for his twin return objectives, Tom retrieves the 401(k) paperwork provided by his human resources manager. He notices the requirement for every employee to indicate what percentage of their financial contributions should flow to which options in their 401(k) investment menu.

Tom grins to himself and is relieved at how easily he can execute his plan through simple math. If he has 100 percentage points to allocate across the menu of investment options, then a total of 50% will be allocated to investment options that satisfy his traditional asset allocation plan while the other 50% will be allocated to investments offering high social justice returns.

Poised to begin allocating his assets across his two buckets, he pauses. Then freezes altogether. The menu of options isn't organized into traditional investments versus social justice investments. The list of options includes descriptions of product types (equities versus fixed income), geographical footprint (US-based versus international markets), associated fees and expense ratios, and performance history.

With his chin in his palm, Tom sighs and returns his pencil to his desk. He needs more information to make a decision.

We'll pick up Tom's story again in the next few chapters.

Energy Boost: A Contrarian with Impact Convictions

Fran Seegull

A contrarian by nature, I was well practiced at questioning the status quo as I began my graduate studies. And after two years in the male-dominated culture of Harvard Business School (HBS), I had developed the thick skin and rugged perseverance needed to voice my opinion with confidence.

I needed all the confidence I could muster to make counterarguments against the reigning beliefs about business, finance, and investment in the late 1990s. Everyone at school had fully bought into the credence that profit maximization is king.

A decade earlier, Michael Douglas (portraying Gordon Gecko in the 1987 blockbuster *Wall Street*) had famously declared that "Greed is good." I'm pretty sure more than half of my classmates could recite that whole speech by heart. I'm *positive* the dramatic speech influenced their worldviews on finance and investment.

Our professors echoed the sentiment through a more polished academic lens. Students learned that a corporation's primary objective is to maximize financial value for its shareholders through high profits and enriched valuations.

But I approached my education with a different perspective. Coming from a foundation and nonprofit background, I understood how a charitable grant delivered both financial value and impact. I was at business school to explore, instead, how investments could generate financial returns alongside social and environmental returns.

In business management courses, I challenged the prevailing logic that short-term staff cuts would lead to long-term efficiency. In investment courses, I asked guest speakers why so few dollars found their way to women entrepreneurs let alone women of color.

When I argued that investors could find solid financial returns in funds and businesses that also generated powerful impact returns, my classmates raised their eyebrows and exchanged sidelong glances with each other.

I understood quickly that, while my courses might not teach me what I wanted to learn, I could still acquire the tools and experiences needed to figure it out for myself.

So, I took traditional coursework in finance, investing, management, and venture capital. I rounded that out with a yearlong field study analyzing the flow of venture capital to women entrepreneurs. Really, I should call it the trickle of capital. At that time, women entrepreneurs gained access to a paltry 2% of early-stage capital required to grow a startup business into a successful venture. It's an issue that hasn't improved much since 1998.

During the field study, I interviewed dozens of experts about the severe gender disparity in access to critical early-stage investments. I talked to individuals at venture capital firms and angel networks, as well as women entrepreneurs, researchers, and national thought leaders.

While the reasons were complex, the pattern was undeniable: women received far fewer and far smaller early-stage investments than their male counterparts.

Conventional investors were leaving so much value on the table by dismissing these entrepreneurs, and I suspected that the same was occurring with entrepreneurs of color. People with great ideas and the grit to pull off ambitious strategies. People who would thrive if given access to the same resources and capital as their white, male counterparts.

The culmination of my coursework and field study was a series of papers arguing for investments to deliver both financial and impact returns.

But first, I had to argue my position to my venture capital professor, who was widely acknowledged as the brightest, most revered scholar of the field—Professor Josh Lerner.

I'll admit that I was intimidated. Plus, I had considered the possibility that I could flunk my last semester if my series of papers were rejected at face value.

If I could make it past this gatekeeper of a professor, maybe it would spread to my other professors as well. It turns out our conversation set me on a defining course for my career.

I remember my nervous energy falling away as we debated my unconventional approach to investments. I argued that investors could generate healthy financial returns alongside and maybe even because of their social and environmental impact. He disagreed and assertively let me know that, contending that any impact consideration would, by definition, suboptimize financial returns. We argued whether a returns curve (with financial on one axis and impact on the other) would be convex or concave.

I pushed back based on my experiences and research findings, but I didn't have the data or empirical evidence to prove my claims at that time. It was 10 years before the term "impact investing" was even coined.

"Show me the financial returns of a social impact investment. Then we'll see," he offered as we concluded our conversation.

To my utter surprise, he returned my paper with an excellent grade.

"I disagree with your theory," he told me. "But your points were well argued."

What I remember most is the respect I felt for this revered professor. Even while I was arguing against the very intellectual principles at the center of HBS, he never dismissed my ideas.

What's more, I accepted Professor Lerner's offer to come back every so often with the empirical evidence I gathered throughout my career directing capital to investments that offered impact alongside financial returns.

At my five-year reunion, I reintroduced myself to Professor Lerner and asked if he had given any more thought to whether investments could deliver solid financial returns alongside impact.

He wasn't convinced and said, "Get back to me when you have your financial returns."

I got the same response at my 10-year reunion.

At my 15-year reunion, when I shared my returns findings validating my theory, he spent a few minutes considering the results, scratched his chin, and said, "Maybe."

Just shy of my 20-year reunion, I was invited to participate in a working session at HBS with a group of the leading impact venture and private equity managers in the country. There were 30 or so people in an executive education classroom, all seated in the shape of a "U." I looked around to find familiar faces from top investment firms. I saw colleagues from Bain Capital, Bridges Ventures, DBL Partners, and KKR, among others.

But the high point of the event was when I discovered Professor Lerner was delivering the keynote address at dinner later that day. At the predinner reception, I sought out my former professor and reminded him of my thesis, asking if his opinion had changed since last we spoke.

Professor Lerner smiled at me before gathering his notes and walking to the podium.

"Thank you for inviting me this evening. Before I begin presenting my research about the merits of impact investing, I need to make an acknowledgment. I have been pushed in my thinking over the years by a persistent student of mine in this room."

He turned to me and said my name. At long last, he validated and credited my early thinking as a student around the value of generating impact as part of an investment's total returns.

I still don't know how I maintained my composure to calmy reply, "Thank you, Professor." However, I don't think I processed a single word of his keynote address. When my mind wasn't busy turning cartwheels, it was shouting "I knew that curve would be convex!"

In the years since, I've continued to build on those early convictions, strengthened by the years of learnings and conversations with great thinkers like Professor Lerner. I'm incredibly proud of the work my team and I at ImpactAssets and now at the US Impact Investing Alliance and the Tipping Point Fund on Impact Investing have accomplished in institutionalizing a new perspective on investing. We've been fortunate to partner with other leaders and organizations who wanted something more than what conventional thinking and practice could offer.

More than 20 years later, we've finally been validated by being adopted as part of the mainstream investment industry. As I like to say, the future of all investing is impact investing.

We still have work to do. But it sure does feel good to see your convictions validated. Even if it takes 20 years.

Contributing Author Biography

After graduating from Harvard Business School in 1998, Fran Seegull went on to become the chief investment officer and managing director at Impact Assets, where she headed investment management for The Giving Fund—now a $2-billion impact investing donor-advised fund. At the time of writing, Fran is the president of the US Impact Investing Alliance, which works to increase awareness of impact investing in the United States, foster deployment of impact capital across asset classes globally, and partner with stakeholders, including government, to build a national impact investing ecosystem. She also serves as executive director of the Tipping Point Fund on Impact Investing—a donor collaborative focused on growing the field. True to her contrarian roots, Fran continues to question the status quo and find new and innovative ways to drive capital to people and planet.

17.

Financial Detox

After you've identified your financial partners, designed an investment strategy, and created an asset allocation budget, you're ready to consider the individual investments that comprise your portfolio. Because you've laid out all the groundwork in advance, selecting investments for your portfolio is remarkably straightforward:

Sell any investments that deteriorate social justice.
Purchase investments that follow your IPS.

Consider it a financial detox. Out with the bad investments, in with the good.

Of course, it won't always be cut and dry. No company is perfect. Even nonprofit organizations laser-focused on balancing financial sustainability with community-defined social justice hit wrong notes from time to time.

To that end, social justice investors will be wise to remember: balance requires tradeoffs. Sometimes you'll have to accept a company's indifference to the prison–industrial complex in order to reap the benefits of the significant gender equity returns it generates. Perhaps you discover a tremendous investment opportunity in a local nonprofit, but you'll have to work with an attorney to execute a private loan agreement in order to make an investment.

Either way, just remember: Money talks. *You* have power. It's been in your wallet this whole time. Now you have the tools and resources needed to use it.

SELL ANY INVESTMENTS THAT DETERIORATE SOCIAL JUSTICE

To begin your financial detox, first you must determine whether your existing investments are worth preserving or should be sold at the first opportunity. To begin, start by obtaining a list of all your existing investments.

401(k) investors request an itemized list of investments

Employer-sponsored retirement plans like 401(k)s are highly regulated entities that are required to provide detailed information about the securities in any investment option within your menu of choices.

This is fantastic news if you need an itemized list of your investments—someone else has already done all the hard work on your behalf. Simply ask your human resources manager for the latest statements about all the options on your company's 401(k) investment menu.

Investors working with a financial advisor ask for help

If you're working with a financial advisor, you'll have a paid partner to help you sort through and scrub the data. Even better, financial advisors are required by law to have transparent investment data easily accessible to clients.

To proceed, ask your advisor for a time to discuss the existing investments in the portfolio. Since you've talked with your advisor several times already to update your investment strategy and to create an asset allocation budget, they'll know where you're headed next: assessing your existing investment's performance related to your updated IPS.

Below is an example script to guide your conversation.

> **You:** Good morning! Now that we've created my investment strategy and my asset allocation budget, I'd like to start scrubbing my portfolio of any securities that are incompatible with my social justice goals.
>
> **Financial advisor:** Ok. Which securities do you want to sell?
>
> **You:** I need your help with this. Could you please point me to my latest statement that lists my investments?
>
> **Financial advisor:** Yes, I will send it to you now.

You: Thank you. Do you happen to have a tool that will help me conduct research to assess the social justice impact of each investment?

(Note: Your financial advisor likely does not have such a tool and will not until there is sufficient client demand to justify the expense. By asking for a tool to apply a social justice lens to your portfolio, you are creating client demand. When enough people express a desire for a research tool, investment firms will develop one to retain their clients.)

Financial advisor: Unfortunately, I don't have a tool that could help with that.

You: Ok. There are a few publicly available resources we can use.

You've just completed an essential step by collecting the raw data. In this case, the raw data is your portfolio's listing of investments.

DIY investors get organized

If you're acting as your own financial advisor through a DIY approach, you'll need to spend some time locating an itemized list of your investments. If you're just starting out, your list of investments will likely be short. If you have a long history of investing, you'll want to search your investment platform for an itemized accounting of your portfolio.

You have every right to ask for the information you need to make a well-informed investment decision. In fact, investment platforms have a regulatory duty to provide updated information to their clients in a reasonable time frame. If you need help locating your itemized list of investments, consider troubleshooting through the chat feature within your online platform.

Once you have the list of your investment holdings, download it into a format on which you can take notes and organize through different filters. I personally prefer Microsoft Excel, but to each their own. You may prefer printing off your list of investments and writing your notes by hand. Or perhaps you found an app that helps organize your list into different categories.

Once your data is organized, you can start analyzing your investments for their ability to deliver both sustainable financial earnings *and* positive social justice returns.

What if I don't have any investments yet?

If you're taking your first steps as an investor, congratulations!! You have a fresh canvas on which to work. While your fellow social justice investors may need to sell investments that don't reflect their personal values, you'll be starting strong by purchasing investments that reflect your personal values from the outset.

I strongly encourage you to continue reading through this chapter, as you'll need these same processes and tools when you start researching and assessing investments you're considering for purchase.

RESEARCH YOUR EXISTING INVESTMENTS

With your itemized list in hand, it's time to start researching your existing investments. Your ultimate goal is to use the research you accumulate to assess whether the investments align with the objectives and constraints identified in your investor roadmap.

How to research an investment's financial performance

Researching investments can help you evaluate a company, initiative, or project to decide whether it's worth adding to your portfolio.

How you research the financial performance of an investment will vary widely based on whether you're a 401(k) investor, an investor working with a financial advisor, or a DIY investor.

401(k) investors can assess the performance of each of the options on the preset investment menu by reviewing the statements available through their 401(k) administrator. Today, investors can usually download the statements from an online portal provided through their employer. Many companies hire investment consultants and financial advisors to help employees better understand their investment options. Ask your human resources manager for help understanding the tools and resources available to you as an employee.

Investors working with a financial advisor can simply request information about the financial performance of any investment from their advisor, who should be able to provide copious research within a few days after the request.

DIY investors selecting investments without the support of a professional advisor will need to follow a methodical research and assessment process to evaluate the financial performance of any identified investments. Fortunately, many of the most popular online investment platforms offer free research tools and analytics designed to deliver relevant information to your fingertips.

Research questions for every investor

No matter how you gather your information, you should assess your research through a consistent approach, which enables you to compare investments on an apples-to-apples basis.

To start, each investor can address the following questions:

How is the investment typically identified? If applicable, what is the ticker symbol?

How has the investment performed over the past 12 months? Has the price increased or decreased?

How did it perform relative to the general market over that same time period?

If an ETF or mutual fund, what is the expense ratio?

What type of company does the stock or bond support? If an ETF or mutual fund, what types of companies are selected to be included in the basket of stocks and/or bonds?

How does the underlying company(s) make money?

Does the company make more money than it spends? In other words, is the company profitable?

Does the company(s) have a competitive advantage?

How good is the company's management team?

What risks is the investment susceptible to? In other words, what could go wrong?

When you're considering many different investments, it will likely be helpful to keep a dedicated research notebook to help you organize your thoughts. As you gather information on more and more investments, you'll want a single source of notes to compare research over time and across different investments. Trust me when I say that getting organized in the beginning can save you many headaches in the long run.

Either way, researching investments is just a matter of gathering the right resources and materials from the right financial partners, looking at the financial performance, asking important questions, and considering how a company compares to the market as well as its industry peers.

As you grow more confident in your ability to research investments, you can begin expanding your knowledge and asking more technical research questions. Before you know it, you'll be calculating a company's trailing price-to-earnings ratio and comparing its return on equity to that of its industry peers.

How investors screen for their social justice priorities

Investors use a process called "investment screening" to determine whether a product aligns with their investor roadmap.

For example, Nicole uses an investment screening tool called "Invest Your Values," a tool developed by As You Sow, to assess the investments within her portfolio based on their contributions to climate justice, racial justice, and gender justice. When Nicole types the name of her investment into the search field, the "Invest Your Values" screening tool provides a rating (A–F) grading the investment's portfolio against her values. Over several years, Nicole sells the investments with poor grades and purchases investments with high ratings.

About As You Sow (asyousow.org)

As You Sow is the nation's nonprofit leader in shareholder advocacy. Founded in 1992, As You Sow harnesses shareholder power to create lasting change by protecting human rights, reducing toxic waste, and aligning investments with values. As You Sow offers several tools and resources that social justice investors may find helpful in creating and maintaining their investment portfolios.

The "Invest Your Values" tool (InvestYourValues.org) enables investors to evaluate the social responsibility of 3,000 mutual funds and ETFs, from their fossil fuel impact to gender equality and racial justice. With a list of what you currently own in hand, type the name, ticket, or manager of a fund into the search box. The result will show how that fund scores on an A through F scale for the screen you choose.

As You Sow's tools dive deeper into the specific impacts of your investment decisions. Beyond rating your investment's performance related to major social

---

justice issues, As You Sow delivers an expanded analysis of each issue, assesses the investment's carbon footprint, and compares the investment's financial performance against other investments that offer similar social justice returns.

In addition to screening out poorly performing funds, As You Sow provides investors with search tools designed to identify investments that most closely match your return objectives organized by performance related both to financial earnings and social justice returns.

Today's social justice investors have access to many publicly available and easy-to-use resources designed to identify investments that reflect our values. From researched lists of socially responsible companies to searchable online databases, we have resources that industry pioneers could only dream about.

As more and more tools come online, you can use the one that feels most comfortable to you. The tool or resource you use is not important in and of itself. What's important is that it delivers reliable research and enables you to make well-informed decisions about your investment portfolio.

For the purposes of simplicity, the rest of this chapter will rely on the "Invest Your Values" tool to help us assess whether an investment adequately reflects your values.

I feel comfortable using the "Invest Your Values" tool because it was created by experienced investors who value and prioritize both social and environmental factors in investments, while maintaining the rigor and precision required for credible data collection. I wish the tool better or more explicitly articulated feedback from impacted communities, but its creators haven't yet incorporated this feature. Still, at least at the time of writing, the current iteration offers the closest precision available in the market.

For information on other tools and resources available to today's social justice investors, please refer to the following sections at the end of this book: Online Resources & Tools; Social Justice Investing Organizations.

HOW TO USE AN INVESTMENT SCREENING TOOL

With your portfolio listing in hand, enter the name or ticker of each investment into the "Invest Your Values" database. The tool provides investment scorecards that rate investments on their performance related to seven filters. The scorecard assigns a letter grade (A–F) for the investment's performance against the following values-based initiatives: gender equality, civilian firearms, prison–industrial complex, military weapons, tobacco, fossil fuels, and deforestation.

Record grades for each of your investments. I recommend creating a simple grid to tally the results of each investment in your portfolio:

	Gender equality	Civilian firearms	Prison–industrial complex	Military weapons	Tobacco	Fossil fuels	Deforestation
Investment 1	B	A	A	B	A	B	C
Investment 2	D	D	F	B	C	D	B
Investment 3	B	C	F	B	B	F	B

Tools like the "Invest Your Values" database give us insight into how companies use our investment dollars. The additional transparency gives us the opportunity to make better-informed decisions and select investments based on more than their financial earnings projections. When companies and fund managers realize that investors' money is directed to funds with more As than Fs, they'll have the financial incentive to raise their scores.

Let's consider how Nicole, Tom, and Angela screen their investments.

Nicole receives an unexpected inheritance

Nicole was shocked to learn her aunt, a retired schoolteacher who clipped coupons before braving senior discount days at the local grocery store, left Nicole $20,000 in investments and $5,000 in cash in her will.

She could still hear her aunt's admonishment when Nicole arrived on her aunt's doorstep with two ice-cream concoctions from their favorite creamery.

"A penny saved is a penny earned, Nicole!" she would scold in between slurps of chocolate and caramel. "You shouldn't be spending all this money on me!"

Turns out, she had saved a lot of pennies.

Once it had gone through the various legal channels and processes, the money appeared in Nicole's account. Her heart crunched when she saw the new account "Nicole RB," tagged to show the inheritance from her aunt, Roxie Bugg (RB).

When the inheritance money came through, the financial advisor who managed her account called to discuss her plans for it.

"Nicole, this is Marcia. I'm so sorry for your loss. I know this is a hard time, but I'm required to get your guidance on how to manage these funds. The money was transferred as $20,000 in investments and $5,000 cash. Would you like it to stay as it is or do you have immediate plans to manage it differently?"

Nicole paused as her mind went blank.

"I'm sorry, Marcia. I don't know how to process this right now."

Marcia replied gently. "That's ok. You can take the time you need. If it's okay with you, I'll leave it as is and we can touch base again in a few months. Does that work for you?"

Nicole nodded. "Yes, thank you very much. Could you possibly send me a list of the investments I inherited? Then I can have something tangible to think about."

"Of course," Marcia replied. "I'll send that over via email. I'm here whenever you're ready. Feel free to call anytime if you have any questions. If not, I'll call you again in a few months to check back in."

Nicole heard her inbox ping within a few minutes, but didn't actually open the email until the following week.

When she did, she found a list of 13 investments that comprised the total $20,000 balance. She read each of the tickers, but didn't feel a connection to any of them. If their names meant anything special, Nicole didn't know how to decode the language.

Nicole brought her list to her next book club meeting. One of the group's members, Sara, worked in finance. Maybe she would know.

Her friend Sara reviewed the list and handed it back to Nicole. "These seem pretty generic and harmless to me. Do you have a financial advisor you could ask for guidance?"

Nicole nodded. "Yes, but I'm a little scared to call."

"Why? Did something happen? Has he said something to you?" Sara leaned forward in her seat. She was the only woman in her office and had her fair share of dealing with the antics of ridiculous men.

"No, no. My advisor is a woman named Marcia. She's been incredibly nice and was very helpful in getting paperwork processed every time I roll over my retirement accounts to her. She was really kind every time we spoke about processing the inheritance my aunt left me. I'm just feeling a little intimidated about talking about this inherited money. I feel out of my depth," Nicole confessed.

"Oh, friend. Let's get you sorted." Sara patted the seat next to her and asked if our host had a pen she could borrow.

Sara's laptop materialized. She unfolded Nicole's list of investments, asking if she could write on it.

"It's all yours," Nicole said, releasing the list into her care. "What are you doing?"

Sara's pen was already scratching notes on the paper. "Researching the investments." Sara looked up. "Do you mind?"

"Not at all. Thanks!" Nicole sipped her wine and chatted with the rest of the group while Sara worked.

After a few minutes, Sara resurfaced to ask, "Hey, do you want me to check on the investments' commitment to social responsibility? I know you're really active about social justice."

Nicole set down her wine glass. "You can do that?"

"Sure," Sara said. "My clients ask me all the time if I can screen their investments for environmental and social factors. I'm using a paid service to check on the financial performance of these investments, but I typically use a free tool online to check for social justice issues. You ok with that?"

"Yes! I didn't know you could use investments for that." Nicole looked over Sara's shoulder.

"It's relatively new," Sara said as she typed. "But I have a growing number of clients who ask me to screen for it. They want their investments to match their values."

Now three other women were crowding around Sara's laptop watching the scorecards appear on the screen.

"Whoa! That one had three Fs! Is that normal??"

"Ooh look! That one has two As and three Bs. I can't believe it has an F for prison–industrial complex."

Nicole was getting anxious. "Umm, Sara. Is it normal for investments to have so many failing grades?"

Sara glanced up. "Yes. My clients are almost always shocked by the results. Just like your investments, most perform well financially. In fact, yours performed exceptionally well in the past two years. Your aunt had a good feel for investing."

Nicole smiled. "Aunt Roxie always knew more than she let on."

Sara returned the paper to Nicole. "I organized their performance by financial returns as well as social indicators. If your advisor asks, the grades came from an online tool called 'Invest Your Values.' All you do is type in the investment name and it spits out a scorecard. Pretty cool stuff."

Nicole wrapped her arms around Sara. "Thank you so much! I was feeling so overwhelmed every time I looked at this list."

Sara smiled back at Nicole. "You know, it's not unusual for people who inherit investments to sell off a portion at a time to incorporate the money into their other portfolios. Usually people want to streamline their finances. I know you were close to your aunt and I'm really sorry for your loss. I think she knew you well enough to know you'd manage the money to the best of your ability. Based on my experience managing other people's money, the best way to manage money is to really own your decisions. That means bringing your whole self to the table."

Now Nicole was crying. "Thank you, friend. That means so much to me. Will you manage my money for me?"

Sara laughed. "Absolutely not. I don't mix friends and money."

Tom researches his 401(k) options

When last we left our hero, Tom sat frozen. Staring at his 401(k) investment menu, he was rereading the different options without understanding what any of the words meant. Did he want a value fund or an index fund? Should he include a mix of international companies in addition to the US-based companies? What on earth was the difference between small cap and large cap and how did it make a difference in his ability to build wealth?

Fortunately, his fiancée, Emily, chose that moment to shuffle into the kitchen for her nightly cup of tea.

"Sweetheart, you look miserable. What's going on?" she asked.

"Hi, love. I've got to pick my 401(k) investments as part of starting my new job. I just don't know where to start. I'm not sure what most of this means," Tom explained, pulling a hand through his hair.

Emily pulled up a chair next to Tom. "What are you trying to accomplish?"

Tom's shoulders relaxed as he slid his paperwork closer to Emily. After planting a kiss on her cheek, Tom explained, "I'm trying to make investment choices that align with two goals of mine. The first goal is to build financial wealth. I want to take care of you and any children that you and I may have together."

Emily leaned forward, reviewing his notes. After a few moments, she spoke again. "What's the second goal?"

Tom jumped. While Emily read his paperwork, Tom had made the mistake of inhaling near her freshly washed hair. He wasn't sure what scents were in her new shampoo, but he found them intoxicating. Something floral.

"I'm sorry," Tom said, shaking his head to refocus on the paperwork in front of him. "What did you say?"

Emily grinned and leaned her shoulder against his arm. "You explained a moment ago how you had two investment goals. The first was to build financial wealth. What's the second goal?"

"Ah," Tom said. "My second goal is to invest according to my values. I want my investments to generate both financial earnings and social justice returns. I've decided to allocate 50% of my selections toward investment choices that focus on aggressively building financial wealth. The second 50% of my selections will focus on supporting companies and initiatives that create social justice returns. I'm specifically focused on racial justice, but I'm very receptive to other approaches to social justice."

Emily's eyes lit up with excitement. "Oh! I know how to help! I was at a book club last year where my friends Nicole and Sara were discussing a great new tool to help people do exactly that. It's called 'Invest Your Values.' I've used it to research my own investments and really like it."

Emily leaned over Tom to access his laptop and typed the website's name: InvestYourValues.org. "It's pretty straightforward. Just type in the names of these investment options and you get so much information about their financial and impact performance."

Emily turned in her seat, eager to show Tom the first results. "Hey now! Get your nose out of my hair and do your homework. I'll be in our room reading my new book club novel."

With that, Emily scooped up her tea, kissed Tom's forehead, and tapped his list of investments before retreating from the kitchen.

Watching her leave, Tom reminded himself of the impending HR deadline to select investment options. Reluctantly, he returned to his research and focused on his laptop screen.

He typed the name of the target-date fund he was curious about into the search field at the top of the page. A scorecard appeared.

Whoa, thought Tom. *That's a lot of red. Two Fs, three Ds, and two Cs.*

He typed in the default fund he would be automatically enrolled in if he didn't submit his paperwork on time.

Even more red. This time, the scorecard revealed three Fs, three Ds, and one C.

Genuinely shocked by the poor showing, Tom systematically typed in the names of each of the nine options. The highest-graded option was a fund with one D, two Cs, three Bs, and even one glorious A.

After half an hour of research, he closed his laptop and resolved to discuss the investment options with his HR manager this week.

"Hey Emily," he called as he walked up the stairs. "Are you at a stopping place in that book?"

Angela starts with a blank canvas

Angela rubbed her eyebrows and tapped her pencil on the notepad in front of her. Since she's starting fresh with her DIY account, she doesn't have any investments to research.

Shrugging, she smiles and leans back into her chair.

"Easy peasy lemon squeezy!" she sings to the family dog asleep at her feet. "Guess I get to skip this step!" Her dog lifts one sleepy eye as Angela continues, "Now for the fun part! Time to start researching new investments . . ."

SELL ANY INVESTMENTS THAT DETERIORATE SOCIAL JUSTICE

Now that you've researched your existing investments, the next step is to sell any investments that support socially unjust practices.

However, before you start selling off investments, please be aware that sales can trigger capital gains taxes and leave you with unexpectedly large tax bills. You may need to unload socially unjust investments slowly over time to withstand the tax implications. Consider talking to a financial advisor or CPA about a strategy that will point you in the right direction while considering tax implications.

With that important caveat, let's start unloading investments we're not proud of.

Yup, we're going to Marie Kondo your 401(k). If an investment sparks joy, keep it. If it exacerbates social injustice, get ready to toss it to the curb.

Let's return to Nicole and Tom to see how to take the next step.

Nicole sells her inherited wealth in stages

Two weeks after book club, Nicole called her financial advisor, Marcia, to ask about selling the investments her aunt left her.

"Hi Marcia, thanks so much for calling me a few weeks ago about the money I inherited from my aunt. I researched the list you sent me and have a few questions."

"Of course!" Marcia replied. "What are your questions?"

"Well, it's less a question and more of a request." Nicole looked down at the request she had written down as a script. She raced through the words before she could lose her nerve. "I think I want to sell them. My friend and I researched their social and environmental performance using a tool called 'Invest Your Values' and they're completely against my personal values."

"We can do that," Marcia stated simply. "Why don't you tell me a little bit more about what you found. I've used that tool before. If you don't mind, I'd really like to hear what components you feel most strongly about."

Nicole's eyes flickered to her long list of notes detailing her desire to pick investments that financed social justice. Then she sighed. She hadn't prepared to have a big talk with her advisor and didn't have the energy to justify her divergence from convention.

"Really, I just want to pick investments that I can feel good about. I want them to match my social justice values, especially around racial justice, gender equality, and LGBTQ+ rights. I have a few ideas on where to get started, but for right now, I want to figure out if I can sell the investments my aunt left me."

"We can do whatever you want to do. They're your assets to do with what you will."

Nicole was shocked. She felt sure that Marcia would push back and try to convince her to retain a conservative viewpoint on her investments. "Really?" she asked incredulously.

"Absolutely. Before I sell these positions, I do want to talk to you about the tax implications. You will pay a tax for any capital gains earned since the time of your aunt's death." Marcia paused. "I know this is an emotional conversation. I'm going to talk for a while so you can listen and process. Feel free to interrupt me at any point."

"Okay," Nicole said quietly.

"Capital gains describes the rise in value of an investment. If you purchased a stock for $10 but now it's worth $15, you have $5 in capital gains. When you sell the stock, you pay a tax on any profit you gained over time. It's called a capital gains tax. With me so far?"

"I think so," Nicole said. "It's like a tax on an investment's profit that's incurred when the investment is sold."

"That's exactly right. When you receive an investment through an inheritance, the beginning value of the stock is its value on the date the person died. It's only been eight months since your aunt passed away, but we've experienced eight straight months of unprecedented growth since that time. The $20,000 your grandmother left you eight months ago is now $45,000. You would be responsible for paying taxes on the $25,000 capital gains. Assuming a 15% tax rate, you'd be looking at a tax payment of $3,750 during tax season next year."

Marcia had been right. This was an emotional conversation. Nicole wiped her eyes and managed to sound reasonably calm.

"It's okay. We can work out a plan to sell these investments over time. We can wait until the market declines and sell the investments when they're priced lower. I can also capture any interest or dividend payments in a cash account to help offset the cost. Alternatively, we can use the $5,000 in cash your grandmother left you to pay the taxes."

Nicole's response was direct and determined. "No. I have plans for the $5,000. I have a few investments picked out for that money."

"Excellent! Before you tell me about those investments, let's get your exit plan squared away for the existing investments. What feels right to you?"

Nicole frowned in concentration. "Let's sell the investments little by little, trying to cap any capital gains taxes at $1,000 per year. But I want to use any interest or dividends to start buying other investments."

"You got it, boss. I'll put a plan together and get it in front of you by early next week. In the meantime, tell me about your plans for the $5,000 cash."

Nicole sat down at her laptop and pulled open the file. She couldn't wait to share the investments she had discovered with her friend Sara.

Tom advocates for better options

After discovering that none of the investments offered in his 401(k) menu reflected his personal values, Tom scheduled a follow-up appointment with his human resources manager, Tammi, for help in thinking through next steps.

The following week, Tom returned to her office with uncompleted paperwork.

"Hi Tammi. I don't know how to tell you this, but I don't really feel comfortable with any of these options. After researching the options on the 401(k) menu, I just don't want my investment proceeds supporting any of these funds. They all have failing grades when it comes to social and environmental factors."

Tom handed Tammi the research he collected and asked if there were any other options.

Tammi reviewed his research and returned the paper to Tom. "Thank you for bringing me this research. I hear where you're coming from. Unfortunately, as of today, these are the only options I can offer you. Without a fund selection, we can't contribute any of your retirement benefits to which you're entitled."

Tom's shoulders slumped.

"However," Tammi continued, "you're not the first person to raise these concerns with me. Another group of team members has conducted similar research and happens to be presenting their findings to my boss next month. My understanding is that they will be asking the company to add more sustainable options to our retirement plan."

Tom sat back. "Really? Do you think I could learn more?"

Tammi wrote down a name on a slip of paper and handed it to Tom. "Here is the name of the employee group organizing the materials."

When Tom slipped the paper in his shirt pocket, Tammi continued. "For now, I strongly advise you to select one of the options from the existing investment menu so we get your retirement contributions flowing. When and if we have more options that are a better fit for you, we can update your form with your new selections. This action will effectively exit your position from the first fund so you can start investing in the new fund."

Tom smiled. "Thanks very much!" He selected the fund with the highest grades, signed the form, and slid it across the table to Tammi.

Tom joined the employee group and participated in the meeting advocating for better options in their 401(k) menu.

Six months later, Tammi circulated an updated list of fund options to the entire company. The list included three new funds that prioritized environmental and social values. When Tom ran the fund name through the "Invest Your Values" tool, the lowest score across all three funds was a B. He submitted new paperwork to Tammi requesting his retirement contributions to flow to one of the new funds more closely aligned with his values.

Energy Boost: Big Idea Energy

Janine Firpo

Around 2009, I was sitting in the back of a crowded auditorium at the Global Philanthropy Forum, a premier conference for philanthropists and social investors who want to advance equity and opportunity globally. Surrounding me were the leading thinkers in what was becoming a new way of imagining philanthropy and investment. Terms like "corporate social responsibility," "impact investing," and "blended capital" were being invented, discussed, and formalized as part of a new financial lexicon.

Using money to do well while doing good was one of those Big Ideas being discussed at the forum that I could get behind.

The conversation was focused on how money managers who controlled vast sums of money, either personally or on behalf of others, could move their dollars toward good not only through philanthropic donations, but also by investing for positive impact.

The audience sat in rapt attention as they learned about the work of Charly and Lisa Kleissner, a couple who committed $10 million of their own money to demonstrate and validate that financial investments could generate social and environmental impacts as well as financial returns.

I was right there with them—except that I wasn't.

I was not ultra-wealthy. I did not manage other people's money. I did not have enough assets that I had excess to put at risk, the way the Kleissners did. I was still relatively young, unmarried, and worried that I would not have enough money for retirement. To be honest, I had such serious bag-lady syndrome that I was pretty convinced I would end up at 80 years of age alone, living under a bridge eating cat food.

That is when it hit me—why couldn't someone like me invest my money in a way that aligned with my values? Why not? Why did this conversation start and end with people and institutions that had very deep pockets? What about the rest of us?

Sitting in that auditorium, I realized that while my life was aligned with my values, my money was not. And based on what I was hearing in this room, there was little likelihood that it ever could be.

Seated in the back of the room, I raised my hand for a microphone.

We had just entered the Q&A portion of the session and I wanted to know what others in the room thought about reaching a point where anyone, even those who don't identify as "ultra-high-net-worth individuals," could invest their values.

My heart was pounding as the microphone found its way into my hand. My face was known in this room. People respected me. Was I about to make a fool out of myself? I took a deep breath and opened my mouth.

"I want to know if it is possible for the nonwealthy—normal people—to invest this way, too. What would it take to make that happen?"

Heads turned in my direction. There was silence. The attendees met my question with surprised consideration, but offered no answers that day. A few minutes later, the conversation picked up where it had left off.

The idea that regular people could invest in values-aligned financial products was inconceivable in 2009. The impact-investing community at that time was not a place for those without *very* deep pockets.

But I was changed—and committed. In that moment, I made a solemn vow to myself that I would figure out to how to invest my money in a way that made me feel good about what it was doing in the world—what it was supporting and upholding. And I was going to do it without giving up financial return.

I knew I was a smart, successful woman with the experience and perseverance needed to make big changes. I had already done so several times. Plus, I knew a bit about finance because I had started investing in my twenties and bought my first house before I turned 30.

I was determined to figure out how to shift 100% of my financial assets into investments that aligned with my personal values.

I knew there had to be a way that I could *invest for better.*

Since then, I have been working to align all of my assets—from my checking and savings accounts to stocks to real estate—with my values. I want all of my money to support the things I care about—the things I would like to see created, elevated, and empowered.

In late 2017, I retired from my second career and took on this challenge in earnest. Over the past several years, I have taken control of my portfolio and accelerated the movement of my assets into things I feel good about. At this point, I feel good about most of my investments. Some of them make me really happy. They literally give me joy.

This transformation took time and patience. It was often an uphill battle. But it doesn't have to be anymore. Times have changed and there are now values-aligned options available to any investor—and that is true across asset classes.

I still don't have the perfect portfolio, and maybe never will. I still hold legacy investments that have grown so much in value that the capital gains taxes would cripple my cash flow. But I am not giving up and will continue to refine and improve my portfolio over time.

Here's some of what I learned along the way:

One: Smart investing is a marathon, not a sprint. It takes time and attention to build a portfolio that grows your wealth and builds a better world. The sooner you start, the richer and happier you will be. Take your time. Find trusted partners. Create your goals and keep working toward your vision. You'll be amazed by your progress year over year.

Two: For all the women reading this book: I'm here to tell you that women have been misled that we're not good at finance, investments, or even math. Conventional investing is a playbook written by men, for men. We invest differently. We have different goals and different styles. And, when we do invest, we consistently outperform them. So, tear up that old playbook and find one that works for *you*, that speaks to you as a woman.

Three: A community that builds you up is incredibly helpful for long-term success. It is empowering to shift discussions of money from a taboo subject to conversations that build your confidence and your networks of support. Become part of something bigger than yourself, learn with others, and share your wisdom. You will be surprised how much you and the women around you already know—or can find out together.

Almost 15 years into my journey to invest for better, I decided to step into another Big Idea that gives me energy. And that is developing and providing the knowledge, resources, and community other women need to build their values-aligned investment muscles. That is why I wrote *Activate Your Money* and cofounded the nonprofit Invest for Better.

In my experience, one of the joys of money is knowing that it is helping to finance the world you want to live in. Fortunately, there are now socially responsible investment options for all of us. When you are ready to take control of your money, my colleagues and I are here to help.

Contributing Author Biography

Janine Firpo is a seasoned values-aligned investor and social innovator with a long history of working at the intersection of women and their money. From the early years of Apple Computer to senior positions with Hewlett-Packard, the World Bank, and the Bill & Melinda Gates Foundation, Janine has always found herself making an impact. In 2017 she left a successful 35-year career in technology and international development to focus on how women can create a more just and equitable society through their financial investments. Her book, *Activate Your Money: Invest to Grow Your Wealth and Build a Better World*, a collaborative effort that involved almost 150 women (and a few men) was published in May 2021 by Wiley. Later that year, Janine cofounded Invest for Better, a nonprofit organization that helps women invest their money in ways that align with their values.

18.

Purchase Investments That Follow Your Roadmap

Congratulations! You've made it to the most exciting step of social justice investing: shopping for investments.

Before we begin, please take a moment to celebrate your successes leading up to this step: identifying your financial partners, designing an investor roadmap, creating an asset allocation budget, and freeing up cash by selling investments that deteriorate social justice.

Now that you have some cash in hand, it's time to start purchasing investments that follow your investor roadmap. Just like any other purchase, shopping for investments can be broken down into four main components: identify, research, assess, and purchase.

Identify prospective investments

First, identify a list of prospective investments that follow the investor roadmap, or IPS, you designed in chapter 13.

For 401(k) investors, this means reviewing your preset menu of employer-provided investment options to identify any investments that appear to follow your roadmap.

DIY investors, on the other hand, identify prospective investments by following news, blogs, and advertisements through resources like *The Wall Street Journal, Forbes Magazine,* SeekingAlpha.com, ImpactAlpha.com, Morningstar Investor, Sustainalytics, and The Motley Fool (fool.com). DIY investors may also follow investment influencers through social media sites like Facebook and LinkedIn, though one should always remember that just because it's on the internet doesn't mean it's true. While DIY investors can identify prospective investments through myriad sources, they must also do their own research, described below, before making an ultimate purchase.

Investors working with a financial advisor get to lean on the expertise and experience of a trained financial professional who eats, sleeps, and breathes investment opportunities. Their financial advisor's inbox is likely full of reports on new investment trends, performance histories, and hard-to-find investment opportunities. To identify prospective investments, these investors can simply call their financial advisor and ask her to identify investments aligned with your IPS.

Research your list of identified investments

Researching a list of prospective investments is very similar to the process described in the previous chapter for assessing your list of existing investments. Your goal while researching is to uncover the information necessary to determine whether a particular investment follows your investor roadmap.

Just as we discussed in the previous chapter, social justice investors conduct research pertaining to the projected financial performance of an investment as well as its ability to generate social justice advances.

Investors can access financial information with resources available through their DIY investment platform, financial advisor, or employer-provided 401(k) materials available from their HR manager. To assess social justice returns, investors can use free online resources like the "Invest Your Values" investment screen.

Please refer to the previous chapter for a recap on how to research prospective investments.

Assess the research

Using the research you collected in the previous step, assess whether the investments you identified will enable you to fulfill the objectives and constraints defined in your investor roadmap. If it fits, put it in the "buy" pile. If it doesn't, discard it into the "do not buy" pile.

Investors should always remember that no matter how exciting or impactful the investment, if it doesn't fit with your risk–return profile or the financial realities of your life, it's not a good fit for your portfolio. For instance, an investor who needs access to cash in six months should not use their entire fixed income position to purchase a single bond that matures in 18 months, even if presented with a one-time-only opportunity to purchase a bond issued by a nonprofit organization with tremendous social justice returns.

Finally, you'll need to assess whether you have room in your asset allocation budget for any particular investment. For instance, if you have determined that 80% of your investments should be in public equities (also known as stock), and you've already maxed out your budget, then you may need to put that exciting new stock position on ice until you have space in your budget for public equities.

Purchase the investment

After all the planning, preparation, and research, you're finally ready to purchase your social justice investment of choice.

Sadly, after completing all your due diligence, the trade execution itself feels a bit anticlimactic:

401(k) investors purchase investments by updating the appropriate investment allocation paperwork from their human resource manager.

Investors working with a financial advisor need only direct their advisor to make the purchase for a specified amount.

DIY investors follow the purchase procedures outlined by their online investment account to execute the trade.

Nicole taps into the power of accumulated wealth

When last we left our hero, Nicole was on the phone with her advisor, Marcia. During the emotional phone call, Nicole had decided to sell the investments her aunt had left her gradually in order to mitigate any capital gains tax.

With that decision in the rearview mirror, Nicole was about to describe several investments that she felt reflected her social justice values, especially racial justice and gender equity.

Nicole walked to her kitchen table where her laptop sat open. She opened the list she had been compiling with her friend Sara. Sara worked in finance and helped Nicole discover how to use an investment screening tool called "Invest Your Values" to find investments that made her feel good about her money.

"Alright, I've got a list going. Can I share some of these ideas with you?"

"Please do. I'm all ears," Marcia encouraged.

"Ok, I'm going to run through my notes with you. Please stop me if you have questions. The first investment I'd like to consider is called 'IQ Engender Equality ETF.' It's a gender-equality ETF designed to deliver exposure to global companies that promote gender equality and are committed to women's empowerment. The ETF is a basket of stocks representing companies that demonstrate equal compensation and gender balance in leadership and the workforce.

"I found this investment through the 'Invest Your Values' tool and liked it because it scored either A or B on every metric, performed well against the market benchmark, and has a relatively low expense ratio compared to the other ETFs listed as top performers."

Nicole sipped from her water before continuing.

"The second investment I like trades under the ticker named OWNS. It's an ETF that invests in fixed-income securities backed by pools of mortgage loans made to minority families, low- and moderate-income families, and families that live in persistent poverty areas. OWNS seeks to invest in the dignity of homeownership for these traditionally underserved communities.

"My friend Sara found this one through a networking group focused on generating social impact returns for clients. OWNS is managed by a group called Community Capital Management, or CCM. CCM spent time listening to groups that finance mortgages in low-wealth communities and designed an investment to keep the flow of capital open. I couldn't find it on the 'Invest Your Values' tool, but I like its mission and my Google research shows it performed well against the market. Could you please investigate this one for me?"

Marcia responded quickly. "Yes, of course we can. Do you have any other investments you're considering?"

Nicole nodded to herself before answering. "Yes, the last one is an ETF trading under the ticker symbol JSTC. It's an ETF composed of equity securities of companies across all major asset classes screened for social justice criteria including racial justice, climate justice, and gender equity.

"I found this one through a Facebook feed I follow about social justice investing. I learned how a social justice investment firm created this structure to enable investors to align their portfolios with their social justice values and of course I was interested. I especially like how the firm that manages the ETF explicitly states how we need to listen to the people in whom we invest. It's important to me and I don't see it in as many investments as I'd like.

"Anyway, this investment also performed well relative to the market, though I was disappointed that it scored so low on gender equity on the 'Invest Your Values' tool. I'm hoping this was a blip as it's managed by a women-owned investment firm and I have to imagine gender equity hits home for them. I've sent them an email to ask about this just so I feel informed. I know JSTC has a higher-than-average expense ratio of 0.89%, but I'm comfortable with the higher cost if it pays for them to engage directly with the communities in which they're directing investments."

Nicole looked down at her phone. She'd been talking for eight minutes straight. "Marcia, you still there?"

"Yes, and I'm taking notes. Thank you so much for doing all this research. I haven't recommended these particular investments to my clients before, so I want to spend some time doing my own research before purchasing them. My priority, as we discussed in our initial calls together, is to follow your IPS, which strikes a balance between generating sustainable financial earnings and social justice advances. On the surface level, these are excellent examples. I want to send these to my research team for an in-depth review and then get back to you in a few days. Sound okay to you?"

Nicole had been nodding her head the whole time Marcia had been talking. "Yes, that makes perfect sense. Can I ask what you'll be looking for?"

"I want to see what happens to your portfolio's projected performance if we fold in these investments to your existing portfolio. Assuming your research checks out and they perform well against the market, then it's very likely these won't negatively impact your financial performance. Still, I want to double-check."

Nicole pursed her lips. "You know, Marcia, since I'll be purchasing them with the cash my aunt left me, it kind of feels like found money. I feel like I can put more emphasis on social justice returns than financial earnings on this $5,000 I wouldn't have otherwise had."

"Fair enough. We can do that. I'd still advise you to give my research team a few days to review. We like to cross the 't's and dot the 'i's. It should really only take a few days. A week, max."

"Yes, I agree. I'm all for more in-depth research than I sleuthed out."

On the other end of the line, Marcia was joyfully tapping out an email to her research team. She loved it when her clients expressed what they wanted and why they wanted it. It made her job so much more fun.

One week later, Marcia tapped another email to Nicole. "Research came back with an all clear on your three recommended investments. Want me to purchase equal amounts of all three?"

The response was prompt and brief. "Yes, please proceed."

Nicole had just purchased her first investments in the account her aunt Roxie left her. She had asked Marcia to preserve the portfolio's name as "Nicole RB" for sentimental reasons. She was proud to put her aunt's money to work for people and places they both cared about.

Angela confers with her brother

While we've covered how to research an investment's performance related to social justice advances through the "Invest Your Values" tool, Angela's story demonstrates how to assess financial strength and earnings performance.

As you'll recall, Angela recently left her professional job at 40 years old to take on the full-time role of managing a household and small circus of three children and one miniature schnauzer.

Armed with a cup of coffee in her favorite mug, her daughter's Chromebook, and a notebook of ideas, Angela settled into her kitchen chair, poised to take on the world while her son was napping and her daughters were at school. Well, the world of investments, anyway.

She logged onto the web-based investment portal she had activated the week prior and confirmed that her account was active. What's more, she had selected an investment platform that would deposit $3,000 in her account after she made an initial $100 in investment purchases.

Angela was ready to achieve her wealth-building goals.

That is, until the screen prompted her for an investment selection.

The cursor blinked at her expectantly.

Angela stared back.

The cursor blinked again. And again and again until the screen went dark.

Cursing under her breath, Angela opened a new tab and found her favorite search portal: "how to select social justice investments."

Sadly, Google didn't provide a ready-made list of investment options.

It did, however, provide a few links to articles written about social justice investments. She read about companies that support their local communities, financial institutions that drive affordable capital to low-wealth communities, and fixed income bonds that finance affordable housing in underserved locations.

Still, she needed an investment she could purchase through her web-based investment platform. She needed an investment that she could purchase through a stock ticker (abbreviation for a company's stock) or CUSIP (unique nine-digit identification number assigned to all stocks and registered bonds in the United States and Canada).

So far, she was coming up empty. Also, she was recognizing how hard it would be to purchase meaningful amounts of stocks or bonds at $15 per week. Those suckers can be expensive! That particular morning, a single share of Apple cost $130, a share of Amazon cost $90, and Netflix cost over $300 per share.

Frustrated, Angela dialed her brother, Andrew, who she knew had been managing his family's investments for years.

Andrew answered on the third ring.

"Hey Sis," he said quickly. "What's up? You ok?"

"Hi Andrew, I'm good. Do you have a minute to talk about investments?"

Silence on the line.

Finally, Andrew spoke. "Did I hear you correctly? You want to talk about investments?"

Angela grabbed her mug and moved into the kitchen. If she was giving up latte runs to finance her investment portfolio, she was going to have two or three cups of her home-brewed substitute on the regular.

"Yep," she replied, popping the "p" as only sisters can. She always turned into a teenager around her brother.

"Ok," Andrew laughed. "What do you want to know?"

Angela sighed and added cream to her coffee. "You know how I left my job this summer? Well, I've decided to offset my loss in pension contributions by investing a small amount each week. Trouble is, I don't know how to identify the right investments to pick. Even more, I'm stressed about affording reasonable amounts of these stocks. I mean, some of these are expensive! A share of Netflix costs a lot more than my monthly subscription! It's not chill."

Andrew's a good brother and always laughs at his sister's terrible jokes.

"Well, have you considered an ETF? It's short for exchange-traded fund and is like a basket of stocks. For a single cost, you can purchase smaller portions of a large number of individual shares. Then those fragments trade like a single investment purchase—including for a single price. ETFs sell for different prices, but there's generally something for every budget."

Angela set down her coffee and started scribbling ideas in her notebook. "Ooh! Tell me more. Where can I find them?"

Angela took careful notes as Andrew described how you can find ETFs that reflect any number of characteristics—from industry type (technological services versus consumer products versus car manufacturers) to geographic location (US-based versus international focus) to company size (large cap versus small cap).

A few minutes in, Angela interrupted her brother to ask about the ability to select ETFs that focus on social justice returns.

Andrew didn't have an immediate answer, but pointed her to a website he'd recently begun following. "It's called SeekingAlpha.com. It's a website that provides information about all kinds of different investment opportunities. I've noticed they're covering more and more impact investments. Seems like it's an investment type that's growing in popularity. Anyway, I read about a cool ETF that only invests in companies that support diversity and inclusion, sustainability, and social justice. Here, I'll send it to you."

Angela's laptop pinged.

"Ooh, I see it! It's called the Nia Impact Solutions Fund. And it has a ticker symbol!"

Andrew agreed. "Yep, and it's currently trading at $10 per share. That's within your budget, yeah?"

For the first time all morning, Angela smiled as she typed the ticker into her investment platform. "Yes! I can buy it!"

Andrew practically yelled into the phone. "Wait, Angie! You need to research it first. Find out how well it's performed against its peers, what companies it contains, and what the expense ratio looks like."

Now it was Angela's turn to laugh. "I know, little bro. I was just so excited to have found a potential solution that would work with my investment platform. Did I tell you about my research system?"

Angela proceeded to explain how she had worked up a checklist of research to investigate before moving forward with any investment purchase.

First, Angela would write the name of the investment and where she discovered the opportunity. Then she would answer the following questions:

What is the ticker symbol?

How has the investment performed over the past 12 months? Has the price increased or decreased?

How did it perform relative to the general market over that same time period?

What is the expense ratio?

What type of company does the stock or bond support? If an ETF or mutual fund, what types of companies are selected to be included in the basket of stocks and/or bonds?

What types of social justice returns are generated?

What risks is the investment susceptible to?

When she finished explaining her research system, Andrew was clapping his hands on the other end of the phone call. "You're a natural, Sis. Call me whenever you like, but you've got this."

With renewed confidence, Angela started researching the investment Andrew had identified for her. While Angela can't predict the future, she can get comfortable with the potential risks and keep tabs on her investments in case a risk factor increases over time.

Several days later, once she'd had time to assess whether the investment followed her roadmap, she entered the trade information into her DIY investment account.

She called Andrew when she was about to click on the button marked *Confirm Trade.* "I'm about to execute my first trade! I feel like such a grown-up right now."

Andrew chuckled and congratulated his sister. "I'm proud of you, big sister. Listen, I just emailed you a Starbucks gift card. Get yourself a Peppermint Mocha. It doesn't feel like the holidays until you send me your annual selfie with that green cup."

Energy Boost: Courage Is a Muscle

Dr. Stephanie Gripne

My life changed with a handshake and an introduction: "Hi Stephanie, this is Sonya."

Sonya and I were in a national leadership program together, and she and her husband had saved me a month earlier when my dad had unexpectedly passed a few days before a five-day retreat I was hosting in Wyoming. They had stepped up to run the leadership retreat.

Two years earlier, I had lost my mom to pancreatic cancer at 56 years old and now dad at 58 years old. A team of family and friends had pulled and pushed me to the finish line to complete my PhD a week earlier. I was exhausted.

"Hi Sonya," I said. Sonya knew I had a student position with the US Forest Service that would convert to a permanent position now that I had completed my doctoral degree in forestry.

In the early 2000s, Sonya Newenhouse, a nationally recognized green-building expert, had had a front row seat to our family establishing a small affordable housing program, through which we had supported families going through medical bankruptcy during the previous four years.

I had actively been running away from a career in business. I wanted impact. Then, I discovered my aptitude for impact investing transactions, as well as the realization that if I wanted to have the meaningful career that I desired, I would have to overcome my dislike of capitalism and dive into the belly of the beast.

What started as a retirement encore career for my dad quickly escalated into a small portfolio of single-family homes. When possible, we would partner with families who had experienced medical bankruptcy and set up a lease option to purchase with them. It was a "win–win" for all of us. They were able to move into what would become their home two or three years early, gain dignity and partial equity, and enjoy the upside when the houses appreciated above a 10% return. I created an encore job for my dad, had a great tenant and a great investment, and experienced the joy of philanthropy.

It's one thing to experience the rush of doing well by doing good. It's another thing to walk away from a career in which you had spent 12 years in higher education.

"Steph, I've been thinking," Sonya said. "You need to switch your career to real estate."

"Excuse me?" Did she mean I should be a real estate agent? She does know I *just* graduated with a PhD in forestry, right?

"I'm not exactly sure what your job would be, but I've been watching you and believe you need to switch careers. And you need to quit your job. You will not have the urgency and courage to change careers without quitting your job."

After many, many sleepless nights, I decided to take Sonya's advice. It's been a wild ride ever since.

Contributing Author Biography

Dr. Stephanie Gripne is the creative force behind the Impact Finance Center, which she founded in 2012. As an academic entrepreneur, impact investor, speaker, and writer in the field of impact investing, Steph sets the vision for Impact Finance Center. Steph has 25 years of experience at the intersection of business and natural resources, working in private equity and for the Nature Conservancy, the USDA Forest Service, DOE Oak Ridge National Laboratory, the *Journal of Wildlife Management*, and several universities. Stephanie received her PhD from the Boone and Crockett Wildlife Conservation Program at the University of Montana.

19.

Beware the Wolf in Sheep's Clothing

A "Wolf in Sheep's Clothing" (WISC) investment is when a company fraudulently spins its initiatives as "socially just," while the actual impact has a neutral or even negative impact on the ability of a person or community to reach their full potential. WISC investments are the social equivalent of "greenwashing" products to make them appear environmentally friendly when the products are actually neutral or damaging to the environment.

For example, a financial company named FinCo advertises its lending products and services to a low-wealth community that does not have another form of financial access. FinCo mails flyers and pays for radio commercials to market itself as a company that is "meeting the financial needs of an underserved community." On closer inspection, the lender charges exorbitant rates and drags the borrowers into a vicious borrowing cycle.

Social justice investors must be on their guard constantly about discerning reality from marketing spin. Every issuer (company or organization selling you an investment product) has a dedicated sales and marketing team that is hyperaware of market activity and investor preferences.

The sales and marketing teams absorb the prevailing undercurrent of investor interest and spin their own products to reflect that interest. For instance, when Americans are feeling particularly patriotic, marketing directors tout the number of their companies' factories located in the United States and upload pictures of red, white, and blue fireworks on the company's social media platform.

As a social justice investor, you will need to discern which investments are *genuinely* aligned with your values from those that spin their stories to make them *appear* aligned with your values.

For instance, Home Depot landed itself in hot water for over-spinning its commitment to environmentalism.

In his *New York Times* article, "At Home Depot, How Green Is That Chainsaw?" (June 25, 2007), Clifford Krauss observed:

Home Depot sent a note to the companies that supply 176,000 products it sells, inviting them to make a pitch to have their products included in its new Eco Options marketing campaign. More than 60,000 products—far more than the obvious candidates like organic gardening products and high-efficiency lightbulbs—suddenly developed environmental star power.

Plastic-handled paint brushes were touted as nature-friendly because they were not made of wood. Wood-handled paint brushes were promoted as better for the planet because they were not made of plastic.

An electric chainsaw? Green, because it was not gas-powered. A bug zapper? Ditto, because it was not a poisonous spray. Manufacturers of paint thinners, electrical screwdrivers, and interior overhead lights claimed similar bragging rights simply because their plastic or cardboard packaging was recyclable.

This is a classic example of greenwashing: a company markets itself as environmentally friendly (thus the "green") when its actual environmental impact is neutral, or worse, negative.

No one likes the feeling of being hoodwinked. Social justice investors must be wary of any investment product marketed as "socially responsible." Regardless of the organization—nonprofit or for-profit—you must do your homework to ensure the company culture and impact align with your values.

For instance, the social justice investor should be wary of investments that seem to be ethically motivated (i.e., driving capital to low-cost communities), but deeper research leads you to conclude that the investment is actually predatory to low-income communities (e.g., predatory payday lenders).

It takes time to trust your gut instinct about an organization's authenticity of alignment to social justice values. Below is a curated list to guide you on your path.

SIGNS THAT YOU'VE ENCOUNTERED A WISC INVESTMENT

The organization in which you are considering investing does not have a mission or impact statement.

Most mission-centered organizations doggedly pursue a vision, mission, impact, or some other clarifying statement that guides an organization's decisions—like a ship's captain finds its direction by following the North Star. Note that the vision statement may not be written or published on a website, but the organization's leadership will be able to point to an informal motto or verbal commitment that is reflected in the organization's initiatives and impacts. Every decision is filtered through a clarifying question: Does this effectively contribute to our mission? Employees at profit-focused organizations, by contrast, are driven through a profit lens: to improve the company's bottom line, either by increasing revenue or decreasing expenses.

The organization in which you are considering investing uses negative, patronizing, or blaming language to describe the community it targets.

In a real-life example, a household-name food and beverage company currently touts its commitment to social impact by "addressing America's obesity epidemic." A telltale indicator of its WISC status is the blaming language used when offering "portion control" as the single, global solution. The food and beverage company valiantly announced its plan to educate obese individuals on the importance of measuring their food and beverage intake in sensible portion sizes. I had a jaw-dropping sanity check moment when I watched a representative from this particular food and beverage company launch into a sermon about how people just need to embrace personal responsibility in order to reach a weight range deemed acceptable by this company. Since he found it appropriate to lecture in front of an image of a plate of vegetables and grilled fish, I was sorely tempted to ask about the appropriate portion size of the company's signature candy bars or cheese curls—on which it earns a significant portion of its revenue. I managed to hold my tongue and my snark in that moment, but I haven't been able to normalize the blaming and patronizing language used by the WISC to describe its impacted community. By contrast, a genuine social justice investor speaks about the impacted community with respect as valued partners.

The organization in which you are considering investing does not partner with the communities it targets.

A WISC will make decisions that impact a community without incorporating—or sometimes even seeking—feedback from the impacted community. By comparison, respect is a guiding principle to social justice investors. Respect is demonstrated through a *partnership* with the impacted communities—by listening to impacted communities, positioning their leadership in the driver's seat of decisions, and measuring the investment's success by the community's success. A genuine social justice investment views the communities it serves as valued, respected partners. It will meet with the community, learn its specific nuances, and have its finger on the pulse of the community's culture and evolving priorities. A social justice investor puts the community it serves in the driver's seat of the decisions. You will observe this in the form of board seats filled by members from the community, town halls in the targeted neighborhoods, and community feedback sections of internally circulated decision memos.

The organization in which you are considering investing prioritizes financial return at the expense of social justice returns.

When push comes to shove, WISC investments lean into profit-maximizing decisions at the expense of initiatives that sustainably deliver social justice returns. A genuine social justice investor wrestles with the balance of sustaining financial requirements while delivering social justice returns. A social justice investor drives forward positive social change while keeping an eye toward financial sustainability. After all, the organization wants to deliver social justice returns not just today, but also five years from today. In order to detect a true social justice investment, you must identify this inherent tension in a prospective investment and explore how the organization finds its balance.

The organization in which you are considering investing does not have a detailed "Go Deeper" list of products and services it would offer should money be no issue.

If asked, the leadership team at a true social justice investment organization would be able to recite a specific wish list of all the social justice strategies and tactics it would employ were it to have more resources. Any mission-centered organization worth its salt would describe how it would "go deeper" or "reach more people" if it could raise more capital or shift the current political landscape. A WISC organization, on the other hand, may struggle to identify the social justice strategies and tactics it would implement if it were to magically receive additional resources. While mission-centered organizations wake up at night with ideas about how to drive additional resources into their communities, WISC leadership teams are more likely to wake up at night brainstorming additional revenue sources.

As you deepen your practice as a social justice investor, you will learn to ask the right questions, locate the answers in audited statements and annual reports, and trust your instincts. If you're feeling uncomfortable in the initial learning curve, find a trusted advisor or mentor to help navigate your course.

You have authority to make decisions over your own assets. Use it well.

Energy Boost: The Path Is Made by Walking

Monique Aiken

Never in my wildest dreams did I imagine I'd be a podcast host. I studied International Politics, got an MBA, and worked in finance and impact investing. Media? Journalism? Storytelling? Narrative change? Those things were not even in my consciousness. But, sometimes, when an opportunity comes your way, you take it, on behalf of the others you represent who might not have gotten the same chance.

In October 2019, I attended an impact investment conference called "SOCAP19." With my seven-month-old son and nanny in tow, I ran into David Bank, the editor of ImpactAlpha, a digital news magazine for the impact investing sector. I had met David a handful of times previously. I felt comfortable sharing him with what I thought would be a compelling suggestion, nothing more, during the brief chat we had about how the session went, among other topics, after the panel discussion:

"You need more women's voices at ImpactAlpha, particularly on the podcast," I said.

"You're hired!" he said and reached out to shake my hand.

I laughed as I shook his hand, and replied, "If you can't find anyone else, I'll do it."

Fast forward to the next spring, when the COVID-19 pandemic had just begun and relentless police brutality in the United States seared the global consciousness ever deeper with the murder of George Floyd on May 25, 2020. The dual crises caused a collective bubbling over of grief, fear, and rage.

David followed up on our conversation and asked me if I would be willing to host a podcast called *Impact Briefing* to discuss the experience and share perspectives of Black people in the finance field. The podcast team knew it was an important conversation to have but, given the composition of their staff, thought that someone else should lead it. I brought in leaders I deeply respected in the field to join me for what turned out to be a raw, cathartic, and powerful conversation: Demetric Duckett of Living Cities, Angela Matheny of Crewcial Partners, and Donray Von of Castleberry and Elevator City Partners.

Our success at *Impact Briefing* led to a longform interview podcast, dubbed *The Reconstruction*, which focused on moving capital toward justice. During 2021, an amazing team delivered 24 podcasts and corresponding written articles for ImpactAlpha's website. Because it was all unfolding in the middle of a pandemic, and we were all working from home, it was difficult to know who was listening (if anyone!) and we were learning by doing. But with the guiding hand of our producers, mentors, and dedicated steering committee, we sounded official and had branding to match. As it turns out, many people were indeed listening, and were not just being entertained, but were being deeply affected by the conversations we were having.

One senior executive at a major consulting firm reached out to me saying, "Thank you for *The Reconstruction*. The conversations are powerful, reflective yet forward-thinking. Your questions are profound and provocative. They have forced me to rethink my own mission and legacy. I hope to continue to learn and grow through your podcast."

A university professor friend of mine made the podcast required listening for their Social Impact class.

We were on to something. But we knew that the podcast was only one medium and not for everyone. We needed a separate vehicle to further deliver the thoughts around justice and narrative change we had been exploring.

Enter experiment number two, where we formed a nonprofit collective focused on narrative change.

Over the course of a few months, we brainstormed a few ideas that just didn't fit. As I meditated on our "Why?" and the urgent need for narrative change that animated us, I asked myself, "What are we really trying to do?" And then the answer came to me, clear as day: we're trying to *make justice normal*. Not just in impact investing or finance. Indeed, if you had asked me 20 years ago if justice and finance could be in the same sentence, I would have said no. But, since systems are complex and inextricably interconnected, we could not possibly begin to "move capital toward justice" if we did not move everything, in every domain, including finance, toward justice.

Calling something "Make Justice Normal" could be an organizational mission—and a personal manifesto—in one. Making justice normal had to be something we wanted desperately and authentically for our own bodies and lives, as much as we did for the systems that governed us: democratic systems, health systems, financial systems, and environmental ecosystems. In other words, the entire planet.

But also, who was I, a first-generation Jamaican American woman, daughter of immigrants, to think that I could influence anything at all?

Could we really set a bar so high, knowing that we alone couldn't possibly reach it, and that we would very likely be setting ourselves up for failure? After all, in our current truth, injustice is normal and we, collectively, have no idea what the world would look like if justice were normalized. Could we embrace the emergence of it all?

With all the above tumbling around in my brain, I almost didn't share the name idea with my other cofounders.

However, knowing that there were amazing projects naming big ideas like "Made With Black Culture" and "End Poverty Make Trillions" made me think . . . maybe it *could* work.

I knew that something abstract that would require paragraphs of explanation to understand just wouldn't do.

In the end, when I told my cofounders the name, they embraced it. We were electrified by the possibility that by working together we could influence even just a few people to rethink capital, finance, and power; even with just that, we would have done a lot. Together, we could help inspire people to imagine a world in which liberation was indeed possible and help unshackle mental narratives that are the first barrier to change.

Our contribution is to add our energy to the relentless striving toward the goal of normalizing justice that preceded us and will continue long after we are gone. Truly, is there a cause more worthwhile?

We are working toward a world that is more just, where power and wealth are decoupled, and capital shifts more equitably into new hands, causing less harm and more good for more people and the planet. A world where people have more codified rights, and sovereignty and more access to true democracy. A world that defaults to anti-bias and pro-Earth, instead of what we have now, among other goals. We humbly acknowledge that we are not original or unique, but stand on the shoulders of giants. In the words of the late, great

Dr. Martin Luther King Jr.: "Change does not roll in on the wheels of inevitability, but comes through continuous struggle."

A few months after agreeing on the name for our new project, Make Justice Normal, I was asked by a friend and mentor in front of numerous colleagues: "What is your purpose?" And in that moment, after having struggled for months with what to call our fledgling collective, it dawned on me that while we were naming the organization, I was also discovering my purpose at the age of 45.

So, when it was my turn to answer, I said clearly, "My purpose is to make justice normal."

Contributing Author Biography

Monique Aiken is the managing director of The Investment Integration Project, a consulting services and applied research firm that provides advice, thought leadership, and a turnkey solution, Systems Aware Investing Launchpad (SAIL), to help investors manage systemic risks and opportunities. She hosted *The Reconstruction*, a 24-episode podcast series about "moving capital toward justice," and is a contributing editor at ImpactAlpha, where she hosts the *Impact Briefing* podcast. She is a cofounder of Make Justice Normal and host of their podcast, *Into the Record*. She is also a cofounder of the ReStarter Fund. Monique is a Toigo Fellow, Sponsors for Educational Opportunity (SEO) and INROADS alum, and holds an MBA from NYU Stern School of Business and a BSc in Foreign Service from Georgetown University.

20.

Monitor Your Investment Performance

Unless you have a magic wand lying around, you can't force the investments to perform the way you initially envisioned. The recipients of your investment proceeds do the best they can to deliver what they promised, but cannot guarantee the results they promised.

It's our job as investors to monitor the performance of our investments over time. From time to time, we may need to sell underperforming investments to make room for higher-performing investments.

Luckily, we don't have to reinvent the wheel on this one. We can borrow best practices for traditional portfolio monitoring (which focuses on financial earnings) and layer in a simple monitoring approach for social justice returns.

When reviewing your portfolio's financial performance, you want answers to the following questions:

How is the portfolio performing?
Does this track with the returns I targeted in my investment strategy?
Do I need to make any adjustments to get my returns back on track?

FOR INVESTORS WORKING WITH A FINANCIAL ADVISOR

Your advisor is well-equipped to answer these questions and should have information summarizing your investments' performance at their fingertips. Rapid technology developments mean that financial advisors can quickly report your total portfolio performance, compare it to the capital market's overall performance, and drill down into the performance of each underlying investment.

Financial advisors can use this information to answer your questions and tailor their responses to your investor personality. Some investors with aggressive risk appetites may feel disgruntled if their investments don't lean into exciting but uncertain market opportunities. Investors with conservative risk appetites would be horrified to learn one of their favorite companies decided to carve out a new business line in an unfamiliar market.

Remember all that time you spent finding a financial advisor you liked? And then all the tense conversations you facilitated to help your advisor understand your twin return objectives of sustainable financial earnings coupled with social justice returns?

All that time and energy you invested in the relationship is now reaping its rewards. Your financial advisor understands your objectives and can help you stay on track, even when market conditions change. They can help you monitor your financial earnings and keep you moving toward your goals.

Nicole and her advisor examine her portfolio's performance

Let's continue following Nicole's investment story, picking up 12 months after she decided to invest $5,000 of her cash inheritance into three different ETFs that reflected her social justice values. Nicole's financial advisor, Marcia, sent Nicole an email in the middle of January to schedule an annual check-in about her portfolio's performance.

"Good morning, Nicole! Thank you so much for scheduling time with me to review your portfolio. As you know, my company follows best practices to call each of our clients at least once per year to discuss your portfolio's performance and check-in on your financial goals. Is now still a good time to talk?"

Nicole had settled into her favorite chair in her living room. With her pen and paper in hand, she was ready to dig in. "Hi, Marcia! Yes, absolutely. *How is the portfolio performing?*"

"Your portfolio is performing well against the market. Your financial returns are tracking slightly higher than the average market returns, which is in line with your moderate risk appetite. As you'll recall from our conversation last year, one of the ETFs you purchased has a higher-than-average expense ratio. The higher expenses pulled down your total portfolio performance by a small amount, but not enough to make a material difference."

Nicole interrupted her. "Was that the expense ratio for the justice-focused ETF? If I remember correctly, the costs required to manage that ETF were higher because of the time their company spends talking to the communities in which they direct the money. Do I remember that right?"

"Yes, that's right. In fact, the managing company included some information about that in the ETF's annual impact report. I'll send that over to you in case you'd like to review it further." Marcia began tapping out an email on her end of the line.

Nicole smiled and continued walking through her notes. "Great. *Does this track with the returns I targeted in my investment strategy?*"

Marcia tapped out a few more keystrokes before answering. "Yes, it does. You've only held these ETFs for a year and they'll need more time to mature so you get the full return you're looking for out of them. With that said, they're on the right trajectory. Per our conversation, I am reinvesting any dividends earned back into the same investments. Still ok with you?"

Nicole nodded. "Yes, that's great. Thank you. *Do we need to make any adjustments to get my returns back on track?*"

Marcia and Nicole spent many phone calls together trying to find the best time to sell off a portion of the investment Nicole had inherited from her aunt. Nicole had researched the investments and wanted to sell them due to their poor scores related to environmental and social justice.

Marcia picked up the conversation now. "I don't see any need for big adjustments right now. Your portfolio is performing well, following your investor roadmap, and within the bounds of your asset allocation budget."

Nicole smiled on her end of the phone call. "Wonderful! Thanks so much for keeping tabs on everything for me."

Marcia interjected with a question of her own. "While we're on the phone, I also like to check in with my clients about any changes to their financial needs. Have you made any plans that will require you to withdraw funds? Any plans to purchase a house, start saving for a big honeymoon, or quit your job to backpack through Europe?"

Nicole laughed, but then thought about her upcoming financial needs. She was planning a girls' trip to California in a few months, but she had set aside some of her last paychecks in a savings account. Other than that, she had no changes to report since the last time she spoke with Marcia.

"Nope. No big changes here. Just trying to put one foot in front of the other."

Marcia and Nicole exchanged their well wishes and goodbyes, each happy with the portfolio's performance. Their relationship reminds us that we don't have to figure this out in a vacuum. Working with a trained financial advisor keeps you evenly balanced so you don't have to stay laser-focused on your investments, day in and day out. It's quite literally their job to monitor and manage your investments on your behalf.

DIY INVESTORS CREATE A DISCIPLINED APPROACH TO MONITOR THEIR PORTFOLIOS

Every 6 to 12 months, DIY investors should set aside a few hours to compare their portfolio's performance against their investor roadmap, as well as its adherence to the asset allocation budget established in chapter 15.

The tools and resources available through online investment accounts make it easy and convenient to monitor the financial performance of your investment portfolio over time, usually through charts and graphs that are designed to visually depict market movements.

Many DIY platforms even provide visual aids to help investors monitor whether their portfolios are maintaining the asset allocation budget.

If you determine that your portfolio has veered off course, you will need to buy or sell products until your investments follow your roadmap and asset allocation budget once again.

Let's consider Angela's approach to portfolio performance.

Angela explains how DIY investors monitor their portfolio performance

Two years into her DIY investing journey, Angela invited her former colleagues (all third-grade teachers) to her home to celebrate the end of the school year. Over wine and pizza, Angela explained how she was obsessed with tracking her investment portfolio through a mobile app on her phone.

"This app is amazing! I'm able to compare my portfolio's performance against the market in real time. Plus, the app recommends different news articles based on my investment preferences. Like yesterday, I read how a big corporation recently invested $3 billion in creating an affordable electric vehicle. Like, an electric vehicle that my parents, who you know watch every penny that squeezes its way out of their pocketbooks, could really consider as affordable. I'm using my next two weeks' worth of budget to purchase a share of the company. Tomorrow I'll conduct my typical research to confirm it's a good fit."

Her friend Rebecca piped in, "Angela, how do you know these investments will perform like you think they will? Isn't this risky? How are you comfortable with using your money like this?"

All eyes turned to Angela.

"Well, you're right. All these investments carry risk. They could all go belly up tomorrow and my portfolio's value could plummet. But the way I figure, I would have already spent the money anyway, fueling my Starbucks addiction." Angela looked around the room. "You know how I love my lattes."

All the ladies chuckled together and bonded over their shared love of caffeine.

Angela continued. "When I started investing, I justified the money by investing my coffee budget instead of spending it. I mean, my lattes are amazing, but they're never going to return my money. It's money down the drain either way.

"With my investments, though, I can see them grow and evolve over time. Sometimes they gain in value; other times they drop in value. There's a lot I can't control."

Rebecca's curiosity was now piqued. "So how do you monitor the portfolio's performance?"

Angela's eyes lit up. She loved describing her new toy to her friends. "Even though I'm watching the ups and downs of my portfolio every time I make my weekly contribution, I've found I get swept away in the small adjustments. So I've trained myself to wait until my annual statements are available to assess the performance over time."

Rebecca held out her hand to her friend. "Wait. You look at your annual statements? Don't you need to be a financial guru to understand documents like that?"

Angela offered a second slice of pizza to her neighbor and answered, "You'd be surprised how easy it is to understand. Plus, I've narrowed down my assessment to three questions:

How is the portfolio performing?
Does this track with the returns I targeted in my investment strategy?
Do I need to make any adjustments to get my returns back on track?

"The first question is easiest to answer. The app compares my portfolio against the market at large. Last year my portfolio performed similarly to the market average. Which makes sense, as I mostly purchase pooled investments like ETFs and mutual funds. They let me purchase small pieces of a whole bunch of stocks and bonds. It's nice because a single company's loss won't take my earnings."

Now everyone was staring at Angela with open mouths.

"No, really!" She protested. "It's all remarkably straightforward. If you can teach 25 eight-year-olds how the water cycle works, you can learn how to compare your portfolio's performance to the market average."

Rebecca found her voice first. "So how do you answer the other questions?"

Angela took a sip of wine and answered, "Those two tend to go hand in hand. When I first started investing, I wrote down my investment goals in an investment strategy document. My goal for financial earnings is a 7% return over time. If my portfolio is achieving those goals, I leave it alone. If its yearly performance is below my benchmark, I research higher-performing investments."

Rebecca offered Angela a slice of pizza and joked with the group, "If teachers find out how much easier it is to build a portfolio rather than managing a classroom, we'll never staff an elementary school again!"

A chorus of moans met Angela's laughter. "Cheers to that, friend!"

HOW 401(K) INVESTORS MONITOR THEIR PORTFOLIOS

401(k) investors benefit from the highly regulated nature of employer-sponsored retirement accounts. Just like investors working with financial advisors, 401(k) investors can rely on their employer-paid investment advisors to provide annual updates on the performance of their investment portfolios.

401(k) investors can use this information to assess the rate at which their portfolio is growing over time, the current value of their investment portfolio, and whether they need to make any adjustments to get their returns back on track.

Let's consider how Tom reviews his portfolio performance.

Tom reviews his 401(k) portfolio performance

Every 12 months, Tom's company requires all its employees to attend an in-person 401(k) performance review meeting. The company's investment consultant leads the meeting and presents the financial performance of each of the investment options in the 401(k) menu to the employees.

Trudging into the largest conference room in the office, Tom scanned the room for a chair next to a friendly face.

"Hey, pal. How's it going?" Ross asked when Tom sat down.

Tom smiled. "Pretty good! Got those budget numbers in for Dianne and looking forward to a day or two before the new usage reports arrive. You ready for this meeting?"

"Always ready to find out how much closer I am to retirement," Ross grinned. "You ever been to one of these 401(k) performance reviews before?"

Ross continued when Tom shook his head. "The company brings in their investment advisor to walk through the menu of 401(k) investment options and describe how the investment performed over the past year, usually comparing it to the market average. If you brought your annual statements with you, he'll walk around and ask folks if they have any questions. I usually ask him to review my personal portfolio before he heads out for the day."

Tom pointed his chin toward a man in a charcoal suit shaking hands with the company's human resources manager. "That must be the investment consultant. What happens if you don't like your portfolio's performance?"

Ross scratched his chin before answering. "Well, there have definitely been a few years with less-than-stellar performance. Sometimes the economy just isn't working for me. I could always make adjustments, but overall my investments are trending upward at a good rate. I really don't like filling out extra paperwork and I tend to have a 'set it and forget it' personality anyway, so I just let it ride."

Tom nodded and replied, "That feels right to me, too. Do you think the company's investment consultant would alert you if your portfolio is underperforming?"

"Yes, I do," Ross explained. "Actually, I don't even think it would get that far. A few years back, the investment advisor used this meeting to explain that he didn't have faith in one of the investment options anymore and let us know that he was removing that option from future contributions. Then I did have to update my paperwork since I had allocated 20% of my contributions toward that one."

Tom leaned back in his chair. "Really? That's big of him to own up to a mistake."

Ross shrugged, "I mean, it's his job to select good investment options for our 401(k) menu. If he didn't stay on top of their individual performances, the company would fire him. Did you know we can actually call him anytime to walk through our portfolio? I called him when I was changing my allocation and he helped me configure the most effective choices to meet my retirement goals."

"Wow," Tom started. "That's an incredible benefit. I already reviewed my statements and am happy with their direction, but I'll plan on giving him a call if my portfolio's performance ever falters."

Ross nodded. "Sounds like a good plan. You're also of the 'avoid paperwork and let it ride' mentality?"

Tom chuckled. "Yes, I guess I am. The way I figure, investments need time to grow and mature. The less I mess with them, the better they can perform."

With that, Tom and Ross spent the next 30 minutes learning how the menu of 401(k) options were performing well against the market. Tom confirmed with the investment advisor that his portfolio's performance tracked well with his objectives and that he didn't need to make any adjustments against his portfolio.

The investment advisor walked Tom to the door and encouraged him to call anytime with questions. "Your 401(k) is set up to meet your objectives, but please don't hesitate to call with any questions. I'm always available to discuss your financial needs."

Tom walked away reassured that his investments were performing well and that he had a new, professionally trained ally in his corner.

MONITORING SOCIAL JUSTICE RETURNS

Social justice investors have experienced massive breakthroughs in the past decade with respect to the ability to track social justice returns and monitor the performance of our portfolios in creating authentic social change. Resources like "Invest Your Values" do the heavy lifting for investors with positions in thousands of stocks, bonds, and exchange-traded funds. You can keep tabs on your investments' social justice grades over time, using the information to increase your contributions to investments that perform well and sell investments that don't perform well.

If you crave more detailed information about the type of social justice advances your investments are creating, you can tap into your internet sleuthing skills to locate investor reports and impact reports from the companies represented in your portfolio.

Energy Boost: We Can't Change What We Don't Measure

Tanay Tatum-Edwards

In 2018, I attended a conference that changed my life. Well, that might be giving too much credit to the event itself.

Instead, the fancy conference hotel was the backdrop for the moment when all the thoughts and fears racing around my head finally crystallized into the concept that would become the company I didn't yet know I would build.

When I look back at that day, a few moments stand out.

First, the panel of middle-aged white people discussing how investors could address gun violence through financial choices.

And how I grew more and more baffled when they failed to make the connection between gun violence and racial equity.

Looking around to discover that, within a sea of faces, only one person looked like me. A hair tie held her box braids in a ponytail, and her blazer contrasted elegantly against her chic teal dress.

I watched as she extended her hand into the air, eyes connecting with the moderator's gaze, to ask the question I was quietly thinking: "Have you considered the link between gun violence and racial equity?"

My new hero paused to listen to some unsatisfactory response about it being outside the scope of the panel's collective methodologies.

"I see. Do you have any recommendations for people seeking to address racial equity through investments?"

Nothing. None of the expert panelists invited to share their insights on financial approaches to reduce gun violence could provide a single example of an investment that addressed racial equity.

When the remainder of the question-and-answer session concluded, I made a beeline to my new friend. I introduced myself and thanked her for bringing a racial equity lens to the conversation. We then walked toward the hotel's ballroom, where conference attendees were encouraged to meet, mingle, and exchange business cards.

But I was uninterested in speaking with anyone else except my new friend. I was absorbed in learning everything I could about this wicked smart, Black Millennial woman who had so expertly navigated a career as an investment analyst, a field dominated by white men.

She shared her story and invited me to share my own.

After providing my general background in international development finance, I began describing my frustration about the prevailing metrics for measuring an investment's social impact. From my perspective, the investment industry had accepted cursory, check-the-box impact measurements that wouldn't and couldn't move the needle toward real change.

"Tell me about the impact measurements you'd *like* to see," she encouraged.

My mind soared, excited to share my dreams for how investment measurements could be shaped to reflect the on-the-ground realities of communities like ours.

"I want measurements grounded in the lived experiences of people who are most impacted by social injustices. I'm tired of measuring impact in terms of 'number of jobs created' or 'square footage of community facilities financed.' Instead, I want to dig deep into a social justice issue and determine authentic metrics against which investors can manage their success."

My new friend peered intently at me before nudging me forward. "It sounds like you're thinking of something specific."

I paused, looked into her eyes, and was honest.

"I can't help but notice a lack of diversity at this conference. All I see is a sea of white. How can we honestly decide what impact issues are most important if we don't have diverse perspectives in the room?

"I don't know about you, but I grew up in a small town in the rural South. We didn't care about the number of low-wage jobs created. Or how many low-income housing units were built. We wanted full ownership of our labor and our homes.

"We wanted freedom. Economic freedom. But also freedom from fear. We were too busy figuring out how to hold our families together without our incarcerated loved ones. And how to break the cycle and protect our kids from the school-to-prison pipeline. We wanted a world where we didn't fear the police.

"I know this is wonky, but I want investments that measure outcomes that measure wealth creation, defund the prison–industrial complex, and move us closer to ending mass incarceration."

I stopped to gauge my friend's reaction. Was I asking too much of our industry?

She looked at me with heavy admiration and let out a sigh. "It won't happen unless someone like us creates it."

Personally and professionally, I was fixated entirely on correcting the problem of inadequate investment measurement metrics. It was the last thing I thought about at night and the first thing I thought about when I woke up in the morning. I was reading Morgan Simon's *Real Impact* for fun and pushing my supervisors to refine our own impact metrics.

So what was holding me back from leading? I was certainly intelligent enough. I was young-ish but well-connected, and as Beyoncé once said, "I don't like to gamble, but if there's one thing I'm willing to bet on, it's myself."

But I still had doubts. How would the industry perceive me?

My friend could tell I was thinking and asked me to share more.

My response revealed, even to me, how much I had let the investment industry infiltrate my understanding of what it took to step out and step forward. I felt like I was confessing a deep secret when I replied:

"I could do it in the future. But I don't have an MBA from an Ivy League or a CFA Charter. You need both to be taken seriously in finance, especially as a Black woman."

A moment of incredulous silence swirled around us.

"Wow," my new friend sighed. "Those are some crazy high standards for people who want to create change."

I blinked, dumbfounded, while I processed this new truth. I had convinced myself that I couldn't create change because I hadn't met the arbitrary, not-quite-relevant success metrics defined by people who benefit from maintaining the status quo.

Yes, I know about the irony.

But in that moment of clarity, new possibilities stretched out before me.

I could use my own lived experiences to define authentic, relevant success metrics grounded for impact investments. Metrics informed by the realities of the very people and communities for which the investments were designed to help.

I didn't lose any time in executing my vision. Within a year, I received seed money from Echoing Green, a prestigious fellowship for social entrepreneurs, which I used to launch FreeCap Financial, an investment research company. Our data and insights make it easier for investors to align their portfolios with the social justice causes they care more about.

Since then, I've refined my approach by listening to communities closest to the problems we hope to solve. My goal is to convert their solutions into measurable investment metrics.

Our first product is a scorecard that helps investors dismantle the prison–industrial complex—a necessary step to end mass incarceration. There are 2.2 million people incarcerated in the United States, representing over 20% of the global incarcerated population. Black and brown communities, immigrants, and those who suffer from mental illness are disproportionately impacted by this crisis.

Companies routinely lobby to keep prisons full and pay below-market rates to access prison labor. To make matters worse, the discrimination justice-involved workers experience in the workplace leads to unfairly high unemployment rates and increases the likelihood of recidivism.

FreeCap monitors and rates companies' impact on the justice system to highlight industry leaders in racial equity and expose those exacerbating the prison–industrial complex. Our company rankings give investors and those who manage their money the information they need to invest according to their values. When investors make decisions to align their money with specific impact objectives, companies take notice, and will often choose to improve their behavior so that they perform better on the benchmark.

In other words, we make it profitable *not* to profit from racial injustice.

We achieve this with data transparency, so that everyday people can invest in a socially equitable future.

Impact measurement requires us to constantly listen and refine our process to accurately measure outcomes that can truly benefit society. It's an iterative process that requires constant listening and vulnerability but will always be needed.

I'm so glad I took a leap of faith to bet on myself. I hope investors can use FreeCap's work to invest in their own vision of a better future.

Contributing Author Biography

Tanay Tatum-Edwards is the founder and CEO of FreeCap Financial Inc., an innovative data company specializing in Environmental, Social, Governance (ESG), and racial equity investing. Tanay has multiple loved ones impacted by mass incarceration and is committed to using her expertise to address it. Prestigious fellowships, including Echoing Green, Fulbright, Halcyon Incubator, and Roddenberry Foundation, have supported her work. Tanay is regularly featured in the media to discuss insights from her research. Before FreeCap, she developed a lifelong commitment to using investment strategies to create systemic social change while working in asset management. A foodie, NBA fan, and lover of hip-hop, Tanay received an MA in Law and Diplomacy from The Fletcher School at Tufts University, where her classmates elected her commencement speaker, and a BA in Africana Studies and Sociology from Vassar College, where she served as student-body president.

Acknowledgments

While my name might be on the cover, *The Social Justice Investor* distills experiences and expertise from an entire community of leaders, mentors, and practitioners who have spent generations investing in the potential of people. Thank you for sharing your lessons and insights with me so that I may share them with others.

There are a few people who deserve a special callout:

To Kyle: I could not have written this book without you. Your unflagging support was the bedrock from which I wrote and rewrote every version of this manuscript. I love you and this beautiful life we've created together.

To Cora, Lucy, and George: I love you forever, no matter what. Thank you for your hugs and kisses, shrieks of laughter, and kind hearts. You are my light and joy—just by being your wonderful selves.

To Adrienne Ingrum, my editor at Broadleaf Books: Working with you is a blessing that grows every day. Thank you for your guidance, collaboration, dedication, expertise, and thoughtfulness. You took a chance on this first-time author and mentored me through every step of the process. You have a gift and I am forever grateful that you shared it with me.

To my agent, Regina Brooks of Serendipity Literary Agency, and the support of her staff, including Emma Loy-Santelli: Thank you for taking this leap of faith with me and for connecting me with the absolute best partners. You continue to set me up for success and I appreciate your thoughtfulness, insights, and sheer tenacity.

To Rachel Reyes, Carlos Esparza, Dr. Jessica Lockrem, and the entire production team at Broadleaf Books: Thank you for your dedication, diligence, and creativity in refining and designing this book. I deeply appreciate how you expertly shepherded *The Social Justice Investor* into the best possible version of itself.

To Elizabeth Gilbert Kaetzel of Narratur Studios: Thank you for being my thought partner and cheerleader in those early months of weaving this book together. Your guidance and insights were invaluable in shaping the book's tone, content, and direction. You are a bright light and a brilliant writer.

To the contributing authors whose "Energy Boosts" encouraged and inspired us to keep taking the next step: Thank you for sharing your stories and experiences with me. I was both inspired and humbled in every single interview with this amazing group of leaders. Thank you for your patience, generosity, and thoughtfulness. I will always be grateful that you entrusted me with your stories.

There are so many other people, in both my personal and professional lives, who have shaped the content and tone of this book. From mentors who shared an encouraging word to friends who met me for coffee when it all got to be too much: thank you. I wouldn't have made it without my community. I appreciate you more than words can say.

Glossary

Aggressive risk: An investment strategy where investors are willing to take on more risk for the possibility of higher financial earnings.

Alpha return: A term used to describe investments that have an advantage in the market, resulting in a high return.

Asset allocation: An investment strategy that organizes a portfolio's assets across different buckets of asset classes (e.g., equities, fixed income, and cash) to best reflect the investor's goals, risk tolerance, and timing needs. Whereas traditional investors allocate their investments across financial asset classes only (e.g., fixed income, equities, and cash), social justice investors also allocate their investments across social justice priorities.

Asset classes: Groupings of investments that exhibit similar characteristics are subject to the same laws and regulations. Common groups can include equities, fixed income, ETFs, mutual funds, and cash.

Assets: A resource with an economic value that an individual owns or controls with the expectation that it will provide a future benefit.

Capital markets: Financial markets that bring buyers and sellers together to trade stocks, bonds, and other financial assets. Capital markets include the stock market and the bond market.

Cash flow: The amount of cash moving into and out of a company.

Community development financial institutions (CDFIs): Financial institutions that focus on lending in underinvested communities, providing capital for those who have been historically excluded from traditional banking. CDFIs finance microenterprises and small businesses, nonprofit organizations, commercial real estate, affordable housing, and more.

Conservative risk: A strategy for investment designed to deliver predictable, consistent financial earnings.

Diversification: A strategy that mixes a wide variety of investments within a portfolio to reduce portfolio risk. The financial equivalent of "don't put all your eggs in one basket."

Divest: To withdraw existing investment in a company or organization.

Dividend: A sum of money paid regularly (typically quarterly) by a company to its equity shareholders out of its profits or reserves.

Donor-advised funds (DAFs): A private fund created for a charitable purpose and administered by a financial institution.

Employer-sponsored retirement plan: A retirement savings plan offered by many American employers that has tax advantages for the saver. These retirement plans are more colloquially referred to as a 401(k), 403(b), pension, or another name describing the retirement savings benefit offered by an employer.

Environmental, social, and governance (ESG): An investment framework that evaluates company behavior for potential risk from unethical practices.

Equities: Equity investments represent an ownership position in the underlying company or organization. Equities provide financial earnings through both price appreciation and dividends.

Exchange-traded fund (ETF): A prepackaged basket of equity stocks and/or fixed income bonds traded as a single investment product. ETFs usually follow a predetermined list of stocks, but they can also include a list of fixed income securities.

Federal deposit insurance corporation (FDIC) insurance: Insurance issued by the FDIC that covers the balance of the depositor's account(s). The credit union equivalent is called NCUA insurance.

FICO scores: A grade for a borrower's projected ability to repay a loan on a scale of 0 to 850. Also known as credit scores.

Fiduciary duty: The legal and ethical obligation of a financial advisor or investment consultant to act for the benefit of their clients and place their clients' interests before their employer's or their own interests.

Financial advisor (also known as financial coach, money manager, wealth manager, investment advisor): A professionally trained partner who provides guidance in how to manage your money according to your financial situation, goals, and investment personality. In the United States, financial advisors must complete specific training and be registered with a regulatory body in order to provide advice.

Fixed income: Commonly referred to as debt securities, bonds, notes, or even certificates of deposit (CDs), fixed-income investments offer investors predictable cash flows based on the instrument's "fixed" (in that it cannot change over time) interest rate.

401(k) investment menu: Similar to a restaurant menu, a 401(k) investment menu is the list of investment options available to the employee. The employee selects which investment option best meets their needs to fund appropriate retirement plans. In most cases, companies are required to offer at least three investments that are diversified and have materially different risk and return characteristics. On average, companies offer 19 investment options to employees through the investment menu. Employees can select multiple investment options, indicating what percentage of their contributions should be allocated to which investment options.

401(k) plan: A retirement savings plan offered by many American employers that has tax advantages for the employee.

Individual retirement account (IRA): An investment account with tax advantages that can be accessed for retirement.

Initial public offering (IPO): When a private company first sells shares of stock to the public, this process is known as an IPO. An IPO means that a company's ownership is transitioning from private ownership to public ownership. Having "gone public," the company is now considered publicly traded.

Interest rate: The financial payment on a fixed income security. The issuer agrees to pay the investor for lending funds. Interest rates are expressed as a percentage of the total loan amount.

Investment: An asset that is purchased in the hopes that it will accrue value over time.

Investment policy statement (IPS): A document outlining an investor's roadmap, including objectives (return and risk targets) and constraints (liquidity, legal considerations, timing, taxes, and unique circumstances). An IPS may also describe strategies an investor strives to adopt to meet the envisioned investment objectives.

Investment portfolio: A collection of financial investments like stocks, bonds, exchange-traded funds, and mutual funds, among other product types. Portfolios may also contain a wide range of assets, including real estate, gold, art, and private investments. Many investors carry a small amount of cash and cash equivalents in their portfolio.

Investment returns: For traditional investors, a return is the money made or lost on an investment over a specified period of time.

Investment risk: All investments, no matter what you select, carry some degree of risk. Risk is the possibility that an investment's *actual* gains will differ from the *expected* return.

Investment screening: The process or tool that determines whether an investment's objectives align with the investor's strategic priorities.

Issuer: The company, organization, or entity that is responsible for generating the financial earnings associated with the interest payments. For instance, General Motors may issue debt securities to expand product lines or finance current operations. Many governments issue bonds to raise capital to pay down debts or fund infrastructure improvements.

Liquidity: How quickly a financial asset can be converted into cash.

Low-wealth communities: A community that faces systemic barriers to building wealth.

Macro asset allocation: The percentage of one's total investment portfolio allocated to social justice investments.

Market value: The total dollar value of a company's equity. Also referred to as market capitalization. This measure of a company's value is calculated by multiplying the current stock price by the total number of outstanding shares.

Maturity: The date when the issuer is obligated to repay the outstanding principal amount of a fixed income security.

Micro asset allocation: The laser-focused allocation of assets across different social justice priorities.

Mutual fund: The financial vehicle that pools assets from shareholders to invest in securities like stocks, bonds, money market instruments, and other assets. Mutual funds are operated by professional money managers, who allocate the fund's assets and attempt to produce capital gains or income for the fund's investors.

Price appreciation: The increase in the value of an asset over time.

Principal: The dollar amount the issuer agrees to repay the bondholders on the maturity date of a fixed income security. Also known as a bond's "par value."

Publicly traded: A position, company, or fund that is available for purchase on a public exchange.

Security: A financial instrument that holds some type of monetary value. There are primarily three types of securities: equity (which provides ownership rights to holders); debt (loans repaid with periodic payments); and hybrids (which combine aspects of debt and equity).

Share: A unit of ownership in a corporation.

Shareholder: An investor who owns shares of a corporation.

Social justice investing: Putting money to work in a project, organization, or undertaking in order to generate wealth and advance social justice. Returns are characterized by the twin goals of sustainable financial earnings and social justice returns, where "social justice" has no set definition but is tailored based on the investor's personal priorities. Common social justice priorities include combatting racism, gender inequity, the inherent inequities of climate crisis, and LGBTQ+ discrimination.

Stock: A security that represents the ownership of a fraction of the issuing corporation. Also known as equity.

Stock market: A public trading platform for buying and selling stocks.

Stock price: The price at which the company's stock is trading.

Target date fund (TDF): An age-based retirement investment that helps you take more risk when you're young and gets more conservative over time.

"Wolf in Sheep's Clothing" (WISC) investment: An investment that is fraudulently marketed as "socially just," while the actual impact has a neutral or even negative impact on the ability of a person or community to reach their full potential.

Online Resources & Tools

Smart and capable social justice investors don't blindly follow claims. We conduct research and double-check.

Luckily, there are publicly available resources to help us on our way. Resources like As You Sow's "Invest Your Values" tool (investyourvalues. org) enables investors to evaluate the social responsibility of more than 3,000 mutual funds, ETFs, and 401(k)s. Other investors may prefer tools like Invest for Better that provide educational videos that teach everyday investors how to apply core financial concepts to social justice priorities.

The following organizations offer tools and resources designed for investors to align their money with their values.

AS YOU SOW (ASYOUSOW.ORG)

As You Sow is the nation's nonprofit leader in shareholder advocacy. Founded in 1992, As You Sow harnesses shareholder power to create lasting change by protecting human rights, reducing toxic waste, and aligning investments with values.

The "Invest Your Values" tool (InvestYourValues.org) enables investors to evaluate the social responsibility of 3,000 mutual funds and ETFs, from their fossil fuel impact to gender equality and racial justice. With a list of what you currently own in hand, type the name, ticket, or manager of a fund into the search box. The result will show how that fund scores on an A through F scale for the screen you choose.

As You Sow also offers issue-specific tools to identify the following: fossil fuel–free funds (https://fossilfreefunds.org), prison-free funds (https://prisonfreefunds.org), tobacco-free funds (https://tobaccofreefunds.

org), deforestation-free funds (https://deforestationfreefunds.org), weapon-free funds (https://weaponfreefunds.org), gender equality funds (https://genderequalityfunds.org), gun-free funds (https://gunfreefunds.org), and the prison-free action toolkit (https://prisonfreefunds.org/action-toolkit).

INVEST FOR BETTER (INVESTFORBETTER.ORG)

Invest for Better is a nonprofit that gives women the confidence, skills, and encouragement they need to take control of their assets and use them to influence the things they care about.

There, you can build your community through Invest for Better Circles, which are small, peer-to-peer learning and activation groups. Circles of peer investors learn step-by-step practices for investing their dollars according to their values.

Other resources include educational videos that teach everyday investors the basics of core investment concepts; guides for investing with a specific lens, like gender, climate, and racial justice; and modules and webinars for aligning your money with your values using stocks, bonds, banking, and more.

INVESTOPEDIA (INVESTOPEDIA.COM)

Investopedia was founded in 1999 with the mission of simplifying financial decisions and information to give readers the confidence to manage every aspect of their financial life. Investors can use its internal search function to explore Investopedia for definitions and strategies related to investment decisions at every stage of an investor's journey.

US SIF: THE FORUM FOR SUSTAINABLE AND RESPONSIBLE INVESTMENT (USSIF.ORG)

US SIF is a nonprofit hub for the sustainable and impact investment sector in the United States. US SIF offers a free online course for individual investors who want to learn the basics of sustainable investing and how to align their portfolios to address their social and environmental priorities.

ADASINA SOCIAL CAPITAL (ADASINA.COM)

Adasina Social Capital is a registered investment advisor dedicated to transforming wealth into a tool that supports the well-being of people and planet. In its Social Justice Impact Datasets (https://adasina.com/education/#impact-datasets), Adasina Social Capital published a list of publicly traded companies that exacerbate racial, gender, economic, and climate inequities. Investors can compare the list against their own portfolio with the goal of selling positions in companies included on the list.

FORCE THE ISSUE (FORCETHEISSUE.ORG)

Force the Issue is a coalition that represents workers, consumers, and investors seeking to end the practice of forced arbitration for sexual harassment, a harmful practice at odds with gender justice. The coalition offers a database of all publicly traded companies and information on whether they definitely, probably, or do not practice forced arbitration for sexual harassment.

CANDIDE GROUP (CANDIDEGROUP.COM)

Candide Group is a registered investment advisor that works with families, foundations, athletes, and cultural influencers who want their money working for justice. Candide Group offers a Financial Activist Playbook for Supporting Black Lives. Written by Jasmine Rashid, the playbook provides a guide to strategies big and small for moving money for racial justice.

SUSTAINALYTICS (SUSTAINALYTICS.COM)

Sustainalytics provides company ESG (environmental, social, and governance) risk ratings for more than 4,500 companies. The ratings highlight

ESG issues that Sustainalytics believes may pose a financially material risk to the company and assess the magnitude of that risk.

Tools and resources include the following:

> Sustainalytics ESG Ratings Tool combines the company's exposure, or its vulnerability, to ESG risks, and the actions taken by the company's management to address the ESG issue. Each investment then gets an overall ESG rating. A lower ESG risk rating indicates a lower overall risk of experiencing negative financial impact from ESG issues.
>
> Morningstar's ESG Screener (www.morningstar.com/esg-screener) uses company ratings developed by the Sustainalytics ESG Ratings Tool (above) to create a database that enables investors to search for funds by their names. Investors can search using a variety of filters. For example, an investor can search for funds that identify "sustainability" or "ESG" in their marketing materials.

THE NATIONAL ASSOCIATION OF PERSONAL FINANCIAL ADVISORS (NAPFA.ORG)

NAPFA makes it easy to find financial advisors near you that fit your needs through its "Find an Advisor" search tool. NAPFA also offers free resources that guide you through the process of choosing a financial advisor, like evaluating potential advisors and fees.

THE CFP BOARD (CFP.NET)

The CFP board provides designation for Certified Financial Planners (CFP), as well as resources for both planners and consumers. Tools and resources include an online search tool (letsmakeaplan.org) to help individual investors find local advisors with the CFP designation. Another resource is the financial topic guides (letsmakeaplan.org/financial-topics/topics-a-z), which offer guidance for financial topics like retirement planning, budgeting, debt management, saving, or for different life stages.

THE ACCREDITED FINANCIAL COUNSELOR WEBSITE (FINDANAFC.ORG)

AFC is a resource for accredited financial counselors focused on serving middle-income families. AFC provides an online search tool to help individual investors find financial counselors in their geographic area by filtering by areas of financial expertise and types of offerings.

THE GARRETT PLANNING NETWORK (GARRETTPLANNINGNETWORK.COM)

The Garrett Planning Network is a community of fee-only financial advisors who keep their costs down to stay accessible for middle-class families. Tools include an Advisor Directory Search (directory.garrettplanningnetwork.com/search-member-profiles), which lists financial advisors by state. The website also offers a financial advisor interview questionnaire (garrettplanningnetwork.com/about/how-to-choose-an-advisor) that can be used when interviewing potential advisors.

XY PLANNING NETWORK (XYPLANNINGNETWORK.COM)

XYPN includes fee-only financial planners that offer services tailored to the everyday investor. Every advisor in the network offers virtual services so you aren't limited by location. Resources include an online search for advisors by location or specialty, as well as personal finance articles.

THE SOCIAL JUSTICE INVESTOR (THESOCIALJUSTICEINVESTOR.COM)

The Social Justice Investor is a woman-led investor education platform for individuals and organizations interested in applying a social justice lens to their portfolio. Tools and resources include the Social Justice Investor's Toolkit and a reading list of reference guides to social justice investing.

MIGHTY DEPOSITS (MIGHTYDEPOSITS.COM)

Might Deposits is an independent, women-owned bank comparison site which aims to make it easy for you to see what your bank does with your money and choose the right bank for you. Tools and resources include online search functions to find banks and credit unions in the United States, or by region, according to their sustainability, diverse ownership, community financing, and more.

RACIAL JUSTICE INVESTING COALITION (RACIALJUSTICEINVESTING.ORG)

The Racial Justice Investing Coalition is a coalition of investors, asset owners, and business leaders who are taking action for racial justice within our own organizations, as well as in our engagements with portfolio companies. RJIC provides a list of racial justice organizations and tools for making investment decisions for racial justice.

OPPORTUNITY FINANCE NETWORK (OFN.ORG)

Opportunity Finance Network (OFN) is a trade association of CDFIs and a financial intermediary. The nonprofit organization partners with investors, funders, and policymakers to align capital with opportunity. Tools include an online CDFI locator (www.ofn.org/cdfi-locator) to identify CDFIs by geographic regions.

Social Justice Investing Organizations

Activest (activest.org): An investment research firm that analyzes municipal finance and bonds for racial, social, and economic factors.

Adasina Social Capital (adasina.com): A registered investment advisor dedicated to transforming wealth into a tool that supports the well-being of people and planet. They offer an exchange-traded fund so everyday investors can easily invest for social justice (adasinaetf.com).

Betterment (betterment.com/socially-responsible-investing): A smart money manager and one of the largest independent online financial advisors that serves one purpose: to help investors make the most of their money. Betterment helps people manage their money through cash management, guided investing, and retirement planning.

Boston Common Asset Management (bostoncommonasset.com): An investment management firm that activates investor capital toward solutions for people and planet.

Bridging Virginia (bridgingvirginia.org): A nonprofit, community development load fund that provides access to affordable capital and technical assistance for historically marginalized small businesses in Virginia.

Calvert Impact Capital (calvertimpact.org): A nonprofit investment firm that helps all types of investors and financial professionals invest in solutions that people and our planet need. Calvert centers gender equity, racial justice, and climate impact throughout the investment process.

Candide Group (candidegroup.com): A registered investment advisor that works with families, foundations, athletes, and cultural influencers who want their money working for justice.

Choir (www.hellochoir.com): Creator of the financial industry's first conference diversity certification and a diversity-tech platform focused on amplifying the voices of women, nonbinary people, and people of color.

Chordata Capital (chordatacapital.com): A wealth management firm for people who have accumulated wealth and want to reallocate their resources for racial and economic justice.

cNote (mycnote.com): A woman-led technology platform that connects investors to CDFIs that lend in underserved communities. cNote offers 26 unique thematic investing targets, ranging from refugee crisis and immigration issues to climate change, affordable housing, and racial equity. cNote's Flagship Fund offers an easy way to start investing in CDFIs, with no minimum investment and competitive returns.

Community Capital Management (ccminvests.com): A fund management firm that specializes in helping clients align their investments for impact.

First Peoples Worldwide (colorado.edu/program/fpw): An organization that translates the impacts of investments on Indigenous communities into research, advocacy, and tools. Through corporate advocacy they work to ensure that outcomes for Indigenous peoples are considered in the design and decision making of investments.

Four Bands Community Fund (fourbands.org): A nonprofit community loan fund that helps Native American entrepreneurs start or expand a business with lending and technical assistance.

Hope Credit Union (hopecu.org): A southern credit union that prioritizes providing resources and capital to people who are often left out of the traditional banking system.

Impact Finance Center (impactfinancecenter.org): A multi-university, nonprofit academic center that identifies, trains, and activates individuals and organizations to become impact investors.

Initiative to Accelerate Charitable Giving (acceleratecharitablegiving.org/about): A coalition of philanthropists, leaders of major foundations, charities and nonprofits, and others that advocates for policies that keep organizational giving accountable.

Invest for Better (investforbetter.org): A nonprofit that gives women the confidence, skills, and encouragement they need to take control of their assets and use them to influence the things they care about.

Investor Advocates for Social Justice (iasj.org): A nonprofit organization using shareholder advocacy to advance social justice on behalf of investors with faith-based values.

Just Futures (justfutures.co): A financial firm that offers social justice retirement plans and investment advising for nonprofits, social movement groups, and small philanthropies.

LISC (https://www.lisc.org): A nonprofit community loan fund that seeks to connect underserved communities with capital. They receive funding from banks, corporations, foundations, and government agencies, then use that funding to provide financing, technical, and management assistance to local partners and developers.

Make Justice Normal (makejusticenormal.org): A growing collective that aims to foster just relationships and collective action among people working to make justice normal. They support collective action by sharing time and resources for projects that move capital toward justice.

Renegade Capital Podcast (http://renegadecapitalpodcast.com): A podcast about finance and investments for social justice investors. Listeners walk away inspired by the podcast guests and armed with actionable tips and tools to use money to create the world in which they want to live.

Resource Generation (resourcegeneration.org): A membership community of young people (18–35) with wealth and/or class privilege committed to the equitable distribution of wealth, land, and power.

Saltbox Financial (saltboxfinancial.co): An independent, fee-only financial planning firm that offers financial, investment, and tax advice to align with clients' values and goals.

The Investment Integration Project (TIIP) (tiiproject.com): TIIP develops tools for pursuing system-level investing, an advanced sustainable investing strategy for managing systemic risks, and investing in solutions to systemic problems (e.g., climate change, income inequality, economic crises).

The Next Egg (thenextegg.org): An online platform providing webinars, resources, and events focused on demystifying retirement savings and investment.

The Public Finance Initiative (publicfinanceinitiative.com): A nonprofit that specializes in developing finance programs that help organizations center equity, sustainability, and inclusive growth in their fiscal decision-making.

US Impact Investing Alliance (impinvalliance.org): A field-building organization raising awareness of impact investing in the United States. The alliance's long-term vision is to place measurable social, economic, and environmental impact alongside financial return and risk at the center of every investment decision.

About the Author

Andrea Longton is an award-winning author and professional social justice investor. She has raised over $1 billion for social justice investments in the United States and has advised on another $1.5 billion worldwide. Throughout all her experiences, Andrea prioritizes listening to and partnering with communities that have been shut out from traditional financial systems.

In addition to her professional experience, Andrea manages her family's finances, including their own social justice investment portfolio.

Her professional experiences include positions at Opportunity Finance Network, Freddie Mac, Capital Impact Partners (now Momentus Capital), and Delphos International. Andrea holds the Chartered Financial Analyst (CFA) charterholder designation from the CFA Institute (Charlottesville, VA), a BA from Centre College (Danville, KY), and an MA from The George Washington University (Washington, DC).

Andrea is the founder and author-administrator of The Social Justice Investor website and cohost of *Renegade Capital: The Activist's Podcast for Finance and Investments*. She lives in Maryland with her husband and three children.

Index